Popular Mechanics

do-it-yourself encyclopedia

HOME IMPROVEMENT COST GUIDE

CONDENSED EDITION

R. S. MEANS COMPANY, INC.
CONSTRUCTION CONSULTANTS & PUBLISHERS

HEARST DIRECT BOOKS

NEW YORK

POPULAR MECHANICS ENCYCLOPEDIA

Editor:
   C. Edward Cavert
Manufacturing:
   Ron Schoenfeld
Production:
   The Bookmaker
   Fairfax, Virginia
Editorial Assistance:
   Nancy Coggins

This book is published with the consent and cooperation of POPULAR MECHANICS Magazine.

POPULAR MECHANICS STAFF:

Editor-in-chief: Joe Oldham
Managing Editor: Bill Hartford
Graphics Director: Bryan Canniff
Automotive Director: Tony Swan
Home and Shop Editor: Steven Willson
Electronics Editor: Stephen A. Booth
Boating/Outdoors Editor: Joe Skorupa
Science Editor: Timothy H. Cole
Editorial Production: John Bostonian Jr.

MEANS HOME IMPROVEMENT COST GUIDE

Publisher & Editor-in Chief
   William D. Mahoney
Senior Editors
   George Ghiorse
   Roger Grant
   Charles Tringale
   David Tringale
Contributing Editors
   Allan Cleveland
   Donald Denzer
   Jeffrey Goldman
   Mary Greene
   Dwayne Lehigh
   Alan Lew
   John Moylan
   Kenneth Randall
   Kornelis Smit
   Edward Wetherill
   Ernest Williams
   Rory Woolsey
   David Zuniga
Illustrations by
   Carl Linde

MEANS HOME IMPROVEMENT COST GUIDE CONDENSED EDITION is published by special arangement between R. S. Means Company, Inc. and the Hearst Corporation for Popular Mechanics Do-it-Yourself Encyclopedia.

ISBN 0-87851-116-4
Library of Congress Catalog Card Number: 85-81760

10 9 8 7 6 5 4 3 2 1
Printed in the United States of America

In keeping with the general policy of R. S. Means Company, Inc., its authors, editors, and engineers apply diligence and judgment in locating and using reliable sources for the information published. However, no guarantee or warranty can be given, and all responsibilitiy for loss or damage are hereby disclaimed by the authors, editors, engineers and publisher of this publication with respect to the accuracy, correctness, value and sufficiency of the data, methods and other information contained herein as applied for any particular purpose or use.

Hearst Direct Books and Popular Mechanics Magazine make no guarantees, stated or implied, nor will they be liable in the event of typographical errors, misinterpretation or human error made by the reader. Plans for projects illustrated in this book may not meet all local zoning and building code requirements for construction. Before beginning any major project, consult with local authorities or see a structural architect. WORK SAFELY WITH HAND AND POWER TOOLS. WEAR EYE PROTECTION, READ MANUFACTURER'S INSTRUCTIONS AND WARNINGS FOR ALL PRODUCTS.

Contents

FOREWORD

The R.S.Means Company, Inc. researches and publishes cost data for the building construction industry. These selected sections from Means' Home Improvement Cost Guide applies that valuable experience to your home improvement projects. The book is designed and written to provide do-it-yourselfers with professional information for the planning of residential improvements. It is a valuable companion volume to your Popular Mechanics Do-It-Yourself Encyclopedia.

The data in this book will acquaint you with the procedures, material costs and contractor's charges required to complete a project you choose to build. Included in each project is a detailed, carefully-researched estimate of costs and installation times. There is also a description of the procedures required to build or install the project. Pointers and precautions are provided to help you organize the project and assess the level of difficulty of its various operations. To help you determine the length of time required to complete the tasks, adjusted man-hour estimates are provided for do-it-yourselfers at three skill levels, beginners, handymen and experts. Each project also includes a clearly labeled and accurately scaled illustration which identifies the material components and shows their relationship.

Use the cost estimates and labor-time estimates in this book as you plan to build projects you find in the Popular Mechanics Encyclopedia. While the project you choose may not be exactly the same as the one costed out in this book, the information should give you the base for a fairly accurate estimate of the investment in both time and money you'll need for your specific home improvement task.

There are plans for all these projects in the various volumes of your Popular Mechanics Encyclopedia along with other designs and detailed step-by-step construction help. If reading this book generates any new ideas, check the Table of Contents in Volume 1 of your Encyclopedia to find where to look for building projects from garages to gazebos and from kitchens to closets.

This book will inform you of not only the cost but also the various factors that affect the planning process. The information also will help you determine which parts of a project you want to take on yourself and which would be better left to a contractor.

At the end of the book you'll find information to adjust the cost given to the part of the country in which you live. The cost of implementing your plan may vary with the particular conditions of your project and your abilities as a do-it-yourselfer, but the benefits of good workmanship, materials and organization will remain for years to come. You may have to adjust cost estimates for inflation. Costs given in this book are based on the value of $1 in 1989-90.

When planning and construction are done with care, the lasting value of your home improvement will be assured and your time and money will be soundly invested. With the right materials properly placed and in keeping with the design and style of your home, any of these remodeling projects will contribute comfort and convenience to your home life while adding value to your house.

HOW TO USE THIS BOOK

The first two sections, "Interiors" and "Exteriors" provide descriptions and cost estimates for complete interior and exterior home improvement projects. Each project plan presented in the "Interiors" and "Exteriors" sections contains three types of information to help you organize the job. The first is a detailed illustration, which shows the finished project and the relationship of its components. The second is a general description of the plan, which includes a review of the materials and the installation process. It also evaluates the level of difficulty of the project. The "What To Watch Out For" section highlights ways to enhance the project or to cope with particularly difficult installation procedures. The third major element is a detailed project estimate chart, which lists the required materials and professional installation times and their corresponding costs. The components of this chart are described in detail below.

Description of the materials used in the project.

Quantity of each material and its standard unit of measure is given in this figure.

Man-Hours represents the estimated time it takes a professional tradesman to perform each of the installations within the project. The total number of contractor's hours for a complete project is given at the bottom of this column.

Key to Abbreviations
C.Y. - cubic yard
Ea. - each
L.F. - linear foot
Pr. - pair
Sq. - square (100 square feet of area)
S.F. - square foot
S.Y. - square yard
V.L.F. - vertical linear foot

GARAGE CONVERSION

Description	Quantity	Man-hours	Material
Flooring, joists 2" × 4", 16" O.C., on existing concrete slab	525 L.F.	7.0	165.15
Plywood, CDX, 5/8" thick, 4' × 8' sheets for floors & 1 exterior wall	22 Sheets	10.0	374.80
Plates, top & bottom, 2" × 4", 12' lengths	40 L.F.	1.0	12.60
Wall studs at door and new windows 2" × 4" × 8' long, 16" O.C.	192 L.F.	3.0	60.40
Headers over openings, double 2" × 6"	28 L.F.	1.5	13.20
Drywall, 1/2" thick, on walls & ceiling, standard taped & finished, 4' × 8' sheets	38 Sheets	22.0	426.70
Trim, casing for windows & door, 11/16" × 2-1/2" wide	50 L.F.	2.0	21.80
Trim, baseboard, 9/16' × 3-1/2'	90 L.F.	3.0	76.25
Flooring, vinyl sheet goods, .125" thick	500 S.F.	17.5	877.25
Painting, walls, ceilings & trim, primer & 1 coat	1200 S.F.	12.0	130.70
Painting, exterior siding, oil base primer & 2 coats, brushwork	185 S.F.	3.0	49.25
Electrical, 8 duplex receptacles, 1 switch	1 Lot	13.5	134.50
Totals		125.0	$4299.95

Project Size	22' × 22'	Contractor's Fee Including Materials	$10,800

Material cost estimated for each item in the "Description" column. This figure represents the price of a single unit, multiplied by the required number of units shown in the "Quantity" column. The prices reflect the national average of what you can expect to pay at a building supply retailer for the components used in the project. The material cost figure for the entire project can be found at the bottom of this column. You may have to adjust for inflation, costs given in this book are based on the value of $1 in 1989–90.

Project Size Gives the basic dimensions of each example project. The cost estimates are based on these measurements

Contractor's Fee Including Materials is the total estimated cost for the project described. It covers the cost of the building materials, as well as the contractor's labor, overhead expenses and profit. This estimate is based on a national average of what you can expect to pay a contractor to complete the entire job.

SECTION ONE INTERIOR IMPROVEMENTS

This section of the book is designed to inform you of the costs of various interior remodeling projects and to point out some practical concerns that will help to determine which parts of the job are appropriate for the do-it-yourselfer, and which are better left to the contractor. Cost is the primary consideration, with figures given for all materials required in a standard renovation. The estimated contractors' charges, also listed, should be weighed against the investment of the homeowner's time and willingness to tolerate the inconveniences which often accompany home remodeling.

The projects in this section share common features which apply specifically to interior remodeling. One is the degree of accuracy required in the layout of the improvement, and the measuring, cutting and assembly of materials. Because of these demands in interior work, do-it-yourselfers should not hesitate to call in contractors when needed. Although the cost of the project will increase with professional help, the long-term benefits of fine workmanship far outweigh the extra initial expense.

Preparation of the site is another factor which has special meaning in interior remodeling. Old fixtures may have to be removed, and floors, walls, and ceilings reconditioned and prepared to receive new coverings. Experienced do-it-yourselfers can handle many of these basic tasks, but beginners may have to spend some extra money for professional help. Correction of structural problems, particularly, should be left to qualified tradesmen and experts.

Heating, ventilating, plumbing and electrical work can also be a bit tricky in interior remodeling, especially in older houses where the heating system, piping or wiring is in questionable condition or inconveniently arranged. The example projects include the cost of basic plumbing and electrical work. Heating system modification costs have not been included. Should your project require changes to the heating and ventilating system, additional costs will be incurred. Time is a major consideration, especially in kitchen and bathroom remodeling projects, where an expedient renovation can minimize the disruption borne by the household.

Another important consideration is the delivery and storage of materials for an interior project. The method of transporting the materials to the site and to the appropriate room in the house should be carefully planned. The size of entryways will have to be taken into account when moving large appliances or building components, and a location arranged for storage of materials, especially those which are not weather resistant.

All of the renovation projects covered in the "Interiors" section start with a space enclosed by walls and under the cover of a roof. If you are interested in building an addition to house your new room, there are cost guides and descriptions for these improvements in the "Exteriors" section of this book.

Remodeling the interior of your home presents some definite challenges, but it also promises rewards which are realized daily in the improved appearance, function, and value of your house. Being aware of what is involved in a project and knowing the costs in advance will help you to plan the best renovation.

DELUXE HALF BATH

Often a half bath is located in an area of your home where more decorative and deluxe features are desired—perhaps off a recreation room or a room where you do most of your entertaining. A deluxe half bath may also be in order simply because you want to upgrade the facility in keeping with other improvements throughout your dwelling.

Materials

The materials used in the deluxe half bath include the same basis plumbing and decorating items of a standard half bath, but they have been upgraded to create a more decorative and deluxe facility. The toilet is a floor-mounted, one-piece unit of colored vitreous china. The lavatory is a trimmed 18″ round porcelain on cast iron model, also in color. If you want white fixtures, you can deduct about 30% of the estimated cost of the toilet and 25% from the price of the sink. Chrome-plated fittings have been selected for the sink and toilet in this model.

The deluxe half bath also features ceramic tile on both the floor and the lower part of the wall. Working with ceramic floor and wall materials requires some skill and the right tools, but with some advice and assistance at the start, beginners can produce pleasing results. Ceramic floor tile is more durable and easily maintained than vinyl and most other floor coverings. Ceramic wainscoting has the same benefits also gives the room a neat look. The ceiling, upper part of walls, and door can be finished with a primer and finish coat of paint.

Washable wallpaper can also enhance the room's appearance.

The choice of the vanity and other accessories for the deluxe half bath should suit your personal taste and coordinate with the style of the room. A deluxe 30″ two-door vanity with plastic laminate top provides extra storage space, and the high quality hardwood cabinet offers an attractive support for the sink. A lighted medicine cabinet with a built-in mirror is another feature. Stainless steel towel bars and tissue dispenser are one option, but other accessories are available in a variety of materials and costs.

Level of Difficulty

The deluxe half bath is a fairly demanding project for even experienced do-it-yourselfers. The two most difficult tasks involved in the renovation are the plumbing procedures and the floor and wall ceramic tile installations. Both of these jobs require specialized skills and a considerable degree of expertise. Beginners can handle the ceramic work, but only if they are given ample instruction beforehand and guidance during the installation. If you have not done any plumbing work in the past, you should leave the fixture installations to professionals, even if you are an accomplished do-it-yourselfer. Handymen and experts should be able to complete a great deal of this project, including tile installation, but they will need to obtain the specialized tools for ceramic work and seek some instruction at the start. In using the professional man-hour estimates, add 100% to the time if you are a beginner, 50% if you are an experienced handyman, and 20% if you are an expert.

DELUXE HALF BATH			
Description	Quantity	Man-hours	Material
Rough in frame for medicine 2″ × 4″ stock	8 L.F.	0.5	2.25
Painting, ceiling walls & door, primer & 1 coat	142 S.F.	1.0	15.45
Medicine cabinet, with mirror, stock, 16″ × 22″, lighted	1 Ea.	1.5	101.65
Deluxe vanity base cabinet, 2 door, 30″ wide	1 Ea.	2.0	186.35
Vanity top, plastic laminated, maximum	1 Ea.	1.0	41.45
Lavatory, with trim, porcelain enamel on cast iron, 18″ round, in color	1 Ea.	2.5	146.70
Fittings for lavatory	1 Set	8.5	66.00
Towel bars, stainless steel, 18″ long	2 Ea.	1.0	41.40
Toilet tissue dispenser, surface mounted, stainless steel	1 Ea.	0.5	21.20
Walls, ceramic tile wainscoting, thin set, 4-1/4″ × 4-1/4″ tile	20 S.F.	4.0	31.45
Flooring, porcelain type, 1 color, color group 2, 1″ × 1″ tile	20 S.F.	4.0	45.75
Toilet, tank type, vitreous china, floor mounted, 1 piece, in color	1 Ea.	3.0	566.30
Fittings for toilet	1 Set	8.5	100.75
	Totals	38.5	$1366.70
Project Size 4′ × 6′	Contractor's Fee Including Materials		$3100

What to Watch Out For

Ceramic tile, like any other wall or floor covering, requires a dry and clean surface for mounting. Be sure to check the condition of the floor underlayment and the sheetrock before laying the tile. The rough floor surface must be cleaned, leveled, and smoothed out before the tile flooring sections are laid. The sheetrock on the walls must be clean, dry, and solid to provide adequate backing for the wall tiles. Bathrooms are notorious collectors of moisture, and the adhesives used in ceramic tile installations will not bond effectively to damp or moist surfaces. The extra cost involved in preparing or replacing the existing floor or walls is money well spent to ensure a quality installation.

Deluxe Half Bath

Upgrading a basic half bath to deluxe standards can enhance the value and overall appearance of your home. Because a half bath is not the major facility in a house, its renovation does not involve as much inconvenience as that of a full bath. As a result, you may be able to perform much of this project yourself to make it a more economical undertaking.

DELUXE FULL BATH

The deluxe full bath includes the amenities and upgraded fixtures to provide an attractive and durable addition to any home. For the additional expense of deluxe features like a one-piece toilet, a sliding shower door, and ceramic tile, this bath offers first quality materials for a relatively modest investment, especially if you opt to do most of the work on your own.

Materials

The deluxe full bath features top-of-the-line fixtures, durable ceramic wall and floor tiling, and quality accessories. The fixtures used in the bath include matching colored 18″ lavatory, single-piece floor-mounted toilet, and porcelain enamel on cast iron recessed tub with a non-skid mat bottom. Complementing the fixtures and included in the estimated cost are quality faucets, valves and diverters, and shower head. The fittings for the fixtures, including the minimum rough plumbing and supply valves, are listed as a separate cost which may vary according to the amount of rearranging and plumbing modifications made for the particular facility. If you're considering doing the deluxe bath remodeling project on your own, you may want to hire a plumber for the removal and installation of the primary fixtures, especially the tub and shower which require thorough plumbing skills.

The wall and flooring systems of the deluxe bath feature ceramic tile. Although the wall area looks relatively small in comparison to, say, a bedroom, don't let it fool you. And even though the ceramic tile covers only the lower portion of the walls outside of the tub area, there is quite a bit of effort and expense involved in tiling this

room. If you haven't done tile work before, check with an experienced person for advice; also, get the right tools for the job. The grouting process alone requires some know-how and patience. Give particular attention to the ceramic work around the tub and shower. As for the floor, the ceramic installation is a little easier and faster because the material comes in sections, usually 1′ x 1′, which can be trimmed and cut where necessary as the floor is laid. The partition between the tub and vanity is constructed of 2″ x 4″s and should be carefully plumbed and set precisely at a right angle to the line /of the tub. If it is out of plumb even slightly, the ensuing drywall and, particularly, ceramic tile installations become more difficult. The upper part of the walls and the ceiling require two coats of paint (one primer and one finish coat) to complete the job correctly. The door and any trim work should also be refinished with paint, or stained and then sealed with two coats of polyurethane.

The vanity and other accessory items for the deluxe bath can vary with individual taste, but a 30″ two-door deluxe vanity cabinet with a first quality top adds an attractive and functional support for the lavatory. The medicine cabinet can include a built-in lighting fixture and twin sliding mirror doors at reasonable cost. The towel bar and tissue dispenser can be of conventional design, and selected from various materials such as stainless steel, chrome and ceramic. Instead of a basic shower curtain and support rod, the deluxe bath also includes a sliding shower door made from tempered glass.

Level of Difficulty

The deluxe full bath poses certain challenges, and expediency is a prime consideration, especially if your home has just one bathroom facility. For all but the expert level of do-it-yourselfers, a plumber should be hired to do the fixture installations. Beginners should also hire someone to do the tile work for this project. In time, a poor tiling job will cost you many times over the installer's fee in leakage and water problems around the tub and shower. Beginners can figure on 150% added to the man-hours

estimate on other parts of the project. They are advised to seek professional assistance along the way. Handymen should contract the plumbing and add 70% to the man-hours estimate for all other operations involved in the renovation. Experts who can handle the plumbing should be able to complete the entire project with about 30% added to the professional time estimate.

What to Watch Out For

There are many critical parts to any bathroom renovation, but perhaps the most important task outside of the actual plumbing work is the dry-walling and ceramic work in the tub and shower area. Be sure to install 1/2" water resistant sheetrock for the tile backing and then tape and finish it thoroughly to eliminate moisture penetration at the seams. Thoroughly taping and finishing the drywall seams and nail or screw head indentations also provides a flush, continuously flat surface for the ceramic tile. Install the tile carefully, following the adhesive manufacturer's instructions and recommendations. After the tile has been installed, grout it thoroughly, paying careful attention to the vertical corner nearest the shower head to make sure that no voids or open spaces exist in the line of grout. If you've included a ceramic soap dish or handle fixture in the tub and shower enclosure, then grout around it carefully as well. A bead of flexible caulking or tub sealer along the seam at the top of the tub will add further protection against water penetration and subsequent damage to the floor and wall in the tub area. Even though these preventive measures may take a little extra time and add a bit to the cost of the project, they will save you considerable expense and aggravation in years of trouble-free use of the tub and shower facility.

DELUXE FULL BATH

Description	Quantity	Man-hours	Material
Partition wall between vanity and tub, 2" x 4" plates and studs, 16" O.C., 8' high	64 L.F.	1.0	20.10
Rough-in frame for medicine cabinet, using 2" x 4" stock	10 L.F.	0.5	3.15
Drywall, 1/2" thick, on walls, water resistant, taped and finished, 4' x 8' sheets	2 Sheets	1.5	27.10
Painting, ceiling, walls, and door, primer and 1 coat	230 S.F.	2.5	25.05
Vanity base cabinet, deluxe, 2 door, 30" wide	1 Ea.	2.0	279.50
Vanity top, Formica covered	1 Ea.	1.0	136.10
Lavatory, with trim, porcelain enamel on cast iron, 18" round, color	1 Ea.	2.5	158.80
Fittings for lavatory	1 Set	8.5	73.30
Bathtub, recessed, porcelain enamel on cast iron, w/trim, mat bottom, 5' long, color	1 Ea.	4.0	317.05
Fittings for tub and shower	1 Set	9.5	85.40
Sliding shower door, deluxe, tempered glass	1 Ea.	2.0	320.65
Medicine cabinet, sliding mirror doors, 34" x 21", lighted	1 Ea.	1.5	242.00
Walls, ceramic tile, shower enclosure and wainscoting, thinset, 4-1/4" x 4-1/4"	140 S.F.	12.5	728.40
Flooring, porcelain tile, 1 color, 1" x 1" tiles	36 S.F.	4.0	135.00
Toilet, tank type, vitreous china, floor mounted, 1 piece, color	1 Ea.	3.0	597.75
Fittings for toilet	1 Set	8.5	100.75
Toilet tissue dispenser, surface mounted, stainless steel	1 Ea.	0.5	23.00
Towel bar, stainless steel, 30" long	1 Ea.	0.5	21.80
Totals		65.5	$3294.90

Project Size	7' x 8'	Contractor's Fee Including Materials	**$6980**

Deluxe Full Bath
Whether you are modernizing an old bath or constructing a new one, the value and comfort of your home will be enhanced. You can save on labor costs while learning and doing some of the work on your own, and the investment of your time and money will be returned in future years.

DELUXE MASTER BATH

The extra accessories and amenities offered in this deluxe master bath are designed to reflect the quality of larger, more expensive homes. The four-fixture project offered in this plan involves a considerable commitment of both money and time. If you plan to accomplish some or all of this renovation on your own, don't hesitate to seek the assistance of knowledgeable people. Good advice can save you money and prevent damage to quality fixtures and materials.

Materials

The fixtures and accessories selected for this room are first quality and appropriate for a deluxe bathroom facility. The four plumbing fixtures include a porcelain on cast iron recessed tub with a non-skid mat bottom and a separate shower stall with a terrazzo receptor. The toilet is a quality one-piece floor-mounted unit made from vitreous china. Both the tub and toilet are available in white or colored styles, with the colored fixtures costing about 25% to 30% more than the white units. The basic rough-in for these fixtures may cost more than the estimated price if relocation or replacement of the existing plumbing is required. Only expert do-it-yourselfers and plumbers should tackle the plumbing tasks encountered in this project. Ceramic tile is the primary wall and floor covering throughout the deluxe master bath. If you are considering doing the tiling in this bath, then be prepared to make a major commitment to the task. All of the walls are wainscoted to a height of about 4', and the shower stall above the terrazzo receptor is completely tiled. If you haven't done any tile work before, you should hire a tilesetter to do the job. A poor tiling job will not only harm the appearance of the bathroom, but also invite major problems from water penetration later on. The shower stall and tub area, in particular, require precise tile installation if they are to remain watertight for a long period of time. Placing the ceramic flooring is a bit easier than installing the ceramic wall tile, but it also requires patience and a reasonable level of skill. Like any other flooring job, one of your first and most important concerns should be the thorough inspection and proper reconditioning and preparation of the subfloor. The accessories and amenities included in the plan for the deluxe master bath can be altered or changed within a wide range of options. Basic items like the tissue dispenser and towel bar, for example, are available in ceramic, chrome, wood, and stainless steel. Different styles of deluxe and standard vanity cabinets can also be purchased at varying costs to suit the decor of your bath. The oversized medicine cabinet unit may be replaced with a half-wall mirror and decorative lighting fixtures.

Level of Difficulty

Installing this bathroom is a major job for even the accomplished remodeler. The extensive tile work and complexity of the plumbing fixtures dictate that even the most experienced worker will need some advice from a professional. In this case, we suggest that the expert add 25% to the man-hours given. The home handyman should opt to have the plumbing contracted and to get assistance on the tile work. Jobs like constructing the partition at the head of the tub and drywalling and finishing the shower stall are well within the realm of most experienced do-it-yourselfers. Handymen should add 60% to the man-hours for these and the other remaining

tasks. Beginners could attempt the medicine cabinet, towel bars, and toilet accessories installation, and can also save on labor costs by painting the walls, ceiling, door, and trim. They should add 100% to the man-hours for these items and leave the rest of the work to professional contractors.

What to Watch Out For

The deluxe master bath includes some specialized items that require careful treatment during installation. Two of these are the cultured marble vanity top and the terrazzo receptor for the shower stall. Both units will provide years of service when properly installed. They are, however, prone to cracking and chipping if they are not handled carefully during placement or if they are improperly supported or fastened. The marble top should be carefully placed and then leveled on the vanity cabinet. Follow the adhesive manufacturer's instructions when securing the top. The terrazzo receptor, or pan for the base of the shower, should be carefully aligned and leveled at the base of the pre-framed shower stall before the drain is permanently set and secured.

DELUXE MASTER BATH

Description	Quantity	Man-hours	Material
Partition wall for shower stall, 2" x 4" plates & studs, 16" O.C., 8' high	152 L.F.	2.5	47.80
Rough in frame for medicine cabinet, 2" x 4" stock	16 L.F.	0.5	5.00
Drywall, 1/2" thick on shower stall walls, water resistant, taped & finished, 4' x 8' sheets	5 Sheets	3.0	67.75
Painting, ceiling, walls & door, primer & 1 coat	330 S.F.	1.5	35.95
Deluxe vanity base cabinet, 2 door, 72" wide	1 Ea.	4.0	626.75
Vanity top, cultured marble, 73" x 22" double bowl	1 Ea.	3.0	210.55
Fittings for lavatory	2 Sets	16.0	146.60
Shower stall, terrazzo receptor, 36" x 36"	1 Ea.	8.0	611.05
Shower door, tempered glass, deluxe	1 Ea.	2.0	183.90
Bathtub, recessed, porcelain enamel on cast iron, w/trim, mat bottom, 5' long, color	1 Ea.	4.0	317.05
Fittings for tub & shower	1 Set	9.5	85.40
Medicine cabinet, center mirror, 2 end cabinets 72" long, lighted	1 Ea.	2.0	266.20
Walls, ceramic tile, shower stall & wainscoating, thin set, 4-1/4" x 4-1/4"	170 S.F.	15.5	884.50
Flooring, porcelain tile, 1 color, color group 2, 1" x 1"	40 S.F.	3.5	208.10
Toilet, tank type, vitreous china, floor mounted, 1 piece, color	1 Ea.	3.0	597.75
Fittings for toilet	1 Set	8.5	101.60
Towel bar, stainless steel, 30" long	2 Ea.	1.0	43.55
Toilet tissue dispenser, surface mounted, stainless steel	1 Ea.	0.5	23.00
	Totals	88.0	$4462.50

Project Size	8' x 10'	Contractor's Fee Including Materials	$9100

Deluxe Master Bath

Renovating a master bath or expanding a full bath to a four-fixture deluxe facility improves the value of your home as well as its comfort. If this plan is in keeping with the size and style of your home, it can be a rewarding remodeling project.

DELUXE BATH

If your home has the space to accommodate a deluxe bath, or if you are building an addition large enough for such a room, this remodeling plan will help you in selecting materials and designing the facility. The project is a costly one, as only top-of-the-line fixtures and materials are recommended to complement the size and intended comfort and luxury of this room. Many different layouts are possible in the design of a five-fixture deluxe bathroom, as long as the available floor area allows for them and for the various amenities and accessories. A deluxe bath requires adequate floor space, and cramming the fixtures into too small an area or reducing the bath's open space will only detract from its intended luxury and spaciousness.

Materials

The materials included in the deluxe bath are of the highest available quality short of custom-made items. The five plumbing fixtures include a one-piece, low-profile, colored toilet and matching bidet, a double-bowl lavatory cast into the cultured marble vanity top, a 5' x 5' ceramic shower stall, and a 46" x 56" molded fiberglass tub with whirlpool. The estimated cost of these fixtures includes the appropriate trim like faucets, valves, diverters, and shower head. Additional expense may be added to the estimated cost of the fittings if the rough plumbing is not in place or requires relocation. Added expense will also be incurred if the deluxe bath project is a renovation of an existing facility and old fixtures have to be removed.

The floor, ceiling, and walls of the deluxe bath also incorporate the best available structural materials and finish coverings. The floor is comprised of 1/2" underlayment-grade plywood over the subfloor and then covered with a high quality wool carpet and pad. If the deluxe bath is a brand new installation or part of a larger renovation project, the ceiling should be leveled and covered with 1/2" drywall. After it is taped and finished, it should be painted with a primer and a finish coat of high quality paint. The walls should also be covered with 1/2" sheetrock. Be sure to use 1/2" water resistant drywall on the wall areas near the tub, on the tub support, and around the shower stall. After the walls have been taped and finished, they can be painted or covered with a washable vinyl wallpaper. Ceramic tile should be installed on all walls in the shower stall and on the tub support. The partition between the shower and tub compartments and the framing for the storage closet, shower stall, and the tub support should be built of construction grade 2" x 4"s. If you are doing some or all of the floor, ceiling, and wall installations yourself, it's best to take the time to do them thoroughly, and seek advice along the way. The deluxe quality of the fixtures and materials should be backed up by solid workmanship in the installation process. Beginners and less experienced handymen should hire a contractor to perform most of these tasks.

The window, door, and vanity installations also include first quality materials. The exterior wall can be enhanced with a plastic-clad thermopane casement or sliding window unit. Six-panel or other decorative solid doors between compartments and on the closet maintain the deluxe character of the facility. Louvered units are also available if more ventilation is desired within the bath and the closet. The prefinished shelving for the closet and the deluxe vanity cabinet offer functional and attractive amenities to the facility. A large mirror on the wall area above the lavatory and vanity unit provides a practical substitute for a mirrored medicine cabinet while contributing to the feeling of spaciousness of the bath.

Level of Difficulty

As noted in the introduction to the plan for this remodeling project, the deluxe bath is a luxurious facility comprised of expensive plumbing fixtures and other costly building materials. If these fixtures and amenities are within your budget and you have a home large enough to accommodate them, you might find it most expedient to hire a contractor to do the installations. Tasks like the painting and wallpapering can be completed by the homeowner to cut some of the cost. Beginners can accomplish these jobs without much difficulty. Handymen and expert do-it-yourselfers who want to have a hand in constructing the facility should leave the plumbing, ceramic, and carpeting installations to the professionals, but they should be able to complete most of the other jobs involved in the project. Experts should add about 30% to the professional time estimates for those tasks which they intend to do; handymen, about 70%.

What To Watch Out For

The finish materials applied to the floor, ceiling, and walls of any bath should be durable, water and moisture-resistant, and easy to maintain. For these reasons, ceramic tile has proven to be one of the most effective coverings for bathroom installations. The portions of walls, ceilings, and trim which require painting should be carefully prepared, primed, and then finish-coated with a high quality paint. Gloss or semi-gloss finishes generally hold up better than flat finishes and are easier to clean. If you prefer wallpaper, select a product that is labeled as washable. Even though vinyl wallcoverings, for example, may cost more than conventional wallpaper, they are worth the extra initial expense because of their durability and low maintenance. Carpeting can be used as a bathroom floor covering, but it has to be cleaned more often than carpeting placed in other locations in your home. Also, if it gets wet constantly and is not given a chance to dry, it is prone to mildew and, under prolonged wet conditions, deterioration. For regular bathroom use, ceramic and resilient floor coverings are more practical but certainly less comfortable under foot than carpeting.

DELUXE BATH			
Description	Quantity	Man-hours	Material
Partition walls, 2" x 4" plates and studs, 16" O.C., 8' high	400 L.F.	6.0	125.85
Framing around tub, 2" x 4" stock	80 L.F.	3.0	25.20
Drywall, 1/2" thick on walls & ceilings, water resistant, taped & finished, 4' x 8' sheets	32 Sheets	18.5	433.65
Sub-flooring underlayment grade, plywood, 1/2" thick, 4' x 8' sheets	6 Sheets	2.5	65.05
Vanity, deluxe base cabinet, 4 doors, 21" x 76"	1 Ea.	4.0	711.50
Vanity top, including basins, cultured marble	1 Ea.	5.0	392.05
Fittings for lavatory	2 Sets	16.5	146.40
Tub, whirlpool, molded fiberglass, 56" x 46"	1 Ea.	16.0	2662.00
Fittings for bathtub	1 Set	9.5	85.40
Shower receptor & fittings	1 Ea.	11.0	297.15
Shower door, tempered glass, deluxe	1 Ea.	2.0	320.65
Window, 4' x 4'-6", plastic clad, casement type	1 Ea.	2.0	469.50
Doors, 6 panel pine doors, 2'-6" wide x 6'-8" high	2 Ea.	2.0	348.50
Trim for doors, window & baseboard, 9/16" x 3-1/2" wide	180 L.F.	6.0	152.45
Painting, ceiling & trim, primer & 1 coat	800 S.F.	3.5	87.15
Tile, ceramic, shower & tub, 4-1/4" x 4-1/4"	210 S.F.	19.0	1092.65
Wallpaper, vinyl, fabric backed, medium weight	560 S.F.	9.5	420.10
Shelving, 10" wide, prefinished, 4' long	4 Ea.	2.0	111.30
Toilet, one piece, low profile	1 Ea.	3.0	732.05
Fittings for toilet	1 Set	8.5	101.60
Bidet, vitreous china, white trim	1 Ea.	3.5	338.80
Fittings for bidet	1 Set	8.5	101.60
Carpet, wool, including pad	24 S.Y.	5.5	828.50
Mirror over vanity, plate glass, 6' x 4'	1 Ea.	1.0	158.25
Totals		168.0	$10,207.35

Project Size	12' x 18'	Contractor's Fee Including Materials	$21,040

Deluxe Bath

Adding or remodeling a bath to deluxe standards is a way to increase your comfort while boosting the overall value and atmosphere of your house. If a deluxe bathroom fits in with your lifestyle and your home is spacious enough to accommodate it, this project can pay dividends in the coming years.

DELUXE STRAIGHT WALL KITCHEN

The deluxe features of this straight wall kitchen facility enhance its appearance and convenience while maintaining the efficiency and durability standards required of all kitchens. This kitchen plan might be appropriate for those who prefer the features of the deluxe projects and whose kitchens are a highly visible area in their homes. Although this plan presents a small and relatively simple renovation design, its materials are expensive, and do-it-yourselfers should use discretion in determining which tasks they will undertake. Nevertheless, the uncomplicated straight wall layout of the facility provides the opportunity for handymen to tackle more of the remodeling tasks than would be practical in larger, more elaborate kitchen plans.

Materials

The materials used in this deluxe kitchen design are top-of-the-line products which will enhance the appearance of the facility and provide many years of reliable service. Some substitutions can be used, but these modifications should be made with discretion and thought given to their aesthetic impact on the kitchen's appearance. Remember that kitchen products are in place for a long time and economizing with lower-grade substitutes may lead to problems in the future. If you feel that you need guidance, consult a professional kitchen planner. The cost of this service may save you unnecessary expense in materials and improve the efficiency of the facility.

The cabinets in this kitchen plan are hardwood units with paneled cabinet doors. Because the cabinets establish the decor of the room, they are its main feature and are worthy of some advance planning and research. Since much of the expense of the new facility is incurred in the cost of the cabinets, you will want to buy units of high quality materials and construction. If you are installing the cabinets on your own, follow acceptable carpentry methods and work slowly and carefully. Rushing this operation can result in misaligned components and, worse, damage to expensive prefinished cabinets. The ceramic

tile used for the counter top and the vinyl tile used for the floor provide durable, easily maintained, and attractive surfaces. The ceramic tiles are available in many colors and designs which can be highlighted with colored epoxy grout to create an attractive and functional work surface and backsplash. If you plan to do the tile work on your own, be sure to fasten the plywood subsurface firmly to the base cabinets, as movement of this support surface subsequent to the tile installation can cause the grout to crack and, eventually, the tiles to loosen. Also, make sure that the plywood surface is clean, dry, and level before the tiles are placed. The vinyl flooring for the facility can be comprised of sheet goods or individual tiles as determined by personal preference or the aesthetic mandates of color, design, and surface texture. Remember that the flooring should be installed after all other kitchen components, except the refrigerator and free-standing stove, have been placed. The vinyl material should cover the floor surface under the plug-in appliances, but not the area under the cabinets. The appliances for this straight wall facility should be placed in locations which will make them conveniently accessible during their use. Before purchasing the refrigerator, for example, determine which design features of the appliance will best suit its location. Size, left- or right-hand door opening, side-by-side or upper and lower freezer/ refrigerator layout are all important considerations, especially in smaller kitchens. If a built-in range is utilized, special cabinet and counter-top planning is required, whereas a free-standing unit requires only a standard opening, so plan accordingly.

Level of Difficulty

This remodeling project provides the opportunity for do-it-yourselfers to accomplish a significant amount of the work on their own. Although the undertaking is challenging because of the wide variety of skills required to complete the installation, its single wall layout and small area make it a reasonable project for experts and competent handymen. Remember that precise measurement, tight fits, and accurate alignment are required in all interior finish operations, especially kitchen cabinet, countertop, and flooring placement. Also, bear in mind that you are working with deluxe materials that are ex-

pensive to replace or repair if you damage them with poor workmanship and carelessness. As a general rule, beginners should not attempt the cabinet installation and should double the estimated professional time for basic tasks. Experts and handymen should add 20% and 50%, respectively to the man-hours estimates for the basic operation, and 50% and 100% for the cabinet placement. Specialized jobs like the tiling, flooring, electrical installation and plumbing should be attempted only by individuals experienced in these areas of construction, or by accomplished do-it-yourselfers.

What to Watch For

Because the cabinet system for this kitchen project is basic in its single wall design and limited in the number of units, its installation is a manageable undertaking for skilled do-it- yourselfers. If you follow a few basic guidelines, work patiently, and seek advice before you start and when any problems develop, your efforts can produce professional results and considerable savings in labor costs.

Here are a few suggestions to get you started. Thoroughly prepare the walls and floor in the cabinet area by making sure that they are solid, free from voids and obstructions, and reasonably plumb and level. Install the wall units first, making all fastenings temporary as you keep a constant check on tight abutments and the alignment of facings. Maintain plumb and level as you proceed, using shims and spacers where needed. Follow the same process for the base cabinets, giving special attention to irregularities or slope of the floor. Make all permanent fastenings with heavy wood screws or lag bolts after the entire system has been placed. Install the valance and trim after the wall units have been permanently placed. At least two workers are needed for the cabinet installation, so plan accordingly.

DELUXE STRAIGHT-WALL KITCHEN

Description	Quantity	Man-hours	Material
Blocking, for mounting cabinets, 2" x 4" stock	18 L.F.	1.0	5.65
Plywood, underlayment grade, 3/8" thick 4' x 8' sheets	4 Sheets	1.5	63.50
Flooring, vinyl sheet goods, .0125" thick	65 S.F.	2.0	93.60
Wall cabinets, 12" deep, hardwood, deluxe	9.5 L.F.	3.0	509.60
Base cabinets, 24" deep, hardwood, deluxe	6.5 L.F.	4.0	839.85
Plywood sub-base for countertop, 1/2" x 4' x 8' sheets	1 Sheet	0.5	17.80
Ceramic tile for countertop and backsplash	30 S.F.	3.0	174.25
Valance board over sink	4 L.F.	0.5	29.05
Trim, crown molding, stock pine, 9/16" x 3-5/8"	28 L.F.	1.0	37.25
Paint, ceiling & walls, primer & 1 coat	185 S.F.	1.5	20.15
Paint, cornice, trim, puttying, primer & 1 coat	28 L.F.	0.5	1.70
Cooking range, built-in, 30" wide, one oven	1 Ea.	8.0	968.00
Hood for range, 2-speed, 30" wide	1 Ea.	5.5	290.40
Refrigerator, no frost, 19 C.F.	1 Ea.	4.0	1331.00
Sink w/faucets & drain, stainless steel, self-rimming, 32" x 22", double bowl	1 Ea.	6.5	371.45
Dishwasher, built-in	1 Ea.	8.0	471.90
Rough-in, supply, waste & vent for sink & dishwasher	2 Ea.	17.5	159.35
Totals		68.0	$5384.50

Project Size	6'-6" x 14'	Contractor's Fee Including Materials	$10,170

Deluxe Straight-Wall Kitchen

This straight wall kitchen plan demonstrates how a small facility can take on an elegant appearance as deluxe products are incorporated into its construction. The additional expense of its top quality materials will be returned in many years of pleasant, practical, and dependable use.

CORRIDOR KITCHEN

Valance Board
Wall Cabinets
Sink W/Faucets
Ceramic Tile
Countertop &
Backsplash
Base Cabinets
Vinyl Flooring
Paint Walls & Ceiling
Dishwasher
Wall Cabinets
Refrigerator
Range Hood
Cooking Range
Base Cabinets

This corridor kitchen project demonstrates how limitations of size can be overcome to create an efficient and attractive facility at a reasonable cost. As in all kitchen projects, many remodeling and building skills are required to complete the renovation. Carpentry, electrical, and plumbing tasks are all involved. Also, because the kitchen area of any home performs a vital function, expediency in completing the project is an important consideration. A long period of renovation work translates into an extended interruption of the routine of home life. If you plan to complete the project on your own, you might want to set a block of time aside to complete most of the work in a concentrated week's effort rather than spreading it out over several weekends.

Materials

The materials used in this kitchen plan are standard grade items, readily available from kitchen suppliers and building supply retailers. To remodel an existing kitchen completely, you may have to modify some of the suggested cabinet and appliance selections to suit your space limitations. Also, your choice of cabinets and appliances should be carefully determined, since the major costs for any kitchen facility are focused on these components. Wise selection of these items can help you to meet your food preparation needs and decorative standards without sacrificing quality. Because the corridor kitchen layout allows for only two walls of work space, the design and arrangement of the cabinet system must be efficient. This plan recommends standard-sized wall and base units with depths of 12″ and 24″, respectively. These depths should be maintained wherever possible because other kitchen plumbing fixtures and appliances are designed around these standard dimensions. Altering the base cabinet depth, particularly, will cost you more money for custom or special order units and can cause additional expense and aggravation in selecting appliances, sinks, and other kitchen fixtures. If your kitchen area is too narrow to accommodate the 24″ deep base

cabinets on both walls, seek advice and suggestions from a professional contractor before you begin the project. When making the choice between giving up floor space and giving up cabinet space, in most cases you will be better off with diminished floor space and standard sized cabinets. The countertop, like the cabinets, should also be designed with efficiency in mind so as to produce a maximum amount of surface area on the two walls. Formica-type counter coverings are durable, easy to clean, and economical, but other more expensive materials like ceramic tile can serve as attractive and functional substitutes. The trim work for the cabinets, including the valance board over the sink and the molding at the top of the wall units, should be selected on the recommendation of the cabinet manufacturer. The valance is usually available as a factory or shop-made part of the cabinet assembly.

Before the cabinets are installed, the ceiling, floor, and walls of the kitchen area have to be reconditioned and prepared. The expense incurred in this step of the project will depend largely on the amount of fundamental restoration required. Tearing out old cabinets and stripping the floors of old linoleum or tile are difficult jobs that take time and require some know-how. Be sure to correct any structural or cosmetic deficiencies in the walls and floor. Any straightening or smoothing of existing rough ceiling, wall, or floor surfaces done at this stage of the project will expedite the rest of the installation. Remember too, that if you plan to continue to use your kitchen during the period of the remodeling work, you will have to move appliances and temporarily rearrange the facility as the job progresses. If you are doing work on your own, plan to have someone available to lend assistance. Like cabinet systems, appliances vary significantly in quality and cost. The price estimates provided in this plan are based on medium priced appliances with a limited number of operational accessories and convenience options. Because the recommended range and refrigerator are free-standing models, just about any standard-sized unit can be installed. The two-speed, 30″ wide, hood and exhaust fan unit is also a common item which can be purchased at most kitchen, electric, or building supply outlets. If possible, duct the exhaust vent to the outside. Remember that the cost for appliance installation will vary if the new unit is to be placed in a different location. Electric or gas ranges, for example, require special supply connections that should be installed by qualified tradesmen.

Level of Difficulty

Kitchen remodeling demands knowledge of and skill in many different building operations. Cabinet installation, plumbing, electrical work, and flooring placement are just some of the tasks that the handyman has to contend with during the renovation process. Most beginners can handle the basic jobs like the ceiling, wall and floor preparation, and the painting and staining; but they should leave the specialized work to the carpenter, plumber, or electrician. Even moderately skilled handymen should hire a professional to install the cabinets and countertop. Because kitchen cabinets involve substantial expense and specialized knowledge of installation procedures, even expert do-it-yourselfers might consider hiring a professional for this job. Handymen and experts should add about 50% and 20%, respectively, to the professional time estimate for all tasks, except the cabinet installation and plumbing work. If they intend to perform these operations, they should add to the man-hours.

What to Watch Out For

If new underlayment cannot be placed directly on the existing floor, the difficult chore of stripping the old resilient floor will have to be accomplished. You can use several methods in performing this task, depending on the amount, type, and condition of the covering to be removed. If the area is relatively small, the old material can be peeled and chipped by hand with a flat bar or other blade-type instrument. If the old material has a backing, and some of it stays on the floor, hand or power sanding may be needed to get it up. Larger floors can be stripped in the same way, but you might look into renting a floor grinder if the job looks too big to do by hand. Before the new covering is laid, be sure that the old underlayment is fastened thoroughly and that all seams and voids have been filled with floor leveler and sanded smooth.

CORRIDOR KITCHEN

Description	Quantity	Man-hours	Material
Blocking, for mounting cabinets, 2″ x 4″, stock	38 L.F.	1.5	11.95
Plywood, underlayment grade, 1/2″ thick, 4′ x 8′ sheets	4 Sheets	1.5	71.25
Flooring, vinyl sheet goods 0.125″ thick	96 S.F.	3.5	377.55
Wall cabinets, hardwood, 12″ deep	18.5 L.F.	4.5	708.70
Base cabinets, hardwood, 24″ deep	18 L.F.	6.5	1270.45
Countertop, 1-1/4″ thick Formica, w/backsplash	18 L.F.	5.0	108.90
Valance board over sink	4 L.F.	0.5	29.05
Trim, crown molding, stock pine 9/16″ x 3-5/8″	42 L.F.	1.0	55.90
Paint, Primer and 1 coat, ceiling & walls	425 S.F.	3.5	46.30
Paint, trim, puttying, primer & 1 coat	42 L.F.	1.0	2.55
Cooking range, free-standing, 30″ wide, one oven	1 Ea.	2.0	314.60
Hood for range, 2-speed, 30″ wide, vented	1 Ea.	3.0	36.30
Refrigerator, no frost, 19 C.F.	1 Ea.	2.0	726.00
Dishwasher, built-in, 2 cycle	1 Ea.	6.5	471.90
Sink w/faucets & drain, stainless steel, self-rimming, 33″ x 22″, double bowl	1 Ea.	6.5	371.45
Rough-in, supply, waste & vent for sink & dishwasher	1 Ea.	9.0	79.70
Totals		57.5	$4682.56
Project Size 11′ x 11′-6″	Contractor's Fee Including Materials		$8810

Corridor Kitchen

Corridor kitchens, because of their two-wall cabinet layout, require both imagination and careful planning in a remodeling design. With the thoughtful arrangement of cabinets and appliances, a stylish and efficient facility can be created.

DELUXE L-SHAPED KITCHEN

Valance Board

Sink W/Faucet

Range Hood

Cooking Range

Wall Cabinets

Ceramic Tile Countertop & Backsplash

Refrigerator

Dishwasher

Base Cabinets

Vinyl Floor Tile

Corner, or L-shaped, kitchen arrangements are often used in situations where the food preparation area is adjacent to or clearly visible from the eating area. For example, in some cases, the open floor area of the kitchen itself is occupied by a table and chairs; in other situations, one or both of the vacant walls may be open to a remote eating or living area. Because of the visibility of the cabinet and appliance area, attractive, deluxe products may be chosen to enhance the kitchen's appearance.

Materials

Like other deluxe kitchen plans included in this section, the L-shaped deluxe kitchen utilizes top-of-the-line products in place of economical, standard-grade components. The homeowner's choice of these top-quality cabinets, appliances, and finish materials should be based on several factors, including budget, the decor and furnishings of other rooms in the house, and personal preference. There is room for compromise, which is to say that a kitchen facility does not have to be exclusively standard or deluxe. However, be sure to make any substitutions carefully so as not to disturb the aesthetic balance.

This L-shaped kitchen plan includes top quality hardwood wall and base cabinets. Paneled doors and drawer facings are common in deluxe cabinet systems, but other options are also available. Formica and other brand name plastic laminates, for example, provide durable, easily-maintained surface coverings for quality cabinets. Remember that kitchen cabinets are permanent installations that you will use daily for many years, so do some research and see what is available before you buy. After you have purchased the cabinets, it is best to have them installed by a professional. Only expert do-it-yourselfers who have done extensive cabinet

work should consider tackling this part of the project. The flooring and countertop surface coverings also involve some important decisions on the part of the homeowner. Like the cabinets, these surfaces require materials which are functional, attractive, and complementary to the color and designof the rest of the kitchen. Many quality resilient flooring materials are available at varying costs, including vinyl tiles and sheet goods and other composition products. The kitchen floor requires more upkeep than any other floor in the house, so keep maintenance and durability in mind when you make your choice. If you plan to lay the floor on your own, and you have a choice between vinyl tiles and vinyl sheet goods in the same pattern, you will find the tile installation the easier of the two. Generally, sheet flooring requires more skill to place, particularly in situations where scribing of the material is needed along skewed or bowed walls in older homes. Ceramic tile provides a deluxe alternative to the commonly-used Formica countertop and backsplash material. Like Formica, it is durable, low in maintenance, and attractive. With the right color grout, ceramic tile gives the countertop a neat, up-to-date appearance. Remember that because tiled counter tops must be fabricated on the site, the charge for their installation is significantly more than for shop-prepared Formica units. The appliances included in the deluxe L-shaped kitchen include a top-of-the-line refrigerator, dishwasher, and built-in range. Many options are available in the selection of these items, depending on the size of the kitchen area and personal preference. Be sure to allow for the additional expense of appliance installations which require relocation of rough-in or new hook ups. Call in a plumber or electrician for all major plumbing or electrical tasks.

Level of Difficulty

Because of the high cost of the deluxe appliances and other expensive materials used in this kitchen, most beginners and handymen should hire a remodeling specialist or general contractor to do the better part of the work. Removing the old cabinets, stripping the floor, and preparing the walls and ceiling are jobs that the homeowner can accomplish to save on labor costs, but even these tasks require knowledge of tools and some remodeling experience. Get some advice from a professional or an experienced do-it-yourselfer before you attempt any operations that are new to you. Also, removal of the old cabinets and appliances usually requires two workers, so plan accordingly and line up some help well in advance of the start of the project. The cabinet and countertop installations for this renovation shouldbe left to experienced tradesmen. Even accomplished do-it-yourselfers should consider restricting their efforts to tasks other than these. As a general rule, beginners should add at least 100% to the man-hours estimates for the jobs which they tackle; handymen, 50%-70%; and experts, 20%.

What to Watch Out For

Corner cabinets can waste considerable space if built and installed in the conventional manner. There are several ways to reclaim some or all of this often wasted cabinet area. One is to install a "lazy susan" or rotating cabinet fixture, to provide shelf and storage space that is immediately accessible. These are commonly installed in base corner units, but they are a special order item and will add to the cost of the cabinets.

DELUXE L-SHAPED KITCHEN

Description	Quantity	Man-hours	Material
Blocking, for mounting cabinets, 2" x 4" stock	32 L.F.	1.0	10.10
Plywood, underlayment grade, 1/2" thick, 4' x 8' sheets	3 Sheets	2.5	53.45
Floor tile, 12" x 12" x 1/8" thick, patterned vinyl	72 S.F.	2.0	261.35
Wall cabinets, 12" deep, hardwood, deluxe	16 L.F.	5.0	858.25
Base cabinets, 24" deep, hardwood, deluxe	12 L.F.	4.0	1185.70
Plywood, sub-base for countertop 1/2" x 4' x 8' sheets	1 Sheet	0.5	17.85
Ceramic tile for countertops and backsplash	53 S.F.	5.0	307.85
Valance board over sink	4 L.F.	0.5	29.05
Trim, cornice molding, stock pine 9/16" x 2-1/4"	20 L.F.	0.5	9.95
Paint, primer & 1 coat, ceiling	96 S.F.	1.0	10.45
Paint cornice trim, puttying, primer & 2 coats	20 L.F.	0.5	1.25
Cooking range, built-in, 30" wide, one oven	1 Ea.	8.0	968.00
Hood for range, 2-speed, 30" wide	1 Ea.	5.5	290.40
Refrigerator, no frost, 19 C.F.	1 Ea.	4.0	1331.00
Sink w/faucets & drain, stainless steel self-rimming, 43" x 22", double bowl	1 Ea.	6.5	423.50
Dishwasher, built-in, 2 cycle	1 Ea.	8.0	471.90
Rough-in, supply, waste & vent for sink & dishwasher	2 Ea.	17.5	159.35
Totals		72.0	$6389.40
Project Size 8' x 12'	Contractor's Fee Including Materials		$11,800

Deluxe L-Shaped Kitchen

If the value of your home is in keeping with this project and the renovation suits your budget, this plan is a good way to increase the efficiency and to improve the appearance of your L-shaped kitchen. The cost of top quality components and professional installation is an investment in a highly visible and heavily utilized area of your home.

DELUXE U-SHAPED KITCHEN

The deluxe facility presented in this plan demonstrates how a basic three wall kitchen layout can take on an elegant appearance while meeting the practical demands of the kitchen. Amenities like a premium-quality range and ceramic tile countertop add to the cost of the renovation, but they return to the homeowner benefits of appearance and efficiency, while increasing the value of the home. Although this kitchen is more expensive to install than a standard facility of comparable size, homeowners can reduce the costs by doing some of the work on their own. Knowing their limits as handymen and taking on the appropriate tasks are the keys to success.

Materials

The selection of materials for the kitchen should begin with the cabinets, since they serve as the focal point of the kitchen's decor. Deluxe kitchens usually include paneled or decorative hardwood cabinets that are durably constructed and carefully finished, but Formica and soft woods are also commonly installed at varying costs. When shopping for the cabinet systems, be sure to get several estimates on the identical or similar units. By reducing the number of variables, you will be able to compare prices more accurately. Be sure to get an itemized written agreement which includes the basic units and all of the auxiliary cabinet materials, like the trim pieces and valance. If installation of the cabinets is part of the contract, be sure to include in the agreement the labor cost for installing any trim items. Unless you are an expert do-it-yourselfer, the cabinets for the U-shaped kitchen should be placed by a professional. The kitchen floor and countertop should match the deluxe quality of thecabinet system. Vinyl flooring is available in a wide range of colors, designs, and surface textures and provides the durability and low maintenance of a proven product. Ceramic and poured composition floors can also be used in deluxe facilities, but they cost more and require

specialized installation skills. The countertop material suggested in this plan is ceramic tile, but Formica is an attractive, less expensive substitute. Remember that the ceramic tiling has to be done on the site after the cabinets are placed and before the sink is installed, so plan the timing carefully to avoid delays. If you are doing the ceramic work on your own, figure on a time-consuming job to cover the three wall surface layout and its backsplash. Selecting the color and design of the tile is an important decision, but you will also want to make sure that the color of the grouting coordinates well with the tile and the room. The preparation and painting of the ceiling and walls should be completed before any other finish materials are placed. Doing these tasks first makes them faster and easier and contributes to a neater end result.

Many different appliance options are open to the homeowner who is planning a deluxe kitchen, including a wide selection of built-in ranges and ovens. Remember that if you are upgrading the present facility from standard to deluxe, additional electrical and, possibly, plumbing work will be required at extra cost. Also, electric-to-gas, and gas-to-electric range conversions involve considerable work by qualified tradesmen, so plan accordingly. The refrigerator and dishwasher should not require additional installation costs, providing that they are not relocated and the rough-in and hook-ups are already in place, The addition of an ice maker or cold water option for a deluxe refrigerator requires extra plumbing to connect the water supply tubing. The conventional range hood can be replaced by an under-counter exhaust and vent system. These units are an expensive option on some built-in ranges, but they work more efficiently than conventional hoods and open up more wall cabinet space above the range. Because all of these appliances demand professional quality installations, do-it-yourselfers who are not experienced in electrical and plumbing work should hire capable people to perform the necessary tasks.

Level of Difficulty

This three wall kitchen project involves a major commitment of both time and money, so tread carefully if you are inclined to do the job on your

own. The basic tasks of removing the old facility, reconditioning and preparing the site for the new products, and applying paint and stain can be accomplished by beginners if they are given ample guidance as they proceed with these operations. They should add 100% to the professional time estimates for these jobs. Handymen should add 50% to the man-hours for the same tasks and plan on doubling the professional time for the flooring, if vinyl tile is the chosen material. The installation of vinyl sheet flooring, ceramic tile, and cabinets should be left to experts and tradesmen. Experts should add 50% to the estimated man-hours for the flooring and ceramic work, at least 75% for the cabinet installation, and 20% for the more basic operations. Except in the case of experts who have had had extensive remodeling experience, the plumbing and electrical work should be performed by professionals.

What to Watch Out For

Ceramic tile provides a durable, attractive, and easily maintained surface for kitchen countertops, but it does have its drawbacks. One is that the material itself is more expensive than Formica and other plastic laminates. Also, because each countertop has to be constructed at the site, the labor costs are higher than shop-fabricated Formica tops. Although ceramic tiles are heat and water resistant, they are prone to chipping and cracking when they are struck by hard objects. The grouting, too, has to be inspected periodically, and repaired, if necessary, to correct cracking that may have developed. Despite these shortcomings, ceramic tile has a neat and elegant appearance which contributes to the overall atmosphere of the deluxe kitchen.

DELUXE U-SHAPED KITCHEN

Description	Quantity	Man -hours	Material
Blocking, for mounting cabinets, 2" x 4" stock	50 L.F.	1.5	15.75
Plywood, underlayment grade, 1/2" thick, 4' x 8' sheets	4 Sheets	1.5	71.25
Flooring, vinyl sheet goods, 0.093" thick	85 S.F.	3.5	241.70
Wall cabinets, 12" deep, hardwood, deluxe	21 L.F.	5.0	1126.43
Base cabinets, 24" deep, hardwood, deluxe	14 L.F.	5.0	1383.30
Plywood sub-base for counter-top, 1/2" x 4' x 8' sheets	2 Sheets	1.0	35.60
Ceramic tile for countertops and backsplash	83 S.F.	7.5	482.05
Valance board over sink	4 L.F.	0.5	29.05
Trim, cornice molding, stock pine, 9/16" x 2-1/4"	30 L.F.	1.0	14.85
Paint, ceiling, primer & 1 coat	100 S.F.	1.0	10.90
Paint, cornice trim, puttying, primer & 1 coat	30 L.F.	0.5	1.85
Cooking range, built-in, 30" wide one oven	1 Ea.	8.0	968.00
Hood for range, 2-speed, 30" wide	1 Ea.	5.5	290.40
Refrigerator, no frost, 19 C.F.	1 Ea.	4.0	1331.00
Sink w/faucets & drain, stainless steel, self-rimming, 43" x 22", double bowl	1 Ea.	6.0	423.50
Dishwasher, built-in	1 Ea.	8.0	471.90
Rough-in, supply, waste & vent for sink & dishwasher	2 Ea.	17.5	159.35
Totals		77.0	$7056.85

Project Size	9'-6" x 10'-6"	Contractor's Fee Including Materials	$15,110

Deluxe U-Shaped Kitchen

Upgrading a U-shaped kitchen to deluxe standards is a challenging undertaking which requires a considerable commitment of both time and money by the homeowner. With some do-it-yourself cost-cutting, however, the renovation can be completed with professional results and at reduced expense.

Deluxe Peninsula Kitchen

The layout of the peninsula kitchen lends itself to being a social and activity center in the home as well as the primary eating and food preparation area. As a result, the installation of deluxe products can be a good investment in an attractive facility. Top quality cabinets, appliances, and surface coverings can turn an old kitchen into a delightful eating and gathering place for family and guests. This model can be used to renovate an existing peninsula design, or to improve a conventional U-shaped layout by adding the peninsula unit. Whatever the case, this plan outlines a remodeling project that is first-rate in appearance, efficiency, and durability. Because of the size of the facility and the cost of its components, do-it-yourselfers should use discretion in tackling the specialized tasks.

Materials

The materials included in the deluxe peninsula kitchen are standard products that have been upgraded. Substitutions of comparable deluxe products are readily available to meet the particular needs and to satisfy the personal taste of the homeowner. Some advance planning and research will get you started. A qualified kitchen expert can help you select the cabinets, surface coverings, and appliances from a range of deluxe components. The large number of cabinets used in the peninsula kitchen, and the complexity of their layout, make them the most important element of the facility. To maintain deluxe standards, the cabinets should be made of quality hard or soft woods with paneled or other decorative features on the doors and drawer facings. Included in the cost of the cabinets in this plan are high quality hardware and the custom features of the peninsula unit. However, the cost for any other cabinet amenities and specialized units must be tacked on to the estimate. A lazy-susan, for example, is a useful device for gaining easier access to the dead storage space found in the corners of both the wall and base units. Cabinet extras like this one are usually expensive, but they complement the other de-

luxe products in the kitchen and add to its operational convenience. The peninsula cabinets can also be imaginatively and attractively customized. Although these modifications may cost more initially, the investment will be returned in the benefits of convenient, personalized use for many years to come. Even if you plan to do some of the work in this kitchen renovation, you should leave the cabinet installation to a professional, unless you are an expert in home remodeling. The cost and magnitude of a four-wall system demand precise installation by a skilled worker.

Like the cabinets, the choices for flooring in this kitchen is top quality. Various options are available, but vinyl tile and sheet goods are among the most popular kitchen floor materials because of their appearance, low maintenance, and durability. Also, because they are manufactured in so many colors, surface textures, and designs, vinyl floor coverings are relatively easy to coordinate with the counter top, cabinets, and appliances. The surface of the countertop for this deluxe kitchen may be covered with a high quality ceramic tile or appropriate Formica veneer. Both of these products are heat and water resistant, durable, and attractive. Although ceramic tile adds to the deluxe appearance of the facility, it is more expensive than Formica and harder to install. If you plan to do this part of the project on your own, be sure to get some advice and installation tips from a knowledgeable person. Also, before you choose tile for the peninsula countertop, consider the intended use of this area. For example, if it is to be used as a writing as well as an eating surface, ceramic tiling might not be a good choice. Formica or even hardwood could be used instead for the peninsula unit surface, and you could still put ceramic tile on the other countertops in the kitchen.

The appliances for the deluxe peninsula kitchen should also complement the other quality products used in the facility. Remember that additional electrical work may have to be completed before the built-in range, dishwasher, and range hood are installed. The sink and dishwasher will also require new plumbing rough-in if they are being relocated. These tasks should be accomplished by qualified professionals or by expert handymen who have considerable electrical and plumbing experience.

Level of Difficulty

Most of the tasks involved in remodeling a peninsula kitchen are highly specialized and require considerable ability in the use of tools. Experts who have extensive remodeling experience should be able to handle most of the work, but they should proceed slowly on highly demanding jobs like hanging the cabinets and installing the ceramic tile. If they plan to complete these tasks, they should allow ample time— perhaps double the professional time estimate— as the materials are expensive and quality workmanship is called for. Experts should add 20% to the man-hours estimate for all other tasks and, depending on the amount of their experience, more for the flooring, plumbing, and electrical work. Handymen and beginners should restrict their involvement to the basic tasks like the removal of the old kitchen, reconditioning of the site, and painting. They should add 50% and 100%, respectively, to the professional time for all of these tasks.

What to Watch Out For

One way to enhance both its appearance and function is to add electrical conveniences and lighting fixtures. There are many possibilities; for example, install one or several duplex outlets in convenient locations on and around the unit, or build direct or indirect lighting into the underside of the overhead unit. Both of these electrical improvements can be done for a reasonable cost, yet they provide a lot of convenience. A warming plate can also be installed in the surface of the base unit, but this electrical amenity will add significantly to the cost. Be sure to have the wiring capacity for the existing kitchen circuits checked before you add these or other new electrical fixtures. These items should be carefully planned in advance, as spur-of-the-moment modifications will cost more for installation after the finished materials are in place.

DELUXE PENINSULA KITCHEN

Description	Quantity	Man-hours	Material
Blocking, for mounting cabinets, 2" x 4" stock	72 L.F.	2.5	22.65
Plywood, underlayment grade, 1/2" thick, 4' x 8' sheets	4 Sheets	1.5	71.25
Flooring, vinyl sheet goods, 0.125" thick	100 S.F.	3.0	393.25
Wall cabinets, 12" deep, hardwood, deluxe	34 L.F.	8.0	1823.75
Base cabinets, 24" deep, hardwood, deluxe	20 L.F.	7.0	1976.20
Peninsula base cabinet, custom-built, 24" deep x 9' long	9 L.F.	4.5	1089.00
Plywood sub-base for counter-top, 1/2" x 4' x 8' sheets	3 Sheets	1.0	53.45
Ceramic tile for countertop and backsplash	106 S.F.	9.5	615.65
Valance board over sink	4 L.F.	0.5	29.05
Trim, cornice molding, stock pine, 9/16" x 2-1/4"	46 L.F.	1.5	22.85
Paint, ceiling, primer & 1 coat	125 S.F.	1.0	13.60
Paint, cornice trim, puttying, primer & 1 coat	46 L.F.	1.0	2.80
Cooking range, built-in, 30" wide, one oven	1 Ea.	8.0	968.00
Hood for range, 2-speed, 30" wide, vented	1 Ea.	5.5	290.40
Refrigerator, no frost, 19 C.F.	1 Ea.	4.0	1331.00
Sink w/faucets & drain, stainless steel self-rimming, 33" x 22", double bowl	1 Ea.	6.0	371.45
Dishwasher, built-in	1 Ea.	8.0	471.90
Rough-in, supply, waste & vent for sink & dishwasher	2 Ea.	17.5	159.35
Totals		**91.0**	**$9705.60**

Project Size	9'-6" x 13'	Contractor's Fee Including Materials	$17,740

Deluxe Peninsula Kitchen
The deluxe peninsula kitchen is an expensive and complex remodeling project which can enhance the quality of life in your home. The high grade of its components can add value to your dwelling, while improving its appearance and versatility.

Deluxe Island Kitchen

Range Hood
Cooking Range
Wall Cabinets
Ceramic Tile Countertop & Backsplash
Base Cabinets
Island Cabinet w/ Laminated Maple Top
Vinyl Floor Tile

Dishwasher
Valance Board
Sink W/Faucet
Wall Cabinets
Base Cabinets
Refrigerator
Shelving - Formica Covered
Formica Desk Top

Like the other deluxe kitchens presented in this section, this facility features the upgrading of standard kitchen materials to top-of-the-line products. If it is within your budget and fits in with your home and lifestyle, a deluxe island kitchen may be the appropriate remodeling design to follow. This plan outlines a luxurious alternative to simpler, more standard arrangements. Good planning and professional workmanship will be rewarded with a beautiful, durable, and functional kitchen area.

Materials

Because this kitchen plan involves deluxe appliances, cabinets, and other materials, its cost is substantially higher than that of a standard facility of the same size. All of the basic components of the kitchen can be replaced by less expensive items, and substitutions can be made to reduce the cost to a compromise level somewhere between that of a standard facility and this one. Remember, though, that any replacements should be made with discretion, as the aesthetic balance of the kitchen's appearance is important. Your personal taste and the decor of your home should serve as your guides when determining the materials for the new facility.

One of the most pleasing features of this kitchen plan is the U-shaped cabinet layout with a convenience island located in the center of the room. This layout requires a fairly large kitchen area to ensure enough floor and counter space without cramming its design and creating a closed-in feeling. The island cabinet puts normally wasted floor space to practical use as a food preparation or utility work surface. Depending on the intended function of the island, a variety of surface materials can be used, from laminated hardwoods in butcher-block design,

to stone, ceramic tile, or Formica-type coverings. The wall and base cabinets which border the island cabinet can be constructed from a variety of hard or soft woods with paneled or decorative drawer and door facings. The valance boards, desk top, and shelving should be included in the design and manufacture of the cabinet system.

The materials used for the floor and countertop of the new kitchen are products which complement the elegance of the cabinets. This plan includes durable vinyl tiles for the floor surface, but sheet goods are also available at varying costs. The ceramic tiling on the countertop and backsplash provide a durable and attractive alternative to plastic laminate coverings. The design and capacity of the appliances to be included in the deluxe island kitchen should be determined by such variables as the size of your family, extent of anticipated use of the kitchen, and food preparation methods. Such considerations as preference for gas or electric range, refrigerator and freezer capacity, and general use of appliances should be carefully weighed before you select the fixtures and decide on their location in the new kitchen. Conversion from an electric to gas range, for example, requires significant rough-in preparation which should be built into both the design and the cost of the overall kitchen plan before the work begins. Other appliance plumbing and electrical relocations should be similarly planned and incorporated into the cost of the facility before you begin the renovation. Changing your mind on such matters after the work has begun will usually cost you more money and aggravation.

Level of Difficulty

The kitchen is a challenging room for the handyman to remodel because carpentry, plumbing, electrical, flooring, and other specialized building skills are required. Also, most of the materials used in kitchen construction are expensive, and many are difficult to install. For example, the planning, measuring, and placing of the

cabinet and counter top systems in this plan involve three walls totaling 30 linear feet, with appropriate allowances for a window, sink, under-counter dishwasher, refrigerator, built-in range, oven and hood, as well as the island unit. Overseeing and accomplishing this cabinet installation requires the skill of a professional. Experts should have prior experience with cabinet installation and tile work if they plan to tackle the project. Beginners and handymen can save on labor costs by removing the old facility, laying the underlayment, and reconditioning and finishing the walls and ceiling, but they should leave the cabinet and appliance installation and the tile work to professionals. They should add 100% and 50% respectively, to the professional time for laying the plywood and painting. Experts should add 20% to the time estimates for these tasks and 50% to 100% to the time for the more specialized jobs within the kitchen.

What to Watch Out For

If you plan to do some or all of the work on this remodeling project, take stock of your building skills and the amount of free time available in your personal schedule. Kitchens, like baths, are difficult facilities to remodel because their operation is vital to the daily routine of home life. Disturbing their function can cause considerable inconvenience, especially if the interruption is prolonged and the work done piecemeal on weekends, evenings, and holidays. In most cases, a concentrated and limited period of remodeling is desirable for kitchen projects. Make plans ahead of time to arrange for alternative meal preparation and to allow for the inconvenience. If you are doing the work on your own, build in some extra time for those hidden problems that always surface.

DELUXE ISLAND KITCHEN

Description	Quantity	Man-hours	Material
Blocking, for mounting cabinets, 2" x 4" stock	68 L.F.	2.5	21.40
Plywood, underlayment grade, 1/2" thick, 4' x 8' sheets	6 sheets	2.5	106.90
Floor tile, 12" x 12" x 1/16" thick, embossed vinyl composition	125 S.F.	3.0	98.30
Wall cabinets, deluxe, hardwood, 12" deep	28 L.F.	6.0	1394.60
Base cabinets, deluxe, hardwood, 24" deep	23 L.F.	10.5	2964.25
Island cabinet, 30" x 48" base	1 Ea.	2.0	726.00
Plywood sub-base for countertops 1/2" x 4' x 8' sheets	3 Sheets	0.5	35.65
Ceramic tile for countertops and backsplash	105 S.F.	9.0	609.85
Island Top, maple, solid laminated 1-1/2" thick	24 L.F.	7.0	871.20
Valance boards over sink & bookshelf	8 L.F.	0.5	58.10
Desk-top, 1-1/4" thick, Formica-covered	1 Ea.	1.0	18.40
Shelving, 3/4" thick, Formica-covered	8 L.F.	1.0	49.35
Trim, cornice molding, stock pine, 9/16" x 2-1/4"	36 L.F.	1.0	17.85
Paint, primer & 1 coat, ceiling & walls	170 S.F.	1.5	18.50
Paint, primer & 1 coat, cornice trim, puttying	36 L.F.	0.5	2.20
Cooking range, built-in, 30" wide, one oven	1 Ea.	8.0	968.00
Hood for range, 2-speed, 30" wide	1 Ea.	5.5	290.40
Refrigerator, no frost, 19 C.F.	1 Ea.	4.0	1331.00
Sink w/faucets & drain, stainless steel, self-rimming, 43" x 22", double bowl	1 Ea.	6.0	371.45
Dishwasher, built-in, 2 cycle	1 Ea.	8.0	471.90
Rough-in, supply, waste & vent for sink and dishwasher	2 Ea.	17.5	159.35
Totals		97.5	$10,584.65
Project Size 11'-6" x 14'-6"		Contractor's Fee Including Materials	$19,060

FREESTANDING FIREPLACE

An alternative to conventional masonry or pre-constructed built-in fireplaces is the freestanding, prefabricated model. These units can be installed economically by the experienced do-it-yourselfer. The hearth in this plan is brick masonry, but prefabricated hearths are also available. Because the fixture stands away from the walls, expensive and time-consuming room preparations are usually not required. Sometimes the walls will need to be treated with fire-proofing materials because of their proximity to the fireplace or local building codes.

Materials

Very few conventional building materials are required for this project, as the installation of a free-standing fireplace involves limited preparation. Besides the fireplace itself, a hearth of some type must be placed under and around the base of the unit, and the flue pipe must be installed with appropriate fittings. The fireplace is available as a preassembled unit or in sections that require assembly before being installed. Many different styles and designs can be purchased at varying costs, but most of the units have a base with a hood to divert smoke and the by-products of combustion into the flue. The base of some models comes factory-equipped with a heat resistant liner, while others require the application of a protective substance or recommend that sand or heat resistant tiles be used to protect the metal base from damage caused by overheating. Some of the units are enclosed except for an access and viewing opening in one section; other designs feature 360° of heat-resistant glass between the hood and base. One of the advantages of free-standing fireplace units is that they are capable of radiating heat in all directions, and, therefore, surpass conventional wall fireplaces in heating efficiency.

A fire-resistant hearth is a vital part of a freestanding stove installation. This plan recommends the use of standard new or used brick placed on a mortar bed and then grouted to form the hearth, but a wide variety of tiles may also be used. An economical hearth can be built with stone fragments or other loose non-combustible materials, placed 2″ to 3″ deep within a framed circular, oval, or square perimeter. Regardless of the type of material and the design used, make sure that you follow the manufacturer's recommendations and local code regulations for safe surface and depth dimensions of the hearth.

The materials used for the flue pipe assembly are normally included as part of the fireplace kit. If they are not included, then check with your retailer or the manufacturer of the unit and purchase approved insulated chimney pipe, high quality stove pipe, and similarly safe and durable fittings and flashings. Make sure that the pipe matches the fireplace unit, as it is one of the bigger investments in this project and replacing it would be costly. Unlike prefabricted built-in fireplace installations, the section of flue pipe which runs from the top of the free-standing fireplace to just below the ceiling does not have to be made of insulated materials. In fact, it is to your advantage to run uninsulated stove pipe in this section because it radiates precious heat.

Above this section, from just below the ceiling through to the top of the flue, you should use the recommended insulated chimney pipe material.

Level of Difficulty

The installation of a free-standing fireplace does not require a high level of ability in the use of tools. Beginners, with help, can handle some of the tasks required to complete the installation. The most difficult operation involves cutting the openings in the ceiling and roof for the flue. Beginners should hire a qualified professional to do this part of the installation and to place the chimney pipe, the flashing unit, the joist shield, and the ceiling support fittings. Handymen should be able to accomplish this entire installation, but they should get some advice and instruction before cutting the openings if they are inexperienced in this task. Experts should be able to complete all parts of the project in 10%

additional time over the man-hours estimate. Handymen should add 30% to the estimated time, and slightly more for the hole-cutting and roof flashing installation. Beginners should add 75% to 100% to the professional time for the fireplace unit and hearth installations and hire a professional for the rest of the job.

What to Watch Out For

One of the problems encountered when installing flue pipe is keeping the line of pipe straight and plumb from the top of the fireplace through to the roof. Because the sections of insulated chimney pipe interlock precisely, they cannot be bent or angled without damaging the connection and creating a fire hazard. It is important, therefore, that you take the time to align the centers of the proposed openings before you make the cuts. After you have determined where the ceiling opening is to be located (midway between joists directly above the location of the fireplace) use a plumb bob to find the center point of the roof opening. Double check your marks and then make your cuts slightly oversize to allow for easier placement of the preassembled chimney pipe.

FREESTANDING FIREPLACE			
Description	Quantity	Man-hours	Material
Cut ceiling & roof opening for flue	2 Ea.	4.0	0.00
Frame through ceiling and roof, 2" x 6"	16 L.F.	0.5	7.55
Fittings, ceiling support, 10" diam.	1 Ea.	1.0	72.60
Fittings, joist shield, 10" diam.	1 Ea.	1.0	41.15
Hearth, 5' x 5', standard size brick	1 Ea.	8.0	108.90
Fireplace, prefab, freestanding, with hood, screen & flue	1 Ea.	6.0	726.00
Flue, 10" diam., additional height needed	5 V.L.F.	5.0	344.85
Fittings, roof flashing, 6" diam.	1 Ea.	0.5	30.55
Fittings, round top, 10" diam.	1 Ea.	1.0	83.50
	Totals	27.0	$1415.10
Project Size 5' x 5' x 13'	Contractor's Fee Including Materials		$2980

Freestanding Fireplace

Free-standing fireplaces provide an economical alternative to conventional and prefabricated built-in fireplaces. They are easier to install and offer the advantages of greater heating efficiency than most built-in installations. With all these features, plus a choice of available styles, these units can fit harmoniously into many homes.

BUILT-IN FIREPLACE

Flue

2-2" x 6" Header

Existing Wall

2" x 4" Studs

Drywall

Mantel Beam

Brick Facing

Brick Support Angle

Prefabricated Freestanding Fireplace

Paint

Baseboard

Brick Hearth

With careful planning and appropriate design, a new fireplace can make a drab room come alive with atmosphere. Conventional fireplaces made of brick and/or other masonry materials are difficult to install in an existing house, but other options are available. One of the most popular alternatives is a prefabricated fireplace unit that comes from the supplier ready for installation. Before placing the unit, the area where it is to be located has to be framed and prepared to receive it. The extent of preliminary work depends on many variables, such as the floor level where it is to be placed, whether it is to be installed on an interior or exterior wall, and, especially in old houses, the amount of leveling and reconditioning required for the support floor surface.

Materials

The materials required to complete the installation include the prefabricated free-standing fireplace unit, its flue-related accessories, a simulated brick chimney top, brick and masonry materials for the facing, and conventional framing and wall supplies. The heart of the project is the prefabricated fireplace, which is an efficient and economical alternative to standard brick and mortar installations. Many different manufacturers produce these units, usually from sheet steel. The structure may look heavy, but it is lightweight enough to be carried and placed by two people. Also, most prefabricated fireplaces do not require additional floor support, as they weigh about as much as a heavy piece of furniture. Make sure that you purchase a unit that complies with the standards of stove and free-standing fireplace approval agencies. Also, follow carefully the manufacturer's instructions and precautions during installation of the fireplace and its flue assembly. Before the unit is placed, the cavity or wall area where it will sit permanently has to be framed with 2" x 4"s. The cost of the framing materials for this operation will depend on the particular location of the fireplace. For example, if the unit is to extend

outside of the house, the exterior wall will have to be built, at more expense, to enclose the fireplace unit and the flue. If the installation is to be located inside the room (as in this example) and backed to an existing partition or wall, the materials cost will be lower. Remember that if the fireplace unit is located in the room, it will take up considerable floor space. The exterior placement may cost you more, but the extra expense may be worth it to save floor space. After the fireplace has been put into position and the flue pipe safely tied in, the new framing should be covered with 1/2" fire resistant drywall which is then taped, finished, and painted or wallpapered to suit the room's decor.

The brick hearth and facing recommended in this plan can enhance the fireplace opening, with other noncombustible veneers providing viable options at varying costs. The laminated hardwood mantel is one of many alternatives available for dressing up the opening. The design and choice of materials for the facing, hearth, and mantel should be given careful consideration before the selections are made. Brick, marble, and stone are among the materials that can be used. Some extra expense may be worthwhile, as the aesthetic appeal of the fireplace is important. Take care in cutting the openings for the flue pipe and be sure to use high quality fittings and flashing where necessary. Joist shields should also be installed where needed for safety. A simulated brick chimney top is a feature which adds to the appearance of the job by hiding the top of the insulated piping. If the pipe extends from a rear-facing or hidden section of your roof or if you are not fussy about the exposed pipe, then omit the simulated chimney as a decorative extra and deduct its cost from the project.

Level of Difficulty

Although the installation of a prefabricated fireplace may appear to be a major undertaking, with the right conditions it can be a fairly uncomplicated project for the capable do-it-yourselfer. The masonry tasks demand specialized skills and should be completed by a professional if you have not had experience in laying stone or brick. Remember that attractive brick work on the hearth and facing are important, so even experts may consider hiring a professional mason. Most of the other tasks, including cutting the ceiling and roof openings, can be completed by handymen and experts. Get some advice from a knowledgeable person if you have not cut ceilings or roof holes before. Beginners should limit themselves to the finish work, the framing, and drywalling. If you are a beginner,

seek some help before you attempt any task that you have not done before. Beginners should also leave the actual fireplace and flue installation to a competent contractor. Experts should add about 10% to the man-hours estimate and more for the masonry operations. Handymen should tack on about 40% to the time for the framing, drywalling, and finish work, excluding the masonry. They should increase the time for hole cutting and fireplace and flue installation by 100% if they have not had prior experience with these tasks. Beginners should not attempt the masonry or the fireplace and flue installation, and they should double the time estimate for any other jobs.

What to Watch Out For

Two aspects of this project should be noted as critical, one affecting materials and labor costs and the other, safety. The expense for both materials and labor will vary significantly from the plan's estimate if the prefabricated fireplace unit will be used as a replacement for an existing fireplace facility or if extensive demolition and alteration of the site are required before the new fireplace is installed. The materials cost will also be increased considerably if an exterior chase has to be built to house the fireplace and flue pipe, especially if the fireplace is to be located on the first floor of a two-story house. Safety is another aspect of this project which has to be monitored carefully throughout the installation process. Follow the manufacturer's safety recommendations closely and observe local building codes which deal with fireplace or wood-burning stove regulations. Most communities require approval of all new fireplace and stove installations, so arrange to have the inspection before you drywall the fireplace enclosure.

BUILT-IN FIREPLACE			
Description	Quantity	Man-hours	Material
Framing, fireplace enclosure, 2" x 4" studs & plates, 16" O.C.	14 L.F.	2.5	50.00
Header over opening, 2" x 6"	12 L.F.	0.5	5.65
Cut ceiling & roof opening for flue	2 Ea.	3.0	0.00
Frame, through ceiling & roof, 2" x 6"	16 L.F.	0.5	7.55
Fittings, ceiling support, 10" diam.	1 Ea.	1.0	72.60
Fittings, joist shield, 10" diam.	1 Ea.	1.0	47.20
Drywall, 1/2" thick on walls, fire resistant, taped & finished, 4' x 8' sheets	4 Sheets	2.5	44.90
Fireplace, prefab, built-in, with hood, screen & flue	1 Ea.	9.0	762.30
Facing, 6' x 5', standard size brick	30 S.F.	11.0	66.15
Hearth, 3' x 6', standard size brick	1 Ea.	8.0	108.90
Mantel beam, laminated hardwood, 2-1/4" x 10-1/2" x 6'	1 Ea.	2.0	102.85
Simulated brick chimney top, 3' high, 16" x 16"	1 Ea.	1.0	151.25
Fittings, roof flashing, 6" diam.	1 Ea.	0.5	30.55
Trim, baseboard, 9/16" x 3-1/2"	10 L.F.	0.5	8.45
Painting, walls & trim, primer & 1 coat	90 S.F.	1.0	98.00
	Totals	44.0	$1556.35
Project Size 5' x 6' x 13'	Contractor's Fee Including Materials		$3780

MASONRY FIREPLACE

Brick Chimney
8" x 12" Flue Lining
Rotary Control Damper
Ash Dump Door
Concrete Hearth Slab
Concrete Block
Concrete Chimney Footing

2" x 4" Studs
Drywall
2-2" x 8" Header
Mantel Beam
Brick Facing
Brick Fireplace Box
Brick Hearth
2-2" x 10" Headers
Cleanout Door

Although the construction of a masonry fireplace involves considerable time, inconvenience, and expense, it is a durable fixture which contributes to the appearance and atmosphere of a room. Both of these features make it a good investment. Masonry work does require some specialized skills and tools, however, and do-it-yourselfers should be cautioned about tackling this project if they do not have any experience in this area. The site preparation, actual construction of the fireplace and chimney, and outside and inside finishing operations should all be carefully planned in the proper sequence so that inconvenience can be kept to a minimum. If you have not done masonry work before, seek advice from a qualified person before you start, and do some reading on the subject.

Materials

The materials used in the installation of a masonry fireplace include conventional masonry products, as well as framing lumber for alternations that need to be made to accommodate the new structure. There are also some incidental materials associated with the fireplace, chimney, and flue. The total cost of these items will vary with each installation, depending on the amount of required site preparation, the height of the chimney, and the extent of finish work needed to receive the new chimney on the side and roof of the house. Costs for materials will also vary with the type of masonry veneer selected for the facing of the fireplace, hearth, and chimney. Before the fireplace and chimney can be put into position, extensive site work is required on the inside and, usually, on the outside of the house. The estimates given in this plan will help you to determine the cost for this work. On the inside of the house, framing materials are required to maintain the floor and exterior wall support system when the openings are cut for the hearth and fireplace. Before cutting the wall opening and installing the headers, be sure to provide temporary ceiling support, as the outside wall may be a load bearing structure. The same precaution should be taken before cutting the floor joists for the hearth. The materials for these temporary 2" x 4" support partitions have not been included in the estimate, but the same lumber used for the ceiling support can be reused for floor support and, possibly, elsewhere in the installation where 2" x 4"s are required. If you have not performed framing and support operations before, get some advice before you tackle them, as mistakes and poor workmanship can cause serious structural damage to the house. Outside of the house, the site must be prepared for the construction of a foundation to bear the weight of the chimney. Because this foundation should extend to the full depth of the house's foundation, a considerable amount of excavating has to be done.

This excavation usually has to be done by hand because of its proximity to the structure and finished landscaping, but excavation by machine can be done at extra cost. After the excavation has been completed, a footing is placed; and later, concrete blocks are laid to serve as the foundation for the fireplace and chimney. Additional labor costs also have to be included for removing the siding and preparing the rake boards or eaves to receive the new chimney. The masonry materials used in this plan include bricks, concrete blocks, flue liner, and mortar. These items are readily available from most building and masonry supply outlets, but it pays to shop around for them. Here are a few suggestions to assist you in the purchase. First, try to buy all of the materials from the same retailer. By consolidating your order, you will get a better price. Second, have the materials delivered to your property, with the delivery charge included in the bill at the time of purchase. Unless the materials have to be transported an excessive distance, most retailers will not charge you for delivery of an order of this size. Third, select the veneer material carefully, as conventional red brick is only one of many options. Field stone, quarry-prepared stone, and cobblestone are other choices that function well and give a different appearance. The costs for these alternative materials will vary, depending on the required preparation of the stone, its quality, and its availability. Concrete block with stucco veneer is an attractive, yet economical option for chimney design. The appropriate fittings, prefabricated firebox, and roof flashing should be selected with the aid of a mason and/or a reputable retailer if you are unfamiliar with these specialty items. Make sure, for example, that you match the size of the cast iron damper unit and firebox and that you install appropriately sized clean-out fittings. The flash-

ing required to join chimney and roof must be carefully installed to assure that the structure is weather-tight. If the new chimney is placed on the gutter side of the roof, a cricket (a sort of diverter) will have to be constructed at extra cost. Additional expense will also be incurred if a chimney cap is needed to avert downdrafts in your fireplace. The rental of staging or scaffolding is one more cost to figure in for work on the chimney construction.

Level of Difficulty

Experts and some experienced handymen should be able to complete the framing tasks, the excavation and footing, and possibly the chimney foundation. Beginners should limit themselves to the excavation and leave the remainder of the project to a professional. Handymen and experts should add about 60% and 30% respectively, to the man-hours estimates for the framing and site preparation operations. If you plan to do the masonry work, and are inexperienced in bricklaying, then double or even triple the professional time, even if you are an expert in other remodeling skills. Plan to work very slowly at first, with a gradual increase in productivity as you gain experience and the project progresses.

What to Watch Out For

One of the most important elements of any fireplace is the firebox. Inaccurate alignment or incorrect sizing of this component can adversely affect the fireplace's operation by causing inefficient draft. Seek advice from a mason before you construct the firebox, as his experience and knowledge can help prevent the incorrect or ineffective placement of this vital fireplace component. It may be worth the expense of hiring a mason for this task if you do not have the skill and know-how to complete it on your own.

MASONRY FIREPLACE

Description	Quantity	Man-hours	Material
Excavating by hand, heavy soil, for chimney foundation	9 C.Y.	18.0	0.00
Concrete chimney footing	0.5 C.Y.	2.0	62.00
Concrete block, 8" thick, for foundation wall, 32" x 60" x 8'	85 S.F.	8.0	140.00
Concrete block, 8" thick, for chimney, 32" x 40" x 8'	70 S.F.	6.5	127.05
Framing, joists, 2" x 10", fireplace foundation opening	30 L.F.	1.0	24.00
Cleanout door & frame, cast iron, 8" x 8"	1 Ea.	1.0	14.50
Framing, walls, header over fireplace opening, 2" x 8" & 2" x 4"	20 L.F.	1.0	13.80
Fireplace box, complete	1 Ea.	8.0	133.10
Damper, rotary control, cast iron, 30" opening	1 Ea.	1.5	54.00
Facing, 6' x 5', standard size brick	30 S.F.	11.0	55.00
Hearth, 3' x 6', standard size brick	1 Ea.	8.0	200.00
Mantel beam, rough texture wood, 4" x 8" x 6'	6 L.F.	1.5	25.00
Demolition, remove siding, cut roof	1 Ea.	8.0	0.00
Chimney, 16" x 20" x 12", standard size brick, 8" x 12" flue	12 V.L.F.	12.0	240.75
Flashing at siding & roof	30 S.F.	2.0	49.00
	Totals	89.5	$1102.20

Project Size	6' x 6' x 20'	Contractor's Fee Including Materials	$4190

DISAPPEARING STAIRWAY

2" x 8" Trimmer Joist

Existing Joists

2-2" x 8" Header

Trim

Disappearing Stairway

The disappearing or fold-down stairway can solve attic and storage area access problems without wasting valuable floor space. The installation of the unit is a moderately difficult operation, but one that advanced beginners could tackle and complete as a weekend project. It must be done to professional standards, however, as it can otherwise become dangerous. The various fittings, screws, nuts, and bolts also tend to loosen and require periodic tightening to keep the structure strong and safe. Because the stairway is very steep with narrow treads, it is really more like a convenient ladder than a set of stairs. On account of these drawbacks, a disappearing stairway should not be installed as an economical substitute for a permanently placed staircase.

Materials

The list of materials needed for the disappearing stairway installation begins with the factory-prepared unit. Conventional framing and support lumber will also be needed to restore the ceiling bracings that are weakened when room is made for the stairway. The unit comes from the supplier fully assembled and with complete instructions and guidelines for the installation procedure. Several manufacturers produce the stairway units in varying levels of quality and cost. Shop around and purchase the one which best suits your needs. Before you place and secure the stairway in its permanent position, check it over carefully by examining the condition of the wood and the tightness of the fittings and fasteners. The treads, rails, and supports should be solid and free of cracks or imperfections. Some of the units come with a built-in handrail, but others require installation of an accompanying safety rail during the stairway's placement. If your stairway is the latter type, make sure that you take the time to attach the handrail carefully, as it is an essential safety item. Regardless of the quality or design of the disappearing stairway which you have selected, follow precisely the manufacturer's installation instructions and guidelines.

The framing and support materials used to strengthen the ceiling openingfor the stairway unit are basically the same as those included for the circular stairway project. A general rule is that the joist materials should match the dimensions of the existing joists on the floor of your attic or storage room. In most newer homes, the joists or stringers are 2″ x 8″s or 2″ x 6″s depending on the structural design of the house and location of the area accessed by the stairway. If the disappearing stairway is to be placed near a supporting wall or partition, the required amount of support lumber will be minimal. However, if the unit has to be placed in the middle of the ceiling, away from partition or wall support, additional joists and blocking may be needed for adequate support. Galvanized joist hangers should also be used where needed for the headers and trimmer joists. The trim pieces used to face the unit should match the design of the trim work in the room or hallway where the stairway is placed. After the unit is installed and trimmed, it can be painted to blend in with the ceiling.

Level of Difficulty

This project places moderate demands on the skill level of the handyman. With some advice and instruction from a professional, advanced beginners can handle most of the tasks. The biggest challenge involved in the installation process is the cutting of the opening and subsequent joist support placement. These are moderately difficult procedures because of the awkward ceiling location and the cutting by power or hand tools overhead or in a stooped position from the attic floor. If you don't have skill with tools, especially the use of a circular or saber saw overhead, then hire a contractor to do the cutting and joist work. Most handymen should be able to complete this project if they have had experience with cutting joists beforehand. If you are reasonably skilled in the use of tools, but have not performed these specific tasks before, then seek some advice before you start the project. Experts should have no trouble in completing all tasks required to install the stairway and should add about 10% to the estimated professional time. Handymen should add about 30% to the man-hours if they are exerienced in cutting and joist support work, and about 50% if they are not. Beginners should not attempt the cutting and joist support operations unless they are advanced enough to use tools in the awkward positions required for this installation. Regardless of your level of remodeling skill,

bear in mind that the installation of a disappearing stairway is a two-man job.

What to Watch Out For

The prefabricated disappearing stairway unit is ready to be placed in the prepared opening as soon as it is uncrated; but it should be handled carefully, because it is heavy and can be put out of square if dropped or mishandled. Take some time to make up temporary guides out of strapping or other scrap lumber, and tack them to the ceiling side of the unit. These guides help to keep the face of the unit flush with the ceiling and can double as temporary supports while the stairway unit is fastened from above. You can also make up a "T" to hold the assembly in place while it is being fastened. If you plan to refinish the ceiling below, you can tack two pieces of strapping across the opening and place the unit on them from above. Two workers are required for the placement of the unit, one above to do the fastening, and one below to position the stairway and to man the temporary supports. When fastening the unit, use shims to keep it square and to avoid bowing of the side pieces of the framer. Before seating the fasteners, double check the stairway box to see that it is square. If it is not, the unit will not seat properly in the fold-up position, and the ends of the stair rails will not sit evenly on the floor when the unit is in fold-down position. Follow the manufacturer's recommendations for trimming the stair rails at the correct length and angle.

DISAPPEARING STAIRWAY			
Description	Quantity	Man-hours	Material
Cut opening for stairway, 30" x 60"	1 Ea.	2.0	0.00
Rough in opening for stairway, headers, double 2" x 8" stock	12 L.F.	1.0	8.30
Trimmer, joists, fastened to existing joists, 2" x 8" stock	28 L.F.	0.5	13.20
Hangers for headers & joists, 18 ga. galv. for 2" x 8" joists	4 Ea.	0.5	2.65
Blocking, miscellaneous to joists, 2" x 8" stock	8 L.F.	0.5	5.35
Stairway, disappearing, custom grade, pine, 8'-6" ceiling	1 Ea.	2.5	121.00
Trim, casing, 11/16" x 2'-2"	16 L.F.	1.0	7.00
Totals		8.0	$157.50
Project Size 16' x 20'	Contractor's Fee Including Materials		$440

Disappearing Stairway

A disappearing staircase is one way of solving access problems to an attic or storage area. The prefabricated unit is moderately difficult to install, but the job can be completed within a workday by most handymen and experts.

CIRCULAR STAIRWAY

Aluminum Railing & Balusters

1" x 12" Pine Trim

Oak Platform

Trimmer Joist 2" x 10"

Existing Floor

2-2" x 10" Header

Spiral Aluminum Stair

Aluminum Balusters & Railing

Oak Treads

While conventional staircases take up a significant area on two levels, circular stairways can be an efficient alternative, particularly in smaller dwellings where space is at a premium. A prefabricated model can simplify the project and provide a new or more efficient stairway between levels of the house.

Materials

The materials used for this project include the factory-made circular stairway unit and the framing and support materials required to maintain the floor and ceiling strength. The stairway itself is spiral in design, consisting of a heavy aluminum or steel center support pole and triangular treads which fan outward from it. Several other tread materials are available at varying costs, including steel and cast iron. The stairway comes from the supplier in a prepackaged kit with instructions and guidelines for installation. After the ceiling opening has been cut to the dimensions specified by the manufacturer, it should be framed. The stairway is then assembled in place by sections, and plumbed, leveled, and fastened in its final location. After the first step, which involves cutting out the required ceiling and floor spaces, the exposed joists will need to be boxed off and framed. The lumber used for the trimmer joists andheaders should match the existing joists, which are usually 2" x 10"s. Additional 2" x 10"s may be required for-blocking near the opening. These and any joist hangers that are needed will add some extra cost to the project.

Because much of the load of the stairway is concentrated on the base plate, additional sup-port should be provided beneath the floor on which the stairway stands. Usually, doubling the existing 2" x 10"s in the area directly under the unit and adding supplementary blocking is enough. Plan on spending some extra time and money for this operation if you have to cut into a finished ceiling below to install these additional floor support members. If you are inexperienced in these tasks, then seek assistance or hire a professional to do the work. Inadequate placement of these structural components can cost you more in the long run because of repairs needed to correct sagging ceilings or floors.

The materials used to finish the ceiling cut-out should match the trim work in the room below. The rough 2" x 10" box should first be faced with pine boards and then finished with one of several available types of trim. Care should be taken at the start in cutting the stairway opening to avoid the extra expense of patching the ceiling material around it later.

Level of Difficulty

The installation of a circular stairway may at first appear to be a routine project, but the consequences of doing the work incorrectly make it a job for accomplished handymen. Beginners may be able to assemble the stairway and do the finish work, but they should hire a professional contractor to cut the opening and reinforce the joists. Experts and handymen who have experience in framing should be able to accomplish most of the work on this project. Handymen without experience in structural carpentry should get some help and guidance before attempting those tasks. Beginners should add 150% to the estimated professional time if they plan to assemble the stairway and secure the permanent installation. They should also seek professional assistance on the task before they tackle it. Handymen should add 90% to the man-hours estimate for the actual stairway installation and 75% to the time for cutting and framing work if they have some experience with these kinds of tasks. They should double the time for the cutting and joist work if they have not performed this task before. Experts should add 20%-30% to the man-hours estimates throughout the project.

What to Watch Out For

There are several considerations that can save you time and money on this project. One is selecting the right location for the new stairway if the choice is open to you. A position near a corner or wall is desirable because it normally involves less reinforcing work. Remember that you have to be aware of head room requirements at the top of the stairway, particularly if it leads to an attic or room with sloped ceilings. If the stairway leads to a second or third story room with a finished floor, extra materials and labor may be required to trim the floor area around the opening. Exercise care when cutting the opening; try to avoid damage to the existing ceiling and floor, as this can add needless cost and time to the finish work on the project.

CIRCULAR STAIRWAY

Description	Quantity	Man-hours	Material
Cut opening for stairway, 5' x 5'	1 Ea.	4.0	0.00
Rough in opening for stairway, headers, double 2" x 10" stock	40 L.F.	2.0	27.60
Trimmer joists, double, 2" x 10" stock	40 L.F.	1.0	18.90
Blocking, miscellaneous to joists, 2" x 10" stock	12 L.F.	0.5	11.35
Reinforcement of first floor, double existing joists, 2" x 10" joists	40 L.F.	1.0	37.75
Hangers for headers & joists, 18 ga galv., 2" x 10" joists	4 Ea.	0.5	2.65
Stairs, spiral aluminum, stack unit, 5' diam. oak treads, 14 treads & platform	1 Ea.	10.5	2631.75
Trim, casing at opening, 11/16" x 2 -1/2"	22 L.F.	1.0	9.60
Trim, pine, 1" x 12" at stair opening	22 L.F.	3.5	43.90
Totals		24.0	$2783.50

Project Size	5' diam. x 13 risers	Contractor's Fee Including Materials	$4990

Circular Stairway

If you are cramped for space and in need of a stairway to the attic or next floor in your house, a circular staircase may provide the solution to your problem. The installation requires only as much floor area as a circle 4' to 5' in diameter, and as long as care is taken in the cutting and framing, the result should be a sturdy and functional stairway.

STANDARD STAIRWAY

Renovating an existing stairway requires a substantial level of carpentry skill and knowledge. For this reason, beginners and handymen with limited experience in this area should plan to hire a carpenter for much of the work in this project. There are many reasons why stairway installations demand specialized building skills, but foremost among them is the precise cutting and fitting of hardwood treads, risers, railings, bannisters, and other milled stairway materials. Despite these very demanding aspects, there are other tasks within this project that the do-it-yourselfer can accomplish. The expense and time put into the renovation, whether the work is done by the homeowner or a professional, will result in a refreshing improvement in your home. Because a stairway is often the focal point of the entryway, hallway, or room that it enters, select your materials with both appearance and function in mind.

Oak Railing

Oak Risers

Oak Treads

Volute

Newel-Landing

Pine Skirt Board

Birch Balusters - Turned

Newel-Starting

Oak Starting Step

Materials

This remodeling project has been planned around the renovation of an existing flight of stairs, measuring 4′ in width and rising to a height of 8′-6″. The installation is typical of those found in many two-story dwellings, but variations in such factors as stairway design, height, width, and tread-to-riser proportion are as numerous as the dwellings themselves. The best course of action for the homeowner is to duplicate as closely as possible the existing stairway. Significantly altering the design, size, or direction of the staircase or attempting to match exactly a plan that differs from the original structure will add to the time and cost of the project.

The materials used in this plan consist primarily of milled wood products typical to most house stairway systems. Oak is the featured wood, but other hard or soft woods may be installed at varying costs. Under normal conditions, it is best to duplicate the material of the existing staircase as well as its design. Oak has

been chosen for this plan because it is the most commonly used material for treads. It is durable, pleasing in appearance, relatively economical, and is readily available in most areas of the country. The risers in this stairway plan are also made from oak, but soft woods like fir and pine can function adequately in its place. If you are looking for a cost-cutting measure, or if the stairway is to be carpeted, the use of softwood treads and risers in place of oak will reduce your materials expense considerably. In addition to the treads and risers, a special starting step and tread nosing will be needed to complete the stairway.

The materials used for the handrail and its support are also constructed of woods milled specifically for stairways. The homeowner has a wide choice of variously priced materials, from economical soft wood bannisters to expensive and ornate hardwood rails, newels, and rail starters. If you want to spruce up or change the design of your stairway, this is the place to do it, as structural alterations usually are not required to modify the stairway's railing system.

In addition to these milled woods, some rough lumber may also be required to replace damaged or warped stringers and other stairway supports. When removing the old stairs, try to avoid chipping or cracking the existing stringers. If they are straight, level, and sound, then leave them in place and save yourself the time and cost of replacement. If you are not sure about their condition, then have a knowledgeable person check them.

Level of Difficulty

The renovation of a stairway demands a considerable level of carpentry skill and know-how. The finish tasks, particularly the cutting and fitting of the risers and treads and the setting of the railings, newel, and bannisters, require precise planning and mastery of woodworking skills. Near perfect accuracy of measurement in all aspects of the project is also necessary to assure quality of appearance and safety in the use of the new stairway. Beginners, therefore, should not attempt any of these advanced carpentry tasks and should restrict their efforts to the removal of the old stairway and finish work, such as the staining or sealing of the stairs. Handymen might be able to accomplish some of the finished carpentry on the stairs, but only if they have worked with hardwoods and have had some experience in finish carpentry. Handymen should stop short of the newel, railing, and bannister installations. Experts should be able to install the treads, risers, and various trim pieces; but they, too, should leave the railing work to a carpenter unless they have the know-how, skill, and correct tools to tackle this part of the installation. Generally, beginners should double the professional time for the removal of the existing stairway and any finish work, like painting and staining. Handymen who want to install the treads, risers, and trim on the stairs should plan to work slowly and deliberately. They should triple the professional time for these tasks and should add 50% to the man-hours estimate for the removal of the old stairway. Experts, unless they are accomplished carpenters or woodworkers, should double the professional time for the installation of the treads and risers and leave the placement of the newels, railings, and bannisters to a professional.

What to Watch Out For

Very often the stairways in older homes bow, twist, or sag out of alignment because of settling. It is important, therefore, to check the condition and alignment of the stringers and other supporting members under the stairway after you have removed the old treads and risers. Before you install any of the new materials, you must correct any problems which will cause the new stairway to tilt, sag, or become poorly aligned. Failure to correct these kinds of problems make the installation more difficult and harm the appearance of the new stairs.

STANDARD STAIRWAY			
Description	Quantity	Man-hours	Material
Removal of existing stairway	1 Ea.	8.0	0.00
Rough stringers, three 2" x 12", 14' long	54 L.F.	4.0	42.70
Treads, oak, 1-1/16" x 9-1/2" wide, 4' long	12 Ea.	6.0	361.80
Risers, oak, 3/4" x 7-1/2" wide, 4' long	13 Ea.	6.0	214.90
Single end starting step, oak	1 Ea.	1.0	35.85
Balusters, turned, 42" high, birch	27 Ea.	7.0	196.05
Newels, 3-1/4" wide, starting and landing	2 Ea.	4.0	235.95
Balusters, turned, 30" high, birch, at landing	6 Ea.	2.0	36.30
Railings, oak, built-up, stair & landing, incl. volute	20 L.F.	3.0	102.85
Skirt board, pine, 1" x 12"	14 L.F.	2.5	29.65
Totals		43.5	$1256.05
Project Size 4' wide x 13 risers	Contractor's Fee Including Materials		$3090

Standard Stairway

A stairway often occupies a central place in the house, and thus its improvement can enhance the overall appearance and comfort of the home. The services of a contractor may be required for this job, as the types of skills involved are not often in the do-it-yourselfer's range of experience. Nevertheless, this project has valuable benefits in terms of added safety and aesthetic appeal.

HALF ATTIC

Wall Studs

Drywall

Ceiling Joists

Insulation

Prehung Door

Baseboard

Bi-folding Doors

Plywood Subfloor

Windows

Carpet

If space is limited in your attic, or if you want to continue using a portion of it for storage, then a partial renovation may accommodate your needs. Follow the same guidelines as in a full attic plan when you consider the feasibility of expanding a half attic space. The prime considerations are a large enough area, adequate head room, and accessibility.

Materials

The materials used for a half attic renovation include the common interior construction components employed in most house systems. The framing members consist of construction grade 2″ × 4″s for the walls and closet, and 2″ × 6″s for ceiling joists. Conventional 1/2″ sheetrock, taped and finished, paneling, or decorative veneers like barnboard may be installed at varying costs for the walls and ceilings. Care should be taken in selecting the R-value of the insulation material so that the attic room and the rest of the house are efficiently protected from heat loss and gain in the winter and summer. You can save money by installing carpeting istead of hardwood floors, even though it requires installing 5/8″ as opposed to 1/2″ plywood subflooring. An alternative subfloor for the carpet, in cases where more strength is needed, consists of a layer of 1/2″ sheathing plywood covered by a layer of 3/8″ particleboard. Try to run the particleboard at right angles to the plywood and avoid coincidental seams of the two layers of material. This two-layer underlayment costs more and takes more time to install, but the extra money and effort will give your carpeting and the new floor a more even and durable surface.

The window unit used in this half attic is a metal-clad casement type, which is more expensive than a conventional all wood uninsulated window; but the extra initial cost will be returned over time in savings on fuel and maintenance. The door on the interior wall of the new room is a standard hollow-core lauan prehung unit, but you can purchase paneled and other solid or decorative doors at additional cost. The closet door used in this plan is a bi-folding, louvered unit which provides total accessibility to the 4′ closet opening.

The electrical materials include five receptacles, two light fixtures, and the wiring required to supply and connect the components. If you want to add to the electrical work, make sure that you plan ahead and do it before the sheetrock is installed. Also, check to see that your electric service has the capacity to allow for the new room's circuit. There is a good chance that the new supply wiring will have to be fished up from the service panel, so unless you are experienced in electrical work, call an electrician to perform this task.

Finishing the room can provide an excellent opportunity to gain some experience in the use of tools, even for novices. The cutting, staining or painting, and installation of trim boards may involve a few mistakes at first, but with a simple miter box, careful measuring, and some patience, you will catch on quickly. You can stain or paint the trim boards in your backyard or cellar before you install them, thus enabling you to paint the walls through to the finish coat. Any marks made during installation of the trim can be easily touched up in the final stage. Taping and finishing the sheetrock may take some time if you have never done it before; but the right tools, sound advice, and a quick lesson from a friend who has done it can give you professional results while saving you money.

Level of Difficulty

A partial or half attic renovation project is a major challenge for homeowners, who are doing much of the work on their own. Although the project appears to be relatively routine, many different building skills are required to complete the job from framing through to the finish work. Beginners should not jump into a project of this size without ample professional assistance and advice. If you are a beginner and want to tackle a half or full attic conversion, plan on adding 100% to the professional man-hours estimate. If you are acquainted with tools and have limited experience in building, add 50% to the professional time. Experts with extensive experience in building should anticipate an additional 15% above the professional time.

What to Watch Out For

The attic space of most old or new dwellings can be used for renovation if there is a minimum of 8' from the floor to the ridge board. If your attic does not have sufficient height and area to accommodate a livable room, then dormers may have to be constructed or other costly structural alterations may have to be made. Accessibility is another major consideration. Remember that a conventional staircase will take up precious living or storage space not only in the new attic room, but also in the floor below. Remember, too, that in most cases building materials will have to be carried to the second or third floor attic site, so carefully measure the stairway or other means of access to the work area to head off any materials access problems. It is also a good idea to check the floor joists in the attic for general condition and spacing. The ceiling joists in many older homes are spaced at odd intervals, rather than at 16", and, therefore, need additional strengthening to support the proposed living space above.

HALF ATTIC			
Description	Quantity	Man-hours	Material
Flooring underlayment grade plywood 4' ×8' sheets, 5/8" thick	9 sheets	3.5	198.65
Ceiling joists, 2" × 6", 16" O.C., 7' long	17 Ea.	1.5	56.20
Plates, top & bottom, 2" × 4" 12' lengths	120 L.F.	2.5	37.75
Knee wall studs, 2" × 4", 16" O.C., 4' long	28 Ea.	2.0	35.25
Wall studs, 2" × 4", 16" O.C., 8' long	34 Ea.	4.5	85.55
Blocking, miscellaneous to wood construction, 2" × 4" × 8'	2 Ea.	0.5	5.00
Insulation, R-11, 3-1/2" thick, 15" wide foil-faced blanket 88 S.F. per roll	8 Rolls	3.5	230.00
Insulation, R-19, 6" thick, 15" wide foil-faced blanket 88 S.F. per roll	2 rolls	1.0	83.05
Window, casement type, metal clad, double window, 4' × 4'	1 Ea.	2.0	355.75
Drywall, 1/2" thick plasterboard, taped and finished, 4' × 8' sheets	28 sheets	16.0	271.05
Door, flush, hollow core, lauan finish, 2'-6" wide × 6'-8" high, prehung with casing and non-keyed lockset	1 Ea.	1.0	137.95
Closet door, bi-folding louvered door 4' wide × 6'-8" high	1 Ea.	1.5	208.75
Trim, for closet jambs 1" × 6"	20 L.F.	1.0	13.30
Trim, casing, for window and closet doors, pines, 11/16" × 2-1/2" wide	40 L.F.	1.5	17.40
Trim, for baseboard, pine, 9/16" × 3-1/2" wide	76 L.F.	2.5	64.40
Handrail, pine, 1-1/2" × 1-3/4", 2 pcs. @ 10' long	20 L.F.	1.0	23.75
Carpet, foam-backed, nylon, medium traffic	32 S.Y.	5.5	512.25
Painting, primer plus 1 coat, including walls & trim	1050 S.F.	10.5	114.35
Electrical, including switched hall and closet lights and 5 plugs	1 Lot	11.0	165.75
	Totals	72.5	$2616.15
Project Size 16' × 20'	Contractor's Fee Including Materials		$5420

Half Attic

If your house meets the basic height, space, and accessibility conditions, a half attic renovation may be an ideal way to convert often misused space to living area. It is the perfect solution if you need to expand, but would like to keep a portion of your attic for storage. Because this space is already under roof and protected from the elements, the construction of a new room can be accomplished easily and economically.

FULL ATTIC

Expanding your home living space by using your attic requires careful consideration. Basic physical restrictions can cause problems or even prohibit attic renovation without major structural changes to the existing house. For example, inadequate head room results in the additional cost of adding dormers or raising the ridge and changing the roof line. Your attic should provide the minimum necessary head room for the area to be converted. If you have this capacity and can give up the floor area required for a staircase, then your attic can be converted into a comfortable, pleasant living area.

Materials

The materials used for attic renovation are basically the same as those used for interior work anywhere in your home. One advantage of attic renovation, assuming that dormers or changes in the roof line are not required, is that the area is weather tight and protected at the start. Standard construction-grade framing materials, including 2″ × 4″s for wall studs and plates, and 2″ × 6″s for ceiling joists, can be used to support 1/2″ sheetrock. If you plan on installing wood floors, economical 1/2″ sheathing plywood can be used for the subflooring. Insulation costs will vary according to recommended R-values for your area and preference for paperfaced, foil-faced, or unfaced fiberglass insulation. Windows for the gable ends of the attic rooms can be simple double-hung units or more expensive thermopaned casement models. Extra money invested at the time of construction for quality windows will be returned to you in energy savings and lower maintenance costs over the years.

The electrical materials used in the project include basic outlets, switches, lighting fixtures, and the wiring required to connect the various components. Make sure that you check local codes for proper installation if you are doing the electrical work on your own. Also, have the work inspected by a qualified person after you have installed it.

The finish work for your attic will vary according to your personal taste and the anticipated use of the living space. Taping and finishing the sheetrock and applying two coats of paint will finish the ceiling and walls. Hardwood flooring, carpeting, or other materials can be used for floor coverings. Basic prehung hollow-core lauan doors or more expensive paneled or louvre units can be used for the doorway and closets. For trim, ranch or colonial casing may be installed around doors, windows, and floors.

Level of Difficulty

Major renovation of an attic is a challenging project for the most experienced handyman, even if dormers or other structural changes are not required. Accessibility alone can cause problems in getting materials to a second- or third-floor attic location. If you are to do some of the work alone, plan ahead as the project progresses and arrange to have someone assist you for an hour or two in carrying sheetrock, plywood, and other bulky items upstairs. Much of the work can be done by the homeowner, from easier jobs for beginners, like insulating and painting, to more skilled operations for experts, like framing, flooring, and window installation. Specialized work, especially electrical, should be left to the experts or contractors. If dormers are required, consider bringing in a professional contractor to build and close in the attic area. (See dormer construction project and costs in the ''Exteriors'' section.) As a general rule, beginners with little or no building experience should double the estimated man-hours for the project; handymen with some experience and skill in the use of tools should add an additional 50% to the man-hours estimate; and experts, about 20%. Beginners should seek professional help and advice throughout the various stages of the construction process.

What to Watch Out For

The primary considerations in any attic remodeling project are space and accessibility. Before you plan the renovation, check to see that the head clearance in your attic will allow for a 7'-6" or higher ceiling at the center of the room and that you have enough floor space to make the project worthwhile. Then, check on the accessibility of the attic. Consider the staircase in terms of additional cost as well as the reduction of living or storage area that it causes in the floor below. As a final preliminary check, make sure that the prospective floor joists for the attic room are sufficient to bear the added weight of the new living area. If they are not adequate, they will have to be strengthened at additional cost and time by adding floor joists before the project is begun.

FULL ATTIC

Description	Quantity	Man-hours	Material
Flooring underlayment grade plywood, 4' ×8' sheets, 1/2" thick	17 sheets	6.0	302.80
Ceiling joists, 2" × 6", 16" O.C., 7' long	29 Ea.	3.0	95.80
Plates, top & bottom, 2" × 4", 12' lengths	252 L.F.	5.0	79.30
Knee wall studs, 2" × 4", 16" O.C., 4' long	58 Ea.	6.0	73.00
Wall studs, 2" × 4", 16" O.C., 8' long	44 Ea.	5.5	110.75
Blocking, miscellaneous to wood construction, 2" × 4" × 8'	5 Ea.	1.5	12.60
Insulation, R-11, 3-1/2" thick, 15" wide foil-faced blanket, 88 S.F. per roll	12 Rolls	5.5	345.00
Insulation, R-19, 6" thick, 15" wide foil-faced blanket, 88 S.F. per roll	3 rolls	1.5	124.60
Windows, double hung, plastic clad, insulating 3' × 4'	2 Ea.	2.0	423.50
Drywall, 1/2" thick plaster board, taped & finished, 4' ×8' sheets	60 sheets	35.0	580.80
Door, flush, hollow core, lauan finish, 2'-6" wide by 6'-8" high, prehung with casing	4 Ea.	3.5	367.85
Trim, casing for window pine, 11/16" × 2-1/2" wide	30 L.F.	1.0	13.10
Trim, for baseboard, pine, 9/16" × 3-1/2" wide	210 L.F.	7.0	177.90
Handrail, pine, 1-1/2" × 1-3/4", 2 pcs. @ 10' long	20 L.F.	2.0	23.70
Flooring, prefinished, white oak, prime grade 2-1/4" wide	550 S.F.	26.0	3327.50
Painting, primer plus 1 coat, including walls & trim	2100 S.F.	21.0	228.70
Lockset, residential, interior door, ordinary	4 Ea.	2.0	43.55
Electrical including hall light, two switched closet lights and 5 plugs per room	1 Lot	20.0	285.85
Totals		153.0	$6616.29

Project Size	16' × 36'	Contractor's Fee Including Materials	$14,510.

STANDARD BASEMENT

Existing Joists

Plywood Paneling

Rigid Insulation

Suspended Ceiling

Newel Post

Railing

Balusters

Skirt Board

Prehung Door

Baseboard

Existing Foundation

Vinyl Tile

Your basement can be converted into efficient living space with a minimum of time, effort, and cost. The existing foundation walls provide a solid backing for a variety of finished wall materials; the floor joists for the room above are ready to support the new ceiling; and, in most cases, a concrete floor is in place to receive the new flooring. As long as the area is dry and the existing walls, ceiling, and floor are in good shape, a basement room is an efficient and cost effective place to expand your home's living space.

Materials

With the house's foundation serving as a solid exterior wall system, a limited amount of partitioning is required to prepare the room for the finished walls. The area under the stairwell requires 2″ × 4″ framing members to back the paneling and to frame the understairs closet. In most cases, you will be able to use the existing cellar stair stringers, but if you have to construct the staircase from scratch, you can figure on extra cost for the stringer material and other staircase support modifications. The concrete walls have to be prepared with 1″ × 3″ furring strips which are placed vertically at 16″ on center and horizontally across the top and bottom of the wall. The furring strips can be fastened to the concrete with masonry nails or by firing special nails into the concrete with a stud gun. This procedure can be tricky and sometimes dangerous, so seek professional advice if you have not done it before. After you have completed all of the partitioning and prepared the walls to receive the paneling, the rough electrical work should be performed. Chances are, especially in new homes, that electrical circuits are readily available from the service panel in the basement. If you are unfamiliar with electrical installations, hire a professional to do the work or seek assistance from a qualified person. The styrofoam insulation material used on the exterior walls should match the thickness of the wall furring strips. You should also insulate the ceiling of the new room with fiberglass batts placed between the joists.

The finished walls, ceiling, and floor can be constructed from prefinished materials, all of them readily available from building supply outlets. The walls can be covered with an average grade prefinished paneling which can be nailed or glued to the furring strips. Cheaper grades of paneling are available, but the additional expense of a good quality paneling will make the finished product more attractive.

The ceiling consists of 2′ × 4′ prefinished fiber tiles which are suspended on a prepackaged system of hangers, carriers, and runners. These systems are usually accompanied by sample instructions and guidelines for installation by homeowners. The resilient tile flooring can be adhered directly to the concrete floor. Take some time to prepare the surface so that it is dry, clean, and smooth. If the concrete floor is sloped or in rough shape, then a subfloor may have to be constructed from 2″ × 4″ sleepers and sheathing. This installation requires some know-how and involves some extra costs, so get some advice and assistance if it has to be done.

Individual tiles or a variety of sheet goods are available for resilient flooring. Check with a flooring contractor or consult someone who has done this kind of work before you select the type of floor for your basement. Also, follow the manufacturers' instructions on the flooring material and adhesives to be used.

Finishing the basement will require extensive work on the staircase. It might be a good idea to hire a carpenter to place the risers, treads, bannisters, and handrail. Even if you are a fairly accomplished handyman, you might need assistance in this part of the project. The materials are expensive, and precision is required in calculations and cutting. For the door under the stairs, you can choose a modest prehung lauan unit, or a more expensive solid core or paneled design. Pine, colonial, or ranch design trim can be used for the facings around the windows and doors and at the base of the walls. Inside and outside corner trim pieces are available at building supply outlets to finish the paneling.

Level of Difficulty

The conversion of basement space to a comfortable living area requires a modest amount of skill and knowledge of remodeling. Except for the staircase and the electrical work, the project can be completed by most homeowners. If you are a beginner, seek the advice and assistance of professionals or experts as the building progresses. If you follow directions, work patiently, and learn from your mistakes, you should get very good results at a modest cost. Make sure that in following the professional man-hours estimates you add 80% to the time if you are a beginner or have very limited building experience. If you are competent with tools and house projects, then add 40% to the estimated professional time. If you are an expert, an additional 10% should do it.

What to Watch Out For

One of the major problems with renovations of standard 75% below grade basements is moisture. Even though the basement may be dry and free from flooding or seepage during the wet times of year, ground moisture or condensation can be trapped in closed basements and cause dampness in your new room. If you sense that present or future moisture problems may affect the basement room, apply a sealer to the walls and floor as the first step in construction. If your basement is prone to occasional flooding, don't despair. Systems are available to correct the problem from both inside and outside the foundation. However, this procedure usually involves a significant expense. If your dwelling does have these problems, be sure to get professional advice and assistance before proceeding with the conversion.

STANDARD BASEMENT			
Description	Quantity	Man-hours	Material
Partition wall for stairway, 2″ × 4″ plates & studs, 16″ O.C., 8′ high	180 L.F.	3.0	56.60
Blocking, miscellaneous, nailers for walls	12 L.F.	0.5	5.65
Furring strips for walls 1″ × 3″, 16″ O.C.	665 L.F.	11.0	88.50
Insulation, rigid molded bead board, 1/2″ thick	615 S.F.	6.5	126.50
Paneling, plywood, 1/4″ thick, 4′ × 8′ sheets, birch faced, average grade	26 sheets	38.0	855.70
Suspended ceiling system, 2′ × 4′ panels	440 S.F.	9.5	436.60
Door, flush, hollow core, lauan finish, 2′-6″ wide × 6′-8″ high, prehung	1 Ea.	1.0	91.95
Lockset, keyed, for flush door	1 Ea.	1.0	39.95
Stairway additions: skirt board, 1″ × 10″	12 L.F.	2.0	21.05
Newel posts, 3″-4″ wide, starting	1 Ea.	1.5	48.40
Balusters, turned, pine, 30″ high	21 Ea.	6.0	88.95
Railing, oak, built-up	24 L.F.	3.5	123.40
Trim, jambs for doors & windows, 1″ × 8″ pine	16 L.F.	1.0	14.50
Trim, for baseboard, pine, 9/16″ × 3-1/2″ wide	96 L.F.	3.5	81.30
Trim, casing, pine, 11/16″ × 2-1/2″ wide	10 L.F.	0.5	4.80
Paint, trim, incl. puttying, primer & 1 coat	125 L.F.	2.5	7.85
Flooring, vinyl composition tile, 12″ × 12″, 1/16″ thick	440 S.F.	11.0	266.20
Electrical, including 2 light fixtures w/wiring 2 switches & 6 duplex receptacles	1 Lot	13.5	180.65
	Total	115.5	$2538.56

Project Size	24′ × 20′	Contractor's Fee Including Materials	$7420

> **Standard Basement**
>
> A dry basement which meets the height and accessibility requirements may be a source of new living area, and its renovation may help you to put this normally under-utilized space to better use. Because the rough walls, ceiling, and floor are already in place, the finishing of a basement room is a good way to expand your environment with a limited amount of cost and effort.

WALK-OUT BASEMENT

Casement Window

Wall Studs

Prehung Door

Sliding Door

Existing Girder

Existing Joists

Drywall

Furring

Carpet & Padding

Baseboard

Like attics, basements can also be economically converted to roomy, comfortable living areas. Basement renovation projects can turn under-utilized space into recreation, home office, or utility rooms. If your basement area is dry and already equipped with a walk-out doorway, a conversion can be easily undertaken, even if you have limited experience.

Materials

The materials used for a basement conversion are the same as those used in common home building construction. Because your foundation can serve as the rough wall system for the new room, 2" × 4" framing members are required only to enclose the entry staircase. Additional framing materials will be necessary at extra cost if you want to add a closet or storage area or to erect a partition for a second room. The support system for 1/2" drywall begins with 1" × 3" furring strips secured vertically at 16" on center to the existing foundation wall. Consult someone who has experience in hammering concrete nails or firing specialized nails with a stud gun. If you plan to use 1/2" sheetrock on the ceiling, it might be a good idea to put the furring on the joists first to offset any settling or bowing that has occurred. The additional cost of this procedure is minimal, and the improvement in the appearance of your ceiling can make it worthwhile. Once the walls and ceiling have been furred, the rough electrical work can be done and the insulation and sheetrock put into place. If you are inexperienced in electrical installa-

tions, call a contractor or arrange to have a qualified person assist you in running the wires and installing the receptacles, switches, and fixtures. Drywalling a basement room is a challenging but reasonable undertaking for even inexperienced homeowners. You will need some help in bringing the sheetrock into the cellar and installing it on the ceiling; but with a little ingenuity, you can hang the sheets on the walls alone.

The taping and painting of the drywall can also be done on your own. If you have not worked with drywall before, seek some assistance and purchase or borrow the correct tools. Some good advice or instruction can head off much time-consuming sanding and finish work and enhance the appearance of the finished product.

If your foundation has been constructed to accommodate sliding doors and large window units, vinyl-clad, aluminum, or paintable wood door and window units can be installed after the old units have been removed. If, as in this example, concrete or block has to be removed in order to enlarge existing openings or to create new ones, you should consult a masonry contractor. When existing openings do not match the desired door and window design, you may choose to modify your plan somewhat for the sake of economy.

The cost of your project will vary according to the amount of professional assistance required. The door for the understairs closet or utility space can be an economical prehung hollow-core lauan model or a more expensive paneled or decorative unit. Pine boards in ranch or colonial trim are available for the jambs, casings, and interior facings of windows and doors. The baseboard can be obtained in the same styles and materials.

As for the carpet, a foam-backed type is used in this model, and can be installed directly on a clean, smooth concrete floor in a dry basement. If you have no experience in carpet laying, it might be a good idea to contact a professional.

Level of Difficulty

A complete basement conversion requires a reasonable level of skill and a basic knowledge of tools and building, but many aspects of this project can be tackled by beginners. Except for the electrical work and the foundation preparation for windows and doors, most of the operations are relatively straightforward and uncomplicated. There is a limited amount of framing involved in the conversion, and, except for ceiling obstacles like existing plumbing and electrical fixtures, there are few problems to keep you from direct and rapid progress. If you are a beginner, double the estimated time for professional man-hours. Add about 40% to the man-hours estimate if you have had some experience with tools and renovation, and 10% if you are thoroughly skilled in these areas.

What to Watch Out For

Walk-out basements are usually accessible, but consider the size of your entranceways, as you will need to bring in some large materials. Also, double check the ceiling height to see that it meets your minimum requirements for head room. Remember that you will lose some height when you add furring to the joists, and more with a layer of sheetrock. Lighting fixtures installed in the ceiling also require safe clearance. If you have to box around low-hanging plumbing, you will lose some head room in those areas too. Lally columns which support the house's primary structural beams are another consideration. They can often be boxed in, but if they have to be removed or relocated, proper support systems must be installed to prevent expensive structural problems. These additional operations can affect remodeling costs significantly. It is best to check with a professional contractor before you make any changes that involve the structural support system.

WALK-OUT BASEMENT

Description	Quantity	Man-hours	Material
Partition wall for stairway, 2" × 4" plates & studs, 16" O.C., 8' high	312 L.F.	5.0	98.15
Blocking miscellaneous, nailers for walls	24 L.F.	1.0	11.30
Cut masonry openings, 6' × 6'-8" and 4' × 4'	2 Ea.	35.0	0.00
Furring strips for ceiling and walls, 1" × 3", 16" O.C.	1400 L.F.	22.5	186.35
Insulation, rigid molded bead board, 1/2" thick, R-3.85	1020 S.F.	11.5	209.80
Drywall, 1/2" thick plasterboard, taped and finished, 4' × 4'	74 Sheets	43.0	716.30
Windows, casement type, metal clad, double window, 4' × 4'	1 Ea.	2.0	474.30
Door, sliding, glass, wood, premium, 6' wide	1 Ea.	4.0	795.00
Door, flush, hollow core, lauan finish, 2'-6" wide × 6'-8" high, prehung	1 Ea.	1.0	91.95
Lockset, keyed, for flush door	1 Ea.	1.0	40.00
Trim, jambs for doors & windows, 1" × 8" pine	50 L.F.	2.0	45.35
Trim, for baseboard, pine, 9/16" × 3-1/2" wide	160 L.F.	5.5	135.55
Trim, casing, pine, 11/16" × 2-1/2" wide	48 L.F.	2.0	20.90
Railing, oak, built-up	24 L.F.	3.5	123.45
Paint, ceiling & walls, primer plus 1 coat	2370 S.F.	21.5	372.80
Paint, trim, wood, incl. putty, primer and 1 coat	260 L.F.	5.0	15.75
Padding for carpet, sponge rubber cushion	910 S.F.	5.5	275.25
Carpet, nylon, 26 oz. medium traffic	910 S.F.	16.5	1893.90
Electrical, including 2 light fixtures w/wiring switches & 10 duplex receptacles	1 Lot	19.0	240.20
Total		206.5	$5746.30
Project Size 24' × 40'	Contractor's Fee Including Materials		$14,980

Walk-Out Basement

A dry and accessible walk-out basement is a good source of new living area. Because the space is already enclosed, much of the project can be accomplished by the do-it-yourselfer for a modest investment.

REDWOOD HOT TUB

6' Dia. x 4'-0" Deep Redwood Hot Tub on Concrete Base

2" x 6" Redwood Decking

1/2" x 6" Redwood Siding

1/2" x 6" Redwood Siding

2" x 6" Redwood Decking

Existing Redwood Deck

2" x 8" Redwood Risers

2-2" x 6" Redwood Treads

Hot tubs can be installed in interior or exterior settings and often complement another facility, such as a deluxe bath, exercise room, sauna, sun deck, or swimming pool. This plan demonstrates how a 6' factory-prepared redwood hot tub can be placed on an existing redwood deck. Although many locations and designs are possible, this project covers the basic materials and procedures for a medium-sized installation.

Materials

The materials list starts with redwood support members and decking. These are required to alter and prepare the existing deck to receive the hot tub. The remaining components are the precut and prefinished 6' hot tub kit and incidental finish products. The framing and decking lumber are available from most lumber yards, as are some of the finish materials. Redwood may have to be special ordered, however, in some areas of the country. The redwood tub kit can be purchased from a specialty retailer, but some general building suppliers may also carry hot tubs and spas on a special-order basis. Because the redwood deck materials and hot tub are expensive products, do-it-yourselfers should thoroughly research their options before finalizing the design of the facility and the materials order.

The 6' hot tub suggested in this plan weighs well over three tons when filled and in use. Consequently, a considerable amount of support must be added to the existing deck if it is to bear the load. Each installation will present a different set of conditions, and the requirements for reinforcing your deck's support system may vary from what is recommended in this plan. Consult local building codes, follow the manufacturer's guidelines, and get a professional opinion before you determine the arrangement and size of the deck joists and supports. In some cases, extra joists and bridging may be enough; in others, additional footings, posts, and supports may be required. Most manufacturers of hot tubs recommend an independent ground support system for the unit, separate from the deck. Whenever possible, this method of installation should be employed, even though it may involve considerable extra work and expense. When placing the knee wall and partial perimeter deck structure around the hot tub, be careful not to drive the fasteners into the side of the unit. Also, leave a small space for expansion and drainage between the tub and the deck frame. Use quality hot-dipped galvanized nails and lag screws for the decking and supports to prevent corrosion and rusting.

Many different sizes, shapes, and material options are open to you when selecting the hot tub kit. The unit in this plan features standard-grade bottom pieces and redwood staves collared with adjustable stainless steel hoops. The kit is precision cut and fitted at the factory and delivered unassembled to the consumer. Also included in the price of the kit are the basic plumbing and electrical support packages for the operation of the facility. Many specialty retailers will provide, at extra charge, an on-site assembly service for the tub itself. Handymen and beginners might consider this service, as the hot tub is fairly complicated and must be accurately fitted together so that it will be sturdy and watertight. The cost of this service covers only the basic tub and its attached components, however, and does not include plumbing and electrical work. As noted earlier, careful planning and research will help you determine the size and design features that meet your practical and aesthetic requirements. In addition to redwood, hot tubs are available in teak, cedar, mahogany, and cyprus. Coated fiberglass, stainless steel, and other materials are also used.

After the support system, perimeter decking, and hot tub are in place, the installation can be left as is or finished with stain or sealer. If left untreated, the redwood will eventually weather to a tanned leather color, but it will not rot or deteriorate. However, because of the dampness, a sealer with a mildewcide additive is recommended for the exposed exterior surfaces of the tub and the surrounding deck. If the deck and tub are made from different materials, one or both may be stained to blend the new and old installations. In most cases, a qualified plumber and electrician should be hired to tie in the support packages to the house utilities.

Level of Difficulty

This project calls for some expensive materials for both the redwood decking and the tub kit. This factor, together with precise installation requirements, makes it a challenge for all do-it-yourselfers. Beginners and most handymen might want to stick to the more basic tasks, like the preliminary site preparation and the surface finishing. Experts who opt to assemble the kit themselves should follow the manufacturer's instructions precisely and consult a professional before tackling the operation. Experts should add 25% to the man-hours for all carpentry tasks. Beginners and handymen should add 100% and 50%, respectively, to the time estimate for the basic tasks which they attempt. All do-it-yourselfers should hire qualified tradesmen to accomplish the electrical and plumbing work.

What to Watch Out For

Provisions should be made in the planning stages of this project for features such as proper drainage piping and protection against the effects of freezing temperatures. The installation should allow for complete drainage during the period when the facility is not in use. In cold climates, where the tub is to be used year-round, an optional freeze protection package can be purchased at additional cost. Floating or attached covers made of wood and plastic are other extras which will reduce heat loss and protect the tub. If the tub is to be used during cooler weather, you might consider installing a wind screen adjacent to the facility for greater comfort and reduced heat loss. All of these components will increase the cost of the project, but they will also extend the length of the season during which the facility can be used.

REDWOOD HOT TUB			
Description	Quantity	Man-hours	Material
Remove portion of existing deck	1 Job	4.0	0.00
Reinforce existing deck, 2" x 8" redwood stock	24 L.F.	1.0	42.40
Base support slab, hand grading	50 S.F.	1.0	0.00
Edge forms for slab	24 L.F.	1.5	5.80
Concrete, ready mix, 3000 psi	1 C.Y.	0.0	67.55
Place & screed concrete	1 C.Y.	1.0	0.00
Platform framing, redwood, construction grade Posts, doubled 2" x 4" stock	48 L.F.	2.0	109.20
Joists, 2" x 6" stock	130 L.F.	4.5	160.45
Decking, 2" x 6" x 12'	252 L.F.	8.0	311.00
Stair stringers, 2" x 8" stock	12 L.F.	1.0	21.20
Stair treads, 2" x 6" stock	18 L.F.	0.5	22.20
Stair risers 2" x 8" stock	14 L.F.	1.0	24.75
Vertical siding, 1/2" x 6"	48 L.F.	1.5	77.85
Redwood hot tub kit, 6' diam. x 4' deep with circulating pump & drain system	1 Ea.	20.0	1609.30
Plumbing rough-in & supply	1 Ea.	9.5	85.40
Electrical rough-in, hook-up	1 Ea.	3.0	68.95
	Totals	59.5	$2606.00
Project Size 12' x 14'	Contractor's Fee Including Materials		$5800

Redwood Hot Tub

Although the installation of a hot tub is a relatively expensive undertaking, the comfort and potential benefits can add a unique luxury to your home life. When carefully designed to complementan existing deck, exercise area, or swimming pool, it can also enhance your home's exterior appearance

SAUNA ROOM

Saunas are a popular home improvement, not only as a health and luxury item, but also because they require little space and are only moderately difficult to install. Other than some basic electrical hook-ups, there is no specialized trade work involved. Unlike a steam bath, no plumbing or floor drain installation is required, and ceramic tile or concrete are the desirable floor coverings. This plan outlines a sauna project that can be completed by most experienced handymen. The installation features a 6' x 6' factory-prepared sauna room which is delivered complete with ready-to-assemble walls, ceiling, benches, heater, and accessories.

Ceiling
2" x 6" Joists
6" Insulation
1/2" Fire-resistant Drywall

Prefabricated Sauna
w/Heater & Controls

Floor:
2" x 2" Ceramic Tile

Wall Framing:
2" x 4" Studs & Plates
2-2" x 6" Header
3-1/2" Insulation
1/2" Fire-resistant Drywall
Each Side

Door w/Tempered Insulated
Glass Window

Materials

In addition to the prefabricated sauna room, standard framing, surface covering, and insulating materials are needed for the exterior shell of the facility. These basic construction products can be purchased from most building supply retailers at competitive prices. The sauna room itself is a specialty item.

The first phase of this project involves determining the location and layout of the sauna room and then constructing its exterior shell. Because the prefabricated units are not that heavy and can be ordered in a wide range of sizes and configurations, they can be located almost anywhere in the house. If you have the space off a bedroom and near a shower area, a second-floor location is ideal. However, first-floor, basement, and even exterior areas can also be utilized. This plan allows for enough material to construct the shell of a sauna room in a corner of a basement where two walls are already in place. The two new walls must be framed with 2" x 4"s and then covered with 1/2" fire-resistant drywall on both sides. A ceiling must also be framed with 2" x 6"s and similarly covered on the interior side.

Insulation is required on the new walls and ceiling to ensure energy savings. Some additional expense may be incurred if the existing walls must also be insulated or covered with fireproof material. During the framing of the shell, follow the manufacturer's recommended rough measurement guidelines and maintain precise level, plumb, and square. Inaccurate framing will cause misalignment of the prefabricated components, and, consequently, heat-losing cracks and spaces at the corners and between panels.

The second phase of the project involves assembling the sauna room and its accessories. Various designs and materials are employed in sauna units, but most of them feature soft-wood walls and ceilings. Economical units may employ pine, spruce, and hemlock, for example; and the more expensive ones, cedar and redwood. The benches, safety heater railing, and optional duckboards and back rests are usually manufactured from wood which matches the ceiling and walls.

At the heart of the installation is the heater, which has been carefully engineered to provide the correct output for its particular size of sauna room. A light fixture, switch, and controls for the heater are also normally included in the basic sauna package. Most manufacturers feature prewiring for these electrical devices within the wall panels of their products. No special electrical service is required for the heater; and under normal conditions, a certified electrician can routinely tie the lead wires from the sauna into your house's electrical supply. Throughout the assembly of the sauna unit, follow the manufacturer's instructions and guidelines. Work patiently and follow accepted carpentry practices, as the naturally finished softwood is particularly susceptible to marks and dents caused by careless hammering or handling.

Once the sauna unit has been assembled and fastened, the finished floor can be laid and the special prehung sauna door installed. This plan includes attractive low maintenance ceramic floor tile. If you intend to install ceramic flooring, be sure to use appropriate grout and to seal it thoroughly, as frequent floor cleaning is recommended by most manufacturers. Duckboards are available as an accessory flooring material at extra cost from most sauna manufacturers. Depending on the brand of sauna, several styles of prehung doors are available. All of them are insulated and have wood interior handles, and some include small or full-size insulated glass windows and exterior decoration. The door is usually included in the sauna unit price, but is sometimes an extra.

Level of Difficulty

This project calls for moderate to advanced carpentry skills and know-how. Although the sauna facility measures only 6' x 6', it requires an accurate layout and a precise fit of both the exterior shell and interior wall and ceiling assembly. Careless workmanship can be problematic if the exterior shell is misaligned or inaccurately plumbed or squared. Beginners, therefore, should seek assistance in the framing phase of the installation. They may also consider hiring a professional for the sauna assembly after weighing the cost of the unit and the chance of damaging it against the potential savings in labor. Beginners should add 100% to the professional time for insulating, finishing the drywall, and painting. If they tackle the ceramic floor installation, they should add slightly more time to allow for careful work. Handymen and experts should add 50% and 20%, respectively, to the estimated time for all basic carpentry procedures, and more for the sauna assembly, door installation, and ceramic floor.

What to Watch Out For

Although this plan is for an economical sauna inside your house, there are several other options, both interior and exterior. Some manufacturers of prefabricated sauna units provide completely finished rooms which can be erected without the need of a shell. These units come with insulated walls, interior and exterior finish, and the full range of electrical and convenience accessories. In some areas of the country, they also provide the services of expert installers at extra cost. Exterior sauna locations are a possibility if interior space is limited or if you prefer an outdoor setting. As long the enclosure for the facility is well insulated and weathertight, interior sauna kits can be safely and effectively adapted to an exterior setting. The complete room kit, and especially the outdoor kit, will increase the cost of the project.

SAUNA ROOM

Description	Quantity	Man-hours	Material
Wall framing, plates, 2″ x 4″, top & bottom	36 L.F.	1.0	11.30
Studs, 2″ x 4″ x 8′, 16″ O.C.	112 L.F.	2.0	35.25
Blocking, misc., 2″ x 4″	20 L.F.	1.0	7.50
Header over door opening, 2″ x 6″, doubled	8 L.F.	0.5	3.80
Ceiling joists, 2″ x 6″, 16″ O.C.	60 L.F.	1.0	28.30
Insulation, walls, 3-1/2″ thick, R-11, 15″ wide	170 S.F.	1.0	55.55
Ceiling, 6″ thick, R-19, 15″ wide	36 S.F.	0.5	17.00
Drywall, gypsum plasterboard, 1/2″ thick on ceiling & both sides of walls, fire-resistant, taped & finished	11 Sheets	6.0	123.52
Sauna, 6′ x 6′ prefabricated kit, including heater & controls	1 Ea.	16.0	3872.00
Door, pre-hung w/tempered insulated glass window, including jambs & hardware	1 Ea.	1.5	229.90
Flooring, ceramic tile, 1 color, 2″ x 2″	36 S.F.	3.5	145.95
Painting, exterior walls, primer & 1 coat	85 S.F.	1.0	9.25
Totals		35.0	$4539.32
Project Size 6′ x 6′	Contractor's Fee Including Materials		$8250

Sauna Room

For a reasonable investment of time and money, the unique pleasure of a sauna room can become part of your home life. Skilled do-it-yourselfers can substantially reduce the cost of this amenity by building it on their own.

GARAGE CONVERSION

Like unfinished attic and basement areas, garages can be economically converted to living, work, or studio space, especially if the garage is attached as an integral part of the existing house. Because the expenses for excavation, foundation work, framing, and closing in the new living area have already been taken care of, your only concerns will be the costs of preparing the interior, adding the windows and a door, and closing in, when necessary, portions of the exterior walls. If you are doing the work on your own, plan on a challenging project, but one that includes the benefits of accessibility and a convenient location.

Existing Roof,
Rafters &
Ceiling Joists

6" Insulation

Drywall

Double Hung Windows

Baseboard

Vinyl Flooring

Plywood Subfloor

3-1/2" Insulation

2" x 4" Sleepers

Existing Concrete Slab

Cedar Bevel Siding
Aluminum Sliding Glass Door
2-2" x 6" Headers
3-1/2" Insulation
1/2" Plywood Sheathing
2" x 4" Studs, Plates, & Shoe

Materials

The primary materials used for the garage conversion consist of framing lumber, various sheet goods for the floor, walls, and ceiling, several windows, sliding glass doors, and the finish materials for the inside and the outside of the exterior walls. Insulation, electrical materials, and various incidentals are also required and will vary in type, amount, and size, depending on such factors as the geographical area of your home and the particular location of the garage in relation to the main structure. The minimum framing and structural lumber required in the garage conversion includes 2″ x 4″s and a few 2″ x 8″s. The 2″ x 4″s used as sleepers for the support system of the new floor should be treated with wood preservative before they are placed. Although it is more expensive, pressure-treated wood can also be used for superior quality sleepers. Conventional 2″ x 4″s are used as studs in the exterior walls to frame in the new windows and sliding glass door unit and to frame the new wall that fills the old garage door opening. Sheathing plywood, 5/8″ in thickness, serves as the rough covering for the sleepers and the exterior of the new wall framing. Be sure to insulate the floor and place a vapor barrier on top of the 2″ x 4″ floor sleepers before laying the

plywood. Additional framing may be required at extra cost if the floor of the new room has to be raised or the ceiling lowered for aesthetic or practical reasons. The wall studs and ceiling joists of the new room can be covered with various types of materials, such as drywall or wood paneling. An economical choice is 1/2″ drywall. If the garage is already drywalled, but not insulated, hire an insulating contractor to blow insulation into the walls, and, if necessary, the ceiling. If your garage is situated under the living area of your house, it may already be insulated. While the walls are open, the rough electrical work should also be installed. As for the exterior, these walls should be finished with matching siding around the new window and door installations and in the wall space which fills the void left by the garage door. Make sure that you lace the new siding into the old, prime all of the new materials, and then put a uniform finish coat on all three sides of the new room's exterior. One general rule to follow when purchasing window and door units is that quality products will usually return the homeowner's investment in energy savings, durability, and low maintenance costs over the life of the unit. The finish work in the new room should reflect its anticipated use. The trim for the windows and door, as well as the baseboard, can be painted, stained, or left natural and finished with a clear sealer. A wide range of flooring materials can be installed, from hardwood to carpeting or, as in this plan, durable vinyl sheet goods. Make sure that you vent the subflooring support system so that it can breathe. Also, if you plan to use vinyl or carpeting for the finished floor, it might be worth the additional expense and time to install a layer of 3/8" particle board underlayment over the sheathing plywood. Not only will the surface material look and wear better, but the floor will be stronger, more even, quieter, and warmer.

Level of Difficulty

The conversion of a garage into living space is a major undertaking; but because of the convenient location and accessibility of the work site,

it is the type of project that can be done in stages, over a longer period of time than other remodeling jobs. Many of the tasks involved in the final stages of the project can be accomplished by beginners who seek advice and assistance from knowledgeable people. Novices, however, should leave the window, door, and filler framing jobs to a professional. The installation of the floor sleepers, too, can be a tricky job, especially in garages with sloped or uneven concrete floors. Shimming is necessary in constructing the support frame, and often the 2" x 4" sleepers have to be ripped to size so that they can be set on the sloped concrete. These operations demand skill in the use of tools and the basic know-how of someone who has done this work before. Beginners and most handymen should leave the electrical work to a competent tradesman. As a general rule, if you are a beginner, add 90% to the man-hours estimate for those tasks which you feel you can handle. If you are a reasonably skilled handyman, add 40% to the estimate and more if you plan to lay the sleeper support system and to rough in the windows, sliding doors, and fill in the garage door opening. Experts should add about 10% to all tasks involved in the conversion.

What to Watch Out For

Problems with the floor and ceiling heights can be corrected with careful design and planning. Garage floors, for example, are often located below grade level or are pitched dramatically for drainage. Take stock of the existing floor's location and slope before you determine the level of the new floor and the design for its support. You should also make provisions to divert surface water via drains or other means so that run-off or icing won't penetrate under the floor of the new room and cause damage. Garage ceilings, too, vary in height, so plan on some additional expense if new ceiling joists have to be installed to decrease the height, or if other modifications have to be made to raise it.

GARAGE CONVERSION

Description	Quantity	Man-hours	Material
Flooring, joists 2" x 4", 16" O.C., on existing concrete slab	525 L.F.	7.0	165.15
Plywood, CDX, 5/8" thick, 4' x 8' sheets for floors & 1 exterior wall	22 Sheets	10.0	374.80
Plates, top & bottom, 2" x 4", 12' lengths	40 L.F.	1.0	12.60
Wall studs at door and new windows 2" x 4" x 8' long, 16" O.C.	192 L.F.	3.0	60.40
Headers over openings, double 2" x 6"	28 L.F.	1.5	13.20
Siding, cedar bevel, A grade, 1/2" x 6"	155 S.F.	5.0	305.70
Insulation, fiberglass blankets, paper backed, 3-1/2" thick, R-11, for floor & walls	1000 S.F.	11.0	266.20
Insulation, fiberglass blankets, paper backed, 6" thick, R-19, for ceiling	500 S.F.	6.5	217.80
Windows, double hung, plastic clad, insulating glass, 3' x 4', w/frame, screen & exterior trim	3 Ea.	3.0	635.25
Doors, sliding glass, aluminum, 5/8" insulated glass, 6' wide, premium	1 Ea.	4.0	532.40
Drywall, 1/2" thick, on walls & ceiling, standard taped & finished, 4' x 8' sheets	38 Sheets	22.0	426.70
Trim, casing for windows & door, 11/16" x 2-1/2" wide	50 L.F.	2.0	21.80
Trim, baseboard, 9/16" x 3-1/2"	90 L.F.	3.0	76.25
Flooring, vinyl sheet goods, .125" thick	500 S.F.	17.5	877.25
Painting, walls, ceilings & trim, primer & 1 coat	1200 S.F.	12.0	130.70
Painting, exterior siding, oil base primer & 2 coats, brushwork	185 S.F.	3.0	49.25
Electrical, 8 duplex receptacles, 1 switch	1 Lot	13.5	134.50
Totals		125.0	$4299.95
Project Size 22' x 22'	Contractor's Fee Including Materials		$10,800

> ### Garage Conversion
> A garage conversion is another way in which you can use an existing sheltered area to create new living space in your home. This often underutilized area can be conveniently remodeled to become a comfortable and functional room.

SECTION TWO EXTERIOR IMPROVEMENTS

This section of the book deals with remodeling projects which take place on the outside or apart from the main structure of your home. As in the "Interiors" section, the goal is to inform you of the costs involved and to point out various factors which affect the planning process. Figures are given for the materials, man-hours, and contractor's fees required for the renovation. With this information, you can determine which tasks within the project you want to accomplish yourself and which ones to leave to a contractor. The example projects make suggestions for materials, but other possibilities also exist.

Exterior remodeling has its own set of challenges, but also offers certain advantages over interior projects. Because you are working primarily on the outside of a structure, you generally will have better access to the work area. Carpentry, and especially framing skills, play an important role in erecting the support system of the new structure. The more complicated framing jobs should probably be handled by a contractor. The electrical and plumbing work is more approachable to the do-it-yourselfer because the walls are open for rough-in work. However, if you are inexperienced in these areas, hiring a professional is advised. General precautions should be taken whenever the exterior of the existing house is penetrated. Extra care during the project will head off the expense of repairing damaged finished walls or support members.

The materials required for outdoor projects tend to be of a quantity and size that require delivery by the supplier. Storage is also a consideration. Another point to keep in mind is the availability of building products.

Because some components may have to be ordered in advance, arrangements should be made as soon as possible. Exterior projects sometimes require extra cost for the rental or purchase of special equipment. For the major renovations, it may be best to subcontract the foundation work and framing to a professional who is properly equipped.

Almost all of the projects should have a master plan drawn up in advance. A detailed floor plan will suffice for many of the projects, but a larger scale structure, such as an addition or garage might require side elevations as well. If this drawing cannot be accomplished by a homeowner, a professional can be hired at extra cost. The benefits can be well worth the investment. Another matter which should be taken care of at the beginning is the application for required building permits and an investigation into zoning regulations.

In figuring your total costs, you may need to include extra expenses for such items as a heating system for the additions. Some of the projects may incur extra costs for related procedures, such as adding a driveway for a new garage, or removing one for a garage conversion. Difficult sites and poor soil conditions can also increase your costs. Keep in mind the fact that modifications may need to be made on the model plans and that the costs will change from those listed according to your special requirements.

The projects in this "Exteriors" section are, for the most part, large scale. Some require considerable planning and involve factors different from those in interior remodeling. Knowing in advance both the costs and the work that are involved should prepare you to make the best choices for your exterior improvements.

ATTACHED SINGLE CARPORT

Aluminum Flashing

Rolled Roofing

Aluminum Drip Edge

2" x 4" Girts
Top & Bottom

Rafters 2" x 6"
24" O.C.

2-2" x 6" Header

4" x 4" Pressure-treated Posts

Cedar Board Screen

Concrete Post Footings

Carports offer a simple and economical alternative to the more costly framing and finish work required for conventional garages. In addition to requiring less material, carports are also easier to build than garages. Their uncomplicated design and structure offer the opportunity for do-it-yourselfers to do all or much of the work on their own. Free-standing carports require considerably more skill and know-how to erect than those that are attached to the house, but both projects can be completed by handymen who have basic construction skills and knowledge. This plan demonstrates how a one-car facility can be built for modest expense. Many do-it-yourselfers can complete the job for the cost of the materials.

Materials

The components of this carport project are standard construction materials that can be purchased at building supply outlets. Try to buy all of the materials at the same place, and be sure to make arrangements for curb delivery as part of the purchase price. Because the carport is attached to the house on one side and open at either end, materials are needed only for the side opposite the house and the roof. Both of these sections are basic in their design. Therefore they are fairly easy to build, providing that you lay them out correctly, follow good carpentry paractices, and work slowly on tasks that are new to you.

The side of the structure serves two purposes: providing the support for one end of the roof and supporting the girts to which the siding is fastened. Because the roof structure is large and heavy, the five 4" x 4" posts which support it must be set in concrete footings at least 3' deep. Precise placement of the posts is important, so take time to space them at even intervals, align them with a stringline, and plumb them with a level. If you place the 4" x 4"s in concrete, be sure to use pressure-treated lumber as recommended in the plan. Standard grade 4" x 4"s can also be used at reduced cost, but they should not be set in concrete and require fastening to anchors preset in the footings.

After the posts have been placed, the roof can be framed with 2" x 6"s, set 24" on center, and doubled headers. This roof framing task is the trickiest operation in the project, so get some help if you have not done it before. Be sure to cut the joists at the correct angle on the house end and at the reverse angle on the other end. Also, prepare the house wall to receive the roof assembly by cutting back the siding to the sheathing and arranging for the roof flashing. The method of installing the flashing will depend on the type of siding, so costs may vary for this operation. At the other end of the roof frame, temporary support should be provided for the first few joists before the headers are positioned and fastened. Be sure to square the frame before laying the 1/2" plywood roof sheathing and to stagger the termination seams of the plywood as you are placing it. Rolled roofing material should be used in place of asphalt shingles because of the flat pitch of the shed roof. The installation of this type of roofing can go quickly with the right methods and equipment. With a little advice and instruction beforehand, and the right tools, most handymen can undertake the job, even if they have no prior experience with rolled roofing. Be sure to place the drip edge on all open sides of the roof before you apply the roofing material and to install flashing on the house side.

Once the roof is completed, the girts can be placed between the posts, and then a 5′ high screen attached to them to make up the side of the carport. This plan suggests rough sawn 1″ x 12″ cedar siding boards, but many options are available to suit the style and decor of the house, including various wood sheet goods, and fiberglass and metal panels. The cost of these products varies widely as does their installation time.

No consideration has been given in the plan for the cost of the floor surface within the carport because it is assumed that a driveway is already in place. If a floor surface is not in place, the cost of asphalt pavement, concrete, or gravel, and the time to install it, will have to be added to the project estimate.

Level of Difficulty

This carport plan is a manageable exterior project for most handymen, including beginners who have the time to work slowly and are willing to learn as they go. Some of the tasks involved in the building process require knowledge that beginners may not have, but the required skills can be learned by trial and error and proper guidance from an experienced builder. Two of the jobs within this project are critical: the precise setting and leveling of the support posts and accurate layout and placement of the roof frame. If these two installations are correct, the rest of the job should go smoothly. If you are a beginner, be sure to get some assistance, particularly on these and other unfamiliar tasks. Handymen and experts should be able to handle all of the tasks required in the project, but may need to learn the details of roll roofing installation before they begin that part of the job. Generally, beginners should double the professional time for all tasks; handymen should add 40%; and experts, about 10%.

What to Watch Out For

With the investment of a little more time and money, carports can be made to double as screened-in sitting and eating enclosures. Once the carport structure, as described in this plan, has been completed, screen panels can be made up to fit the open areas in the rear end and side of the enclosure. The front end of the carport can be fitted with roll-down screening that can be raised when the facility is used to shelter the car. These modifications will increase the cost of the project, but they can be done at any time after the carport itself is finished and will add to the practical use of the enclosure.

ATTACHED SINGLE CARPORT

Description	Quantity	Man-hours	Material
Excavate post holes, incl. layout	5 Ea.	7.5	0.00
Concrete, field mix, 1 C.F. per bag, for posts	5 Bags	2.5	15.30
Posts, pressure-treated, 4″ x 4″ x 10′	50 L.F.	2.0	56.90
Headers, 2″ x 6″, doubled	96 L.F.	3.5	59.25
Joists/rafters, 2″ x 6″ x 12′, 24″ O.C.	132 L.F.	4.5	81.45
Sheathing, 5/8″ plywood, 4′ x 8′ sheets	288 S.F.	3.5	153.35
Roofing, rolled, 30 lb., asphalt-coated felt	3 Sq.	2.5	93.90
Drip edge, aluminum, 5″	48 L.F.	1.0	8.70
Girts, 2″ x 4″, for screening panel	40 L.F.	1.5	16.45
Siding boards, cedar, rough-sawn, 1″ x 12″, board on board	110 S.F.	3.5	150.40
Paint, primer & 2 coats, all exposed wood	625 S.F.	12.0	151.25
Totals		44.0	$786.95
Project Size 11′ x 21′	Contractor's Fee Including Materials		$2380

Attached Single Carport

A carport can serve as a practical alternative to a full garage at a fraction of the cost for both materials and labor. Because of the basic design of this project, most handymen can complete this home improvement for only the cost of the materials.

FREESTANDING DOUBLE CARPORT

This plan demonstrates how a two-car facility can be economically built by using post-and-beam construction methods. Although the carport in this plan is large in size, with over 400 square feet of floor area, the simplicity of its design makes it a reasonable undertaking for handymen who are experienced in the use of tools and have a fundamental knowledge of carpentry. Because of the size of this structure, beginners should leave much of the post-and-beam support installation and roof framing to the professional, but they are encouraged to tackle some of the other tasks in the project. Generally, skilled handymen and experts can complete the entire project with the exception of the concrete floor.

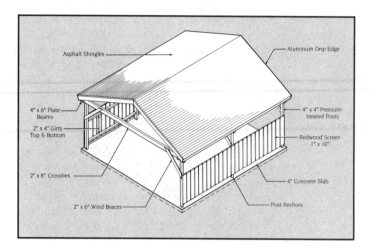

Asphalt Shingles

Aluminum Drip Edge

4" x 6" Plate Beams

2" x 4" Girts Top & Bottom

4" x 4" Pressure-treated Posts

Redwood Screen 1" x 10"

2" x 8" Crossties

4" Concrete Slab

2" x 6" Wind Braces

Post Anchors

Materials

The materials used in this project start with ready-mixed concrete for the floor and the conventional components of post-and-beam construction, including 4" x 6"s and 4" x 8"s (or doubled 2" x 8"s). Standard grade 2" x 6" rafters, plywood sheathing, and asphalt shingles are needed for the roofing, and siding material is required for screening.

The preparation for the wood structure begins with the excavation for and placement of the concrete floor. There are several important aspects in this procedure which, when closely monitored, can help the rest of the project go smoothly. The first is to double check the square and level of the 2" x 6" form before the concrete is placed. The second is to be sure that the post anchors for the 4" x 6"s are set in precise position and alignment as they are imbedded in the concrete. Remember that the wood structure will be supported by the slab and aligned according to the position of the anchors, so measure and square the layout carefully. If you are inexperienced with this type of concrete placement, get some assistance from an experienced person or subcontract this part of the project to a professional.

The post-and-beam construction of the roof support requires basic carpentry know-how and some engineering skills as well. The three post and crosstie assemblies can be laid out and fabricated on the slab before being raised and positioned on the anchors and temporarily braced. Be sure that they are plumb, level, and square before the 4" x 6" plate beams are placed and fastened. Some skilled handymen and experts can tackle this operation, but beginners and handymen with limited building skills should seek the help of a knowledgeable friend or hire a professional for this procedure.

The roof frame is constructed of 2" x 6"rafters, set 24" on center, and a 2" x 8" ridge board. Like the post-and-beam support system, the roof framing requires a fundamental knowledge of carpentry and advanced building skills. If you are unfamiliar with the process of cutting and setting rafters, get some instruction beforehand, and be sure to have some helpers available. Remember, too, that you will be working 8' to 12' off the ground when placing the rafters, so make arrangements to rent or borrow some staging, tressel ladders and planks, or other means of working safely and efficiently at the 12' ridge board height. An alternative to installing the rafters is to purchase manufactured 2" x 4" trusses and place them 24" on center.

The 1/2" plywood sheathing is placed on the rafters after the roof frame has been squared and fastened. The aluminum drip edge, which is installed before the roofing is laid, is an inexpensive but important item, as it provides run-off clearance for rain water and creates a straight, neat, finished edge for the roofing. Experts and most handymen should be able to handle this roofing job, as it consists of straight runs with no valleys, flashing, or other challenging obstacles. Because the finished sides of the carport should conform to the style and decor of your house, you can select from many different materials, including plywood products, siding boards, and metal and fiberglass panels. This plan suggests that the 1" x 10" redwood tongue-and-groove siding be placed on the 2" x 4" girts as screening and then stained or painted. The post-and-beam supports, girts, rafters, underside of the roof deck, and the fascia board are also covered with two coats of stain or paint.

Level of Difficulty

This carport plan calls for a moderate to advanced level of building expertise and carpentry skills. In addition, the size of the structure and the post-and-beam layout requirements involve complex planning that may put parts of the project out of reach for beginners and many handymen.

After the supports and roof frame are in place, most handymen can finish the job, including the installation of the roof sheathing and shingles. Be sure to get some instruction in the roofing process if you have not laid shingles before. Straight roofs are not that hard to install, and a good start can make them a fairly simple installation. Beginners and handymen with no related experience should hire a professional for the concrete slab installation. Experts and handymen should allow extra time for a careful layout of the forms and should arrange to have several helpers on hand when the concrete is placed. Accomplished handymen and experts should add 100% and 50%, respectively, to the professional time for the slab installation, including the form work. They should add 40% and 10%, respectively, for all other tasks.

What to Watch Out For

The concrete surface that serves as the floor of the carport is an important feature of the structure and must be correctly placed. If you are installing it on your own, be sure to set the forms accurately so that the edges of the slab are level and square. Metal rod or wire reinforcement, a sub-base of granular material, and a plastic vapor barrier are also necessary for correct installation. Remember, too, that provisions for surface water drainage should be made by crowning the slab. Wind-driven rain or snow, and water from wet or snow-covered vehicles can collect and puddle in low spots on the surface, but these problems can be avoided with proper finishing of the floor. Seek help from a cement-mason or concrete contractor if you are inexperienced and need assistance in placing the slab.

FREESTANDING DOUBLE CARPORT

Description	Quantity	Man-hours	Material
Grading, by hand, for slab area	53 S.Y.	2.0	0.00
Edge forms for floor slab	86 L.F.	5.0	20.80
Concrete floor slab, 4" thick, 3000 psi complete	460 S.F.	14.5	879.45
Post anchors, embedded in slab	6 Ea.	0.5	2.45
Posts, pressure-treated, 4" x 6" x 8'	48 L.F.	2.5	81.90
Crossties, 2" x 8" x 22'	132 L.F.	5.0	116.60
Plate beams, 4" x 6" x 12'	48 L.F.	2.0	81.90
Ridge board, 2" x 8", x 12'	24 L.F.	1.0	21.20
Fascia board, 2" x 8" x 12'	48 L.F.	2.0	42.40
Rafters, 2" x 6" x 12', 24" O.C.	288 L.F.	9.5	177.75
Sheathing, 1/2" plywood, 4' x 8' sheets	544 S.F.	6.0	269.90
Drip edge, aluminum, 5"	96 L.F.	2.0	17.45
Shingles, asphalt, 235 lb. per square	6 Sq.	9.0	218.90
Braces, 2" x 6" x 4'	40 L.F.	1.5	24.70
Girts, 2" x 4" for screening panels	84 L.F.	2.5	34.55
Screening, redwood channel siding, 1" x 10"	210 S.F.	6.0	304.90
Paint, primer & 2 coats	1100 S.F.	21.0	266.20
Stain, 2 coats, brushwork on screen	420 S.F.	5.0	81.30
Totals		97.0	$2642.35
Project Size 20' x 21'	Contractor's Fee Including Materials		$7200

Freestanding Double Carport
Although this double carport is fairly basic in design, it is a challenging undertaking for most do-it-yourselfers. It is not out of reach, however, with help and guidance. This project is a good way to gain experience while creating a practical addition to your home.

ATTACHED SINGLE CAR GARAGE

A garage can boost the value of a house, as it provides protection for vehicles and sheltered work and storage space. Like carports, garages can be attached or free standing, with single or double bays. They should be carefully planned around such factors as their intended use, and the style and size of your house, as well as the available land and the characteristics of the site. This model is a basic single car garage, attached to the house and built on level ground. Many do-it-yourselfers can accomplish this project with limited assistance and subcontracting. The result is a practical home improvement completed at reasonable cost.

Aluminum Gutters & Downspouts
Aluminum Flashing
Asphalt Shingles
Aluminum Soffit & Fascia
Cedar Bevel Siding
Backfill, Finish Grade & Re-seed
4" Concrete Slab
9' x 7' Wood Garage Door
Wood Double-hung Window
Concrete Block Foundation
Concrete Strip Footing

Materials

Before the foundation and floor are placed, the site for the new garage must be cleared and a perimeter trench excavated to a depth of about 4'. The site conditions of the garage location will have an impact on cost. For example, a severe slope in the grade may require a higher foundation or backfill to raise the grade. If needed, such operations will add to the cost of the project. Generally, if the terrain is level and free of trees and other obstructions, no extra cost will be incurred in the site preparation. The excavation of the 12' x 22' foundation trench should be dug to a level below the frost line and should be deep and wide enough to allow for an 8" x 16" footing and a 3' to 4' foundation. Where no frost line exists, it might be possible to decrease the foundation depth. The estimate for this garage provides for hand excavation and the installation of 8" concrete blocks for the foundation. It is probably best to hire specialty contractors for the foundation work. At the very least, they can will complete the process more rapidly and with less aggravation. The concrete slab can be placed at any time after the foundation has been completed. When excavating for the slab, be sure to allow for several inches of sub-base, 4" of concrete, and at least one exposed course of block

above the floor surface, except in the section that will include the door. If you are installing the floor on your own, be sure to allow a gradual slope toward the door opening for drainage.

Once the foundation has been placed and backfilled, the three walls can be framed and sheathed. Standard grade 2" x 4"s placed 16" on center, with a doubled plate on the top and a single shoe plate on the bottom, make up the walls. Be sure to fasten the shoe plate firmly to the 2" x 6" sill, which is anchored to the top of the foundation wall. The rear wall of this garage is solid, but the side and front partitions require openings for the window and door. The cost for 2" x 8" headers and 2" x 4" jack studs and their installation time have been included in the plan. Remember to include additional time for removing some or all of the siding from the house wall before the framing begins. After the walls are framed, 2" x 6" joists are laid and the roof framing can begin.

The framing of the roof is more difficult than that of the partitions; but this roof is still small enough to provide a good chance for do-it-yourselfers to pick up experience in placing a ridge board and rafter system. With some advice before you start and guidance as you go, your skills will improve as you progress. Consistency of rafter length and accurate angling and notching are the key to a square and level roof frame. Once the rafters have been laid out and cut from a template, the placement and fastening operations usually move quickly. After the frame is complete, the sheathing, drip edge, and roofing are installed. The shingling can be done by most do-it-yourselfers because the roof is straight and basic in its design. Get some assistance on placing the flashing, however, if the process is unfamiliar to you. A poor or incorrect flashing job can cause water damage to the interior of the garage and to the adjacent house wall and ceiling.

There are several options for the exterior finish products to be used on this garage. An economical, standard double-hung model is a good choice for the window. This plan suggests low-maintenance aluminum fascias, soffits, and gutters, but wood products could also be em-

ployed for these components. The design and cost of these items should be considered along with your house's style and your budget limitations. Similarly, garage door units are available in expensive wood-paneled models, as well as in economical fiberglass and hardboard designs.

Level of Difficulty

Foundation, framing, and roofing operations are challenging tasks, regardless of the type of structure being built. Inexperienced do-it-yourselfers should assess their level of skills and the amount of time they can give to the project before taking it on. Because this structure is relatively small, with one side already in place, handymen can improve their building skills while working on the project; but they should seek assistance when they need it. The concrete and masonry work may be out of the reach of many do-it-yourselfers. Digging trenches, constructing forms, and laying concrete blocks are physically demanding, time-consuming operations. Ambitious beginners can complete most of the project once the foundation is in, but they should get instruction at the start and guidance along the way. They should double the man-hours for the tasks they attempt. Handymen and experts should add 40% and 10%, respectively, for the carpentry work, and more for specialty operations like the foundation, floor, and garage door installations.

What to Watch Out For

An automatic garage door opener is a convenient accessory which can be installed by most handymen. These devices can be adapted to all types of door units and garage interiors and installed in just a few hours' time. The cost of an automatic opener has not been included in this plan, but some of the money saved by doing the project on your own might be applied to this convenience item.

ATTACHED SINGLE CAR GARAGE			
Description	Quantity	Man-hours	Material
Site clearing, layout, excavate for footing	1 Lot	6.0	0.00
Footing, 8" thick x 16" wide x 44'	2 C.Y.	5.5	167.00
Foundation, 6" concrete block, 3'-4" high	200 Blocks	18.5	363.00
Edge form at doorway	10 L.F.	0.5	2.45
Floor slab, 4" thick, 300 psi, w/sub-base, reinforcing, finished	265 S.F.	9.0	506.65
Wall framing, 2" x 4" x 10', 16" O.C.	38 L.F.	6.5	139.80
Headers over openings, 2" x 8"	14 L.F.	1.0	9.65
Sheathing for walls, 1/2" thick, 4' x 8' sheets	12 Sheets	5.0	190.50
Ridge board, 1" x 8" x 12'	12 L.F.	0.5	4.10
Roof framing, rafters, 2" x 6" x 14', 16" O.C.	280 L.F.	4.5	132.15
Joists, 2" x 6" x 22', 16" O.C.	220 L.F.	3.0	103.85
Gable framing, 2" x 4"	45 L.F.	1.5	14.15
Sheathing for roof, 1/2" thick, 4' x 8' sheets	11 Sheets	4.0	174.65
Sub-fascia, 2" x 8" x 12'	24 L.F.	2.0	16.55
Felt paper, 15 lb.	340 S.F.	0.5	12.35
Shingles, asphalt, standard strip	4 Sq.	6.5	149.05
Drip edge, aluminum, 5"	52 L.F.	1.0	9.45
Flashing, aluminum	21 S.F.	1.5	16.75
Fascia, aluminum	21 S.F.	1.5	52.85
Soffit, aluminum	38 S.F.	1.5	33.55
Gutters & downspouts, aluminum	44 L.F.	3.0	44.20
Window, wood, standard, 34" x 22"	1 Ea.	1.0	157.30
Garage door, wood, incl. hardware, 9' x 7'	1 Ea.	2.0	453.75
Siding, cedar, rough sawn, stained	400 S.F.	13.5	963.15
Painting, door & window trim, primer & 2 coats	85 S.F.	2.0	7.20
Totals		101.5	$3724.10
Project Size 12' x 22'	Contractor's Fee Including Materials		$9110

Attached Single Car Garage

Adding a garage improves the value of your home while providing shelter for your vehicle and increasing storage and protected work space. By doing some or all of the work on your own, this attached one-car facility can be built at a surprisingly low cost.

FREESTANDING DOUBLE GARAGE

Aluminum Soffit & Fascia

Aluminum Gutters

Asphalt Shingles

Aluminum Downspouts

Wood Double Hung Windows

Aluminum Siding

Wood Pre-hung Entrance Door

4" Concrete Slab

16' x 7' Fiberglass Garage Door

If your house lot is large enough to accommodate the addition of a free-standing garage, you might consider using this model for a two-car facility. This plan is basic in both design and materials; but it is still a major project, and one that will challenge do-it-yourselfers of all ability levels. With patient and careful work, however, handymen can save on labor costs by completing some or all of the project on their own.

Materials

The basic components of this two-car garage are commonly available building materials used in wood frame structures. A 4" reinforced concrete slab with a thickened perimeter comprises the foundation and finished floor of the structure. Standard 2" x 4" framing materials, plywood, and asphalt shingles are employed for the roof. Several specialty products are also included to finish the structure, including aluminum gutters, soffits, and fascias, and a double-width fiberglass garage door. Bear in mind that all of these materials are competitively priced at building supply outlets. With this size order, you have some leverage in getting the best possible price. Arrange for local delivery in the final purchase agreement, as most of these materials require trucking. Cost, quality, and convenience are factors to consider before making your materials purchase.

If the site for the new garage is level and dry, the suggested 4" reinforced concrete slab with a thickened perimeter is generally all that is required for a foundation. Such factors as poor soil conditions, frost, and the possibility of future attachment to an existing structure may require the placement of a footing and foundation wall at extra cost. The site clearing and excavation will

take some time because of the large surface area, so plan accordingly, particularly if you intend to clear and dig by hand. If you are unfamiliar with concrete installations, seek some advice from a knowledgeable person or subcontract the job to a professional. Incorrect slab placement can be the cause of wasted time and materials later on in the construction.

Installing the wall materials for this four-sided structure requires a command of basic carpentry skills. If you have not framed a four-sided structure before, you will need some assistance in the layout, erecting, squaring, and securing of the partitions. After the wall framing is in place, 1/2" exterior plywood sheathing should be installed for support and as a base for the finished siding.

The roof framing is the most difficult task in the entire project, as the 2" x 6" rafters and 1" x 8" ridge board have to be positioned with great accuracy. Poor workmanship can cause wasted time and material, and result in variations in the finished roofing. Like the straight roof in the free-standing carport project, this shingling job can be handled by most do-it-yourselfers. After the drip edge has been placed and the layout established, keep a check on course gain as you go up the roof. Roofing felt is an extra weatherproofing material which is applied under the asphalt shingles in this project. It is not an essential item, however, if you are looking for a way to cut costs.

Once the roof has been completed, the structure is ready to receive the windows, entrance door, siding, garage door, and other finish products. A wide variety of standard prehung window and door units can be used, depending on the style of your home, the garage's visibility, and your budget. The extra expense for insulating glass or deluxe airtight units is unnecessary unless you plan to insulate and heat the facility. This plan features low-maintenance aluminum siding, soffits, and gutters, but standard wood products can be used in their place at varying costs. If you choose the suggested aluminum material, a specialty contractor should be consulted or called in, as these products require particular tools and expertise for fast and efficient installation. Many different types of garage doors are available in a wide range of prices, in both wood and man-made materials.

FREESTANDING DOUBLE GARAGE

Description	Quantity	Man-hours	Material
Grading, by hand, for slab area	576 S.F.	8.5	0.00
Edge forms for floor slab	88 L.F.	5.0	21.30
Concrete floor slab, 4" thick, 3000 psi, complete	484 S.F	4.0	925.30
Anchor bolts, embedded in slab	20 Ea.	1.0	8.25
Wall framing, 2" x 4" x 8', 24" O.C., studs & plates	80 L.F.	10.5	224.60
Headers over openings, 2" x 12"	28 L.F.	1.5	30.85
Sheathing for walls, 1/2" thick, plywood, 4' x 8' sheets	23 Sheets	10.5	365.15
Ridge board, 1" x 8" x 12'	24 L.F.	1.0	8.15
Roof framing, rafters, 2" x 6" x 14', 24" O.C.	336 L.F.	5.5	158.55
Joists, 2" x 6" x 22', 24" O.C.	264 L.F.	3.5	124.60
Gable framing, 2" x 4"	75 L.F.	2.5	23.60
Sheathing for roof, 1/2" thick, plywood, 4' x 8' sheets	21 Sheets	7.5	375.05
Sub-fascia, 2" x 8" x 12'	48 L.F.	3.5	33.10
Felt paper, 15 lb.	625 S.F.	1.0	22.70
Shingles, asphalt, standard strip	7 Sq.	10.5	260.90
Drip edge, aluminum, 5"	100 L.F.	2.0	18.15
Fascia, aluminum	50 S.F.	3.0	125.85
Soffit, aluminum	70 S.F.	3.0	61.85
Gutters & downspouts, aluminum	64 L.F.	4.5	64.30
Windows, wood, standard, 2' x 3'	2 Ea.	2.0	314.60
Garage door, incl. hardware, hardboard, 16' x 7', standard	1 Ea.	3.0	677.60
Entrance door, wood, pre-hung, 2'-8" x 6'-8"	1 Ea.	1.0	199.65
Siding, aluminum, double 4" pattern, 8" wide	680 S.F.	21.5	798.15
Painting, entrance door & window trim, primer & 2 coats	50 S.F.	1.0	4.25
Totals		117.0	$4846.50

Project Size	22' x 22'	Contractor's Fee Including Materials	$12,230

Level of Difficulty

If you are familiar with framing operations and reasonably skilled in exterior home improvements, you should be able to complete this garage project. As noted earlier, it is a major undertaking and will take considerable time to complete, but if you are willing to work slowly and carefully, the results will be worthwhile. Two critical procedures, the slab installation and roof framing, can be costly if they are not done correctly. Seek professional assistance for these tasks if you feel that they are beyond your abilities. Beginners should not attempt the concrete, framing, and specialty installations; and they should add 100% to the professional time for other jobs like the sheathing and roofing. They should get professional help or guidance for all tasks that are new to them. Handymen and experts should add 40% and 10%, respectively, to the man-hours estimates for the jobs they attempt. They should add more for the slab placement and roof framing if they are inexperienced in these operations. Handymen and experts should also consider hiring professionals for the specialty work, like the aluminum siding and garage door installation.

What to Watch Out For

This two-car garage project provides an excellent opportunity for the homeowner to create storage and workshop space in addition to shelter for vehicles. If the peak of the structure is high enough, over 300 square feet of usable storage space exists in the attic above the ceiling joists. Although it will add to the cost and time of the project, decking can be laid over the joists, and an access door can be framed into the gable above the garage door opening. Remember that the ceiling joists suggested in this plan are only 2" x 6"s; 2" x 8"s should be used for the joists if heavy materials are to be stored in this area.

Freestanding Double Garage

If your lot and dwelling can accommodate a large free-standing garage, this economical and practical design might be the right choice. Although it is a major project, handymen who have the time can complete much of the work on their own, with a substantial savings in the cost of construction.

FINISHED BREEZEWAY WITH SCREENS

A screened-in sitting or eating area can add pleasure and comfort to any home. Such a facility can be created without building a separate structure if an existing breezeway is used. Because the roof, side walls, and floor are already in place, the cost of remodeling a breezeway is considerably less than that of a new addition. Also, because breezeways are generally at the first floor level, the project site is easily accessible and can usually be framed and screened with few logistical problems. Like deck projects, breezeway conversions normally cause little or no disruption to the homes routine, and, therefore, can be completed at a slower pace.

Materials

The materials needed to complete this breezeway remodeling project include standard 2″ x 4″s to frame the knee wall and door opening, 2″ x 6″s for the rafters, appropriate coverings for the knee wall, ceiling, and floor, and the screen panels and door. All of these materials are readily available from building supply outlets, so it pays to compare prices from several different retailers. The screen panels are specialty items which have to be custom fitted to the opening created by the knee wall frame. If you hire a contractor to build the panels, it might be a good idea to have him install them as well. If you intend to build the panels on your own, develop a master plan for all of the screening to determine the most cost-effective width for the individual panels, and then base the order for the screening and wood frame on that factor. Plan to include delivery as a part of the purchase order for all of the materials, as the lumber needed to frame the enclosure, the knee wall, and ceiling coverings is cumbersome and will have to be trucked.

Precise framing is required for the knee wall, as it serves as the primary support for the screen panels. If it is not level and plumb, the panels will not seat correctly and openings will result along the abutting edges. If the existing wood or concrete floor of the breezeway is uneven or slanted, you will have to shim or angle the bottom of the knee wall frame to attain a level surface on the top. Do-it-yourselfers who are inexperienced in framing procedures should get some assistance before or during the knee wall construction, as its placement must be correct for the rest of the job to go smoothly. After the knee wall is in place and the doorway has been framed, rough-sawn plywood siding is applied to the exterior.

In this enclosure, the ceiling is prepared with 2″ x 6″ joists, spaced 24″ on center. Although 16″ spacing is the accepted standard in other types of construction, 24″ spacing is adequate for this project. This plan includes 3/8″ rough-sawn fir plywood for the ceiling surface, but other materials can be installed at varying costs. The cost of indoor/outdoor carpeting is also included, though other types of floor materials such as weather resistant tiling and exterior floor paint can also be used. The inside of the knee wall is covered with fir plywood in this model, but once again, other choices are available. Be sure to include additional expense for any electrical work, such as a ceiling light fixture, door lamp, and watertight duplex outlets. Especially if you plan to use the enclosure at night, some provision for lighting should be made in the master plan before construction begins. If you wait until the new materials are in place, the labor cost for electrical work will be higher than if you have it done beforehand.

Particular care should be exercised in the planning, building, and installation of the screen panels. A prefabricated type is included in this estimate, but do-it-yourselfers may consider making their own. Be aware, however, that they are tricky to make and require the proper tools and know-how. Fiberglass and aluminum screening are available in different grades and at varying costs, so shop carefully if you are making the screens yourself. Even tension of the screening is important for both the appearance and longevity of the panels, so get some instruction from a knowledgeable person on the ins and outs of screen panel manufacture before you start. You might consider installing them in such a way that they can be conveniently removed for periodic cleaning, painting, and storage during the off season. Prefabricated aluminum screen panels can also be used as an alternative to the suggested wood-framed units, but they have to be custom made and, therefore, cost more.

Level of Difficulty

This project is a manageable undertaking for most do-it-yourselfers who have a basic knowl-

edge of carpentry and experience in the use of tools. The most challenging task is the planning, building, and installation of the screen panels. As noted earlier, this part of the project should be left to professionals or expert do-it-yourselfers. The hanging of the screen door also requires advanced carpentry skills. Generally, beginners should not attempt the frame, rafter, door, carpeting, and screening tasks; and they should double the professional time estimates for all other jobs. They should seek professional help on unfamiliar tasks. Handymen should stop short of the screen panel fabrication and carpeting; but they should be able to complete the rest of the project with the addition of about 40% to the man-hours estimates. Experts should allow an additional 10% in time for all tasks, and more for the screen panels if they have no experience in this operation.

What to Watch Out For

The details of the wood-framed screen panel installation will vary according to the desired finish appearance of the enclosure. In a basic installation, the panels can be secured at the top and bottom to the interior or exterior face of the new wall. In a more finished installation, the panels can be placed within the framed opening and secured with stops made from trim material, such as quarter-round moulding or 1″ x 1″ pine strips.

Brass or galvanized wood screws can then be used as fasteners to allow for easy removal of the panels for maintenance or storage during the off season. This type of finished installation will require additional materials and more time to accomplish; but the extra cost and effort may prove worthwhile.

FINISHED BREEZEWAY WITH SCREENS

Description	Quantity	Man-hours	Material
Framing for knee wall, plates 2″ x 4″ stock	96 L.F.	2.0	30.20
Framing for knee wall, studs, 2″ x 4″ x 3′	60 L.F.	1.5	14.50
Framing for doorways, 2″ x 4″ x 8′	72 L.F.	1.5	22.65
Ceiling joists, 2″ x 6″ x 24′, 24″ O.C.	240 L.F.	3.5	113.25
Ceiling, rough sawn cedar, plywood, 3/8″ thick, pre-stained	9 Sheets	7.0	372.87
Siding for knee wall, both sides rough sawn cedar, 5/8″ thick, pre-stained	2 Sheets	1.5	82.86
Wood screens, 1-1/8″ frames	200 S.F.	9.0	605.00
Screen door, wood, 2′-8″ x 6′-9″	2 Ea.	2.5	382.35
Painting, inside wall & trim, primer and 2 coats	200 S.F.	2.5	29.05
Indoor/outdoor carpet, 3/8″ thick	32 S.Y.	12.0	818.93
Totals		43.0	$2471.65

Project Size	24′ x 12′	Contractor's Fee Including Materials	$5840

Finished Breezeway With Screens

An existing breezeway already has the basic requirements of a roof and two walls that make it easily convertible to a screened-in porch. It is in a convenient work location, and many of the tasks are within reach of do-it-yourselfers. The costs can be kept down because of the relatively small quantities of materials required and the potential savings on labor.

FINISHED BREEZEWAY WITH WINDOWS

Breezeways are logical areas to convert to interior living space because two walls, the roof, floor, and support structure are already in place. The project requires framing the two open sides and all of the tasks necessary to finish the exterior of the two new walls, including the installation of a door and windows. After the breezeway has been closed in, the necessary interior finish work is completed as in other types of conversion projects. Because the breezeway is usually located on the first floor with immediate accessibility from the yard and garage, the logistics of materials storage and transport are minimal. This plan demonstrates how a 12' x 12' breezeway can be converted to interior living space at reasonable cost.

Aluminum Ridge Vent

Existing Roof Structure

Wood Colonial Door

Red Cedar Shingles

Casement Bay Window

Materials

The materials included in this plan consist of standard construction products available at building supply outlets and lumber yards. First of all, framing materials will be needed for the two open walls. Exterior and interior sheathing is also required, along with a door, windows, and insulation. Floor coverings, trim work, and a minimal electrical installation complete the list of supplies for the interior work.

The framing for the two open walls is constructed from 2" x 4"s set 16" on center with a single bottom and a doubled top plate. The door and window rough openings should be built into the partition using jack studs and 2" x 8" headers. After the framing is in place, 1/2" plywood sheathing is placed on the outside. When the door and windows have been installed, the siding is put on. Try to match closely the siding on the new room to that of the rest of the house by using the same material, following existing course lines, and painting and finishing it in the same style. Additional cost can be anticipated for the matching of expensive sidings and for any special installation techniques required to install them.

The door and window units included in the plan can be altered to meet the style and design of the house. The three-lite bay unit, for example, is an attractive and practical window, but two double-hung windows may be more appropriate. As a general rule, a quality window product is a worthwhile investment. Years of energy efficiency, easy operation, and low maintenance will return the extra initial expense. The same rule holds for the selection of the exterior door unit. Before you attempt to install the door and windows, line up a helper because these items are heavy, can be awkward to manipulate, and are expensive to repair if they are dropped or mishandled.

The materials used in the interior of the remodeled breezeway include new 2" x 6" ceiling joists (if none are in place) and strapping, insulation and drywall for the ceiling and walls, and carpeting for the floor. As in other interior remodeling projects, many alternative materials are available at varying costs to suit your personal tastes and home decor. Remember that if portions of the exterior house and garage walls are included in the new room, they must be stripped of their exterior siding and drywalled or covered with suitable interior wall material. The garage wall may also have to be insulated, and the garage doorway dressed up or relocated. All of these operations will add cost and time to the job.

Before the interior wall and ceiling coverings are installed, the rough electrical wiring and boxes have to be in place. This plan includes the basic electrical service of four wall outlets and a switch box. If you want to put in an overhead fixture, recessed or track lighting, a door lamp, or other electrical facilities, the cost for the project will increase. Hire a qualified electrician to do the work if you are unfamiliar with electrical installation procedures. Do-it-yourselfers should not attempt to tie in the new wiring to the panel, even if they are experienced enough to do all other parts of the electrical installation.

FINISHED BREEZEWAY WITH WINDOWS

Description	Quantity	Man-hours	Material
Wall framing: studs, 2"x 4", 16" O.C., 8' long	240 L.F.	4.0	75.50
Plates, single bottom, double top, 2" x 4"	80 L.F.	2.0	25.20
Headers, over windows & door, 2" x 8"	30 L.F.	1.5	20.70
Sheeting, plywood, 1/2" thick, 4' x 8' sheets	6 Sheets	3.0	95.25
Ceiling joists, 2" x 6", 16" O.C. 12' long	12 Ea.	2.0	67.95
Ceiling furring 1" x 3" strapping, 16" O.C.	150 L.F.	3.5	18.15
Insulation, ceiling, 6" thick, R-19, paperbacked	150 S.F.	1.0	65.35
Insulation, walls, 3-1/2" thick, R-11, paperbacked	200 S.F.	1.0	53.25
Sheetrock, walls & ceilings, 1/2" thick, 4' x 8' sheets taped & finished	18 Sheets	10.0	175.00
Door, exterior, 2 lite, colonial, 2'-8" x 6'-8"	1 Ea.	1.0	296.45
Window, 3 lite bay window, casement type, plastic clad, premium	1 Ea.	2.0	1210.00
Window, 2 lite casement window, plastic clad, premium	2 Ea.	2.0	484.00
Siding, No. 1 red cedar shingles, 7-1/2" exposure	190 S.F.	7.5	183.90
Roof vent, ridge type	12 L.F.	1.0	31.50
Trim, colonial casing, windows, door & base	120 L.F.	4.5	106.00
Paint, walls, ceiling and trim, primer and 2 coats	575 S.F.	7.0	90.45
Carpet, nylon antistatic	16 S.Y.	3.0	296.20
Pad, sponge rubber	16 S.Y.	1.0	43.55
Electrical work, 1 switch, 4 plugs	1 Lot	3.0	74.95
Totals		60.0	$3413.35

Project Size	12' x 12'	Contractor's Fee Including Materials	$7080

Level of Difficulty

Handymen with a command of basic carpentry and remodeling skills and experts should be able to complete most of this project. The site is convenient, the extent of remodeling is fairly limited, and the tasks are routine, with the exception of the electrical and carpeting installations. Specialty contractors should be hired to perform these operations in most cases. Even experts should weigh the savings of doing these jobs on their own against the benefits of fast, high-quality professional work. For all tasks, except the electrical and flooring work, handymen should add 40% to the professional time, and experts 10%. Beginners should hire a contractor to do all of the exterior work, including the window and door installations. With some instruction and guidance, they can perform some of the insulating, drywalling, painting, and trim work. They should, however, leave the placement of the ceiling joists, electrical installation, and carpeting to professionals. For the interior jobs which they do take on, they should add 80% to the professional time estimate.

What to Watch Out For

Although this breezeway project presents an economical means of converting exterior space to interior living area, it contains some potential problems that may add to its cost and increase the installation time. The doorway into the house will require attention because it should be converted into an interior opening and trimmed with the same materials used in the new room. If the doorway is one step above the new floor level, a suitable interior step should be built. The old door can be used for the new exterior installation as a cost-cutting measure.

Finished Breezeway With Windows

Because a breezeway already has a floor, roof, and two walls, it is a practical, convenient source of new interior living space. The tasks involved in its conversion are within the realm of many do-it-yourselfers, and this aspect of the project can make it an economical undertaking as well.

NEW CONSTRUCTION BREEZEWAY

This plan demonstrates how the area between a detached garage and house can be converted to living space. As detailed here, the new structure is connected to the end wall of the house and the side wall of the garage. Depending on the configuration of the existing structures, alternative designs and/or alignments may be required with accompanying variations in cost. Because the breezeway room has to be constructed within established boundaries, it is a challenging project for do-it-yourselfers, but one that can be completed by those who have a reasonable level of remodeling skill. The results of the project will enhance your home's appearance and value, and add considerably to its living area.

Red Cedar Shingles
Zinc & Copper Alloy Valley Flashing
Zinc & Copper Alloy Flashing
Cedar Fascia
Aluminum Gutter
Aluminum Downspouts
Cedar Plywood Soffit
Wood Double-hung Windows, Vinyl-clad
Backfill, Finish Grade, & Re-seed
Cedar Bevel Siding
Concrete Block Foundation
Concrete Strip Footing

Materials

The foundation materials consist of a concrete footing and concrete block wall. Before the footing and wall are placed, excavation of the site is required to make room for the new foundation. Because of the close quarters between the existing structures, much of the digging will probably have to be done by hand, so plan accordingly and allow plenty of time for the job. After the foundation wall is in place, 2″ x 8″ joists and plywood decking are placed to frame the rough floor of the new room. Before installing the joists, cover the area with a vapor barrier, then insulate between the joists before laying the subfloor. The foundation and floor must be correctly installed to ensure a firm and level starting point for the rest of the project. The walls of the breeezeway room are constructed from standard materials, including 2″ x 4″s, sheathing, windows, a sliding glass door, and finished siding. Before the framing begins, allow some time to prepare the adjacent walls of the house and garage to receive the new materials. The siding must be stripped and, in some cases, a door or window may have to be removed or relocated if it will interfere with the framing process. The new partitions should be carefully laid out, since they must be erected to a predetermined height and length as established by the existing garage and house. This plan suggests 25/32″ wood fiberboard for sheathing, but 5/8″ CDX plywood can also be used at a slight increase in cost. Make sure that the wall framing is even with the face of the concrete to allow the siding to extend over the lip of the foundation for proper weather protection. When the rough walls have been erected, the 2″ x 6″ ceiling joists should be installed to keep the new walls in place before the roof is framed. The placing of the rafters is the most challenging part of the project, and advanced framing skills and know-how are required to do the job, so get help if you have not done it before. Be sure that you check the condition of the garage shingles, support, and sheathing before you begin the framing for the new roof. Do not proceed with the installation of the new roof until any deficiencies have been corrected. Additional cost and time will be required if you are careless in stripping the old roofing, so work slowly and remove only as much as you have to. After 1/2″ plywood has been placed on the rafters, the roofing material is installed to make the new structure weathertight. The cost for the roofing material and the time to install it will vary.

After the roof and soffit are in place, the door and windows can be installed, and the exterior walls sided. This plan suggests a high quality vinyl-clad sliding glass door unit and four matching thermopane windows. Both of these products feature the advantages of low maintenance, neat design, and energy savings. Costs will vary considerably with the choice of alternative door and window products, so shop wisely and select quality units which will fit your design standards and budget. Like the roofing, the siding material for the new room should also match or complement the material on the house and garage, and it should be appropriately finished with paint or stain to blend with the existing structures.

New Construction Breezeway

Description	Quantity	Man-hours	Material
Excavate by hand for footing, 4' wide, 4' deep	19 C.Y.	19.0	0.00
Footings, 8" thick x 16" wide x 32'	2 C.Y.	5.5	167.00
Foundation, 8" concrete block, 3'-4" high	120 Block	10.5	181.50
Floor framing, sill plate, 2" x 6"	32 L.F.	1.0	15.10
Joists, 2" x 8" x 10', 16" O.C.,	160 L.F.	2.5	110.35
Insulation, 6" thick, R-19	160 S.F.	1.0	75.50
Subfloor, 5/8" x 4' x 8' plywood	5 Sheets	2.5	85.20
Wall framing, 2" x 4" x 8', 16" O.C. studs and plates	32 L.F.	5.0	99.10
Headers over openings, 2" x 8"	48 L.F.	2.5	33.10
Sheathing for walls, wood fiberboard, 25/32" thick, 4' x 8' sheets	8 Sheets	3.5	92.95
Roof framing, joists, 2" x 6" x 10', 16" O.C.	130 L.F.	2.0	61.35
Ridge board, 1" x 8" x 12',	24 L.F.	1.0	8.15
Rafters, 2" x 6" x 12', 16" O.C.	312 L.F.	5.0	147.25
Valleys rafters, 2" x 6"	32 L.F.	1.0	15.10
Sub-fascia, 2" x 8" x 16'	32 L.F.	2.5	22.05
Sheathing for roof, 1/2" thick, 4' x 8' sheets	15 Sheets	5.5	238.15
Felt paper, 15 lb.	500 S.F.	1.0	16.95
Shingles, #1 red cedar, 5-1/2" exposure, on roof	5 Sq.	16.0	665.50
Flashing, zinc & copper alloy, .020" thick	140 S.F.	7.5	296.45
Fascia, 1" x 8" rough-sawn cedar	32 L.F.	1.0	26.35
Soffit, 3/8" rough-sawn cedar plywood, stained	48 S.F.	1.5	62.15
Gutters & downspouts, aluminum	52 L.F.	3.5	52.25
Windows, wood, plastic-clad, insulated 3' x 4'	4 Ea.	4.0	847.00
Sliding glass door, wood, vinyl-clad, 6' x 6'-10"	1 Ea	4.0	844.60
Siding, cedar-beveled, rough-sawn, stained	220 S.F.	7.5	516.45
Backfill, finish grade & re-seed	1 Lot	13.0	12.10
Totals		**129.0**	**$4691.65**

Project Size	10' x 16'	Contractor's Fee Including Materials	**$11,200**

Level of Difficulty

Building this breezeway project poses a major challenge to all do-it-yourselfers; however, it can serve as an excellent opportunity to advance your building skills. All of the basic operations in exterior house construction are required to complete the job, from foundation work and framing to exterior finish work like siding and gutter installations. Because the foundation involves specialized know-how, inexperienced do-it-yourselfers should consider hiring a qualified tradesman for this part of the project. Beginners should add 100% to the professional time for the basic tasks they take on, such as excavation, installing the sheathing, painting, and landscaping. Handymen should add 40% to the time for the basic tasks and wall framing, and 60% for roof framing. They should seriously consider hiring a tradesman for the foundation and roofing operations if they are inexperienced in these areas. Experts should add 10% to the professional time for all tasks, except the foundation work and roofing. The time increase for these jobs should be gaged according to the amount of experience they have in these areas.

What to Watch Out For

Hiring specialty contractors often makes sense even if you have experience and skill enough to complete the job on your own. The roofing for this project is a good example. A capable roofer can close in this structure quickly and thoroughly, even though there is a considerable amount of flashing involved. The correct installation of the valley is particularly important to prevent leaking and major water damage to the interior later on. A professional roofing job ensures that such problems won't arise.

New Construction Breezeway

This breezeway plan demonstrates how the space between the house and garage can be converted to a comfortable interior living area. If your property is laid out in the appropriate way, much of the work can be done by do-it-yourselfers, with considerable savings in labor costs.

ENCLOSED PORCH WITH WINDOWS

Existing Roof

Vinyl Trim

Wood Combination
Storm & Screen Door

Awning Windows

Vinyl Trim

Walls
2" x 4" Studs & Plates
3-1/2" Insulation
1/2" Drywall
1/2" Plywood Sheathing

Vinyl Embossed Siding

Like breezeways, porches and roofed-over entryways can also be converted into comfortable interior space. If the porch structure already has a good roof and a sturdy floor and support system, the project is that much easier. This plan demonstrates how a 6′ x 12′ porch can become a small, but practical interior room. With the roof, floor, and support system already in place, the conversion can be accomplished quickly and economically by most do-it-yourselfers.

Materials

The materials used in this plan are standard construction products commonly employed in home remodeling. The amount of required material will depend on the dimensions of the existing structure, the style and design of the house, and the extent to which the porch must be prepared and reconditioned. If the porch is large enough to warrant conversion, the materials order will probably be large enough to require trucking. Be sure to work out the conditions of delivery before you finalize the purchase agreement.

Two critical areas of the existing porch should be examined before you begin the construction of the new room. These are the roof and the support system. Especially in older structures, these two vital components may need reconditioning and even replacing if they are to protect the new interior and carry the load of the new materials. Examine the flashing and general condition of the roof covering and rafters for signs of leakage and deterioration. If you can crawl under the structure, make a thorough inspection of the floor joists and decking, as well as the foundation. Rot, insect infestations, moisture, and weakness of the frame and flooring are problems which must be corrected before the

project continues. If you cannot get under the porch the condition of the floor and its frame can be checked by removing some of the floor boards in several places and performing the inspection from above. These preliminary measures take time and may involve expense if reconditioning work is called for. If a problem looks serious, hire a specialist to investigate further and correct the situation. In short, be sure that the existing porch roof, floor, and foundation are in top condition before you install any new material.

After the porch has been reconditioned, the 2″ x 4″ walls are framed and the exterior of the structure is sheathed, equipped with new windows and a door, and then sided. In most cases, the framing will fill areas between the existing roof support posts, so allow extra time, and possibly cost, for extra cutting and measuring. If any of the posts have to be replaced or relocated, be sure to provide temporary roof support posts, during the framing operation. The 1/2″ plywood sheathing and new window and door units are put into place once the framing is complete. This plan includes medium-sized thermopane casement window units, but double-hung or jalousie models may be more appropriate for your home. Embossed vinyl siding is suggested in this model, but cedar, aluminum, or a different style and grade of vinyl may better suit the exterior of your home. Your total cost will vary somewhat with these substitutions. Refurbishing or changing the exterior trim or adding a gutter and downspout, if required, will also add to the time and expense to the project.

Within the enclosure, the old exterior wall must be prepared for new materials. Ceiling joists and insulation must be installed, and finish coverings applied to the ceiling, walls, and floor. The wall preparation involves stripping the old siding and reconditioning the existing entryway for the new interior door. The exterior ends of the new ceiling joists must be tapered to fit the existing roof line and the interior ends plated and lagged into the side of the house. The ceiling and new exterior walls should be insulated to the recommended R-value ratings for your geographical area. Before drywall or paneling is applied, all rough electrical work should be completed. You can place the underlayment for the carpeting or vinyl flooring directly on the old porch floorboards, but be sure to use threaded flooring nails and then level the surface before the finish is applied.

Level of Difficulty

Assuming that only minimum reconditioning is needed, the most challenging operations in the project are the wall framing and ceiling joist placement. If you are unfamiliar with framing, the procedures can be learned from an experienced carpenter. As in other conversion projects, like the breezeway, attic, and garage plans, the work can usually be completed at a comfortable pace without disturbing the routine of the house. Beginners should double the professional time estimates throughout the project. Handymen should add 50% to the estimated man-hours, and experts 20%, for all procedures. All do-it-yourselfers should consider hiring an electrician and a carpet installer for these aspects of the job.

What to Watch Out For

Particularly in colder climates, the floor of the converted room should be insulated for comfort and energy savings. This task can be challenging, however, even if the floor is accessible from underneath the structure. You may have to place the insulation from a prone position and under cramped conditions. Space problems may require that batts, rather than rolled material be used. Once the insulation is in place, some means of permanent support should be installed. Strapping can be nailed across the joists at 16″ intervals, or chicken wire or inexpensive screening can be stapled to the supports to cover the newly insulated area. If the floor is inaccessible from below, styrofoam sheets can be placed between sleepers made from strapping or 2″ x 4″s on the old floor surface. With this method, however, new decking as well as underlayment must be installed before the finished floor is laid. In this case, you may also have to make adjustments for the new floor height at both entryways.

ENCLOSED PORCH WITH WINDOWS			
Description	Quantity	Man-hours	Material
Remove siding & door inside porch	I Ea.	4.0	0.00
Wall framing, studs & plates, 2″ x 4″ x 8′, 16″ O.C.,	24 L.F.	4.0	74.35
Headers over openings, 2″ x 6″ stock	24 L.F.	1.5	11.35
Sheathing, plywood, 1/2″ thick, 4′ x 8′ sheets	6 Sheets	3.0	95.25
Ceiling joists, 2″ x 6″ x 12′, 16″ O.C.	60 L.F.	1.0	28.30
Insulation, ceiling, 6″ thick, R-19, paper-backed	72 S.F.	0.5	34.00
Walls, 3-1/2″ thick, R-11, paper-backed	160 S.F.	1.0	52.30
Sheetrock, walls & ceilings, 1/2″ thick, 4′ x 8′ sheets, taped & finished	12 Sheets	6.5	116.15
Door, wood entrance, birch solid core, 2′-8″ x 6′-8″	I Ea.	1.0	145.20
Lockset, exterior	I Ea.	1.0	116.20
Door, prehung exterior, combination storm & screen, 6′-9″ x 2′-8″	I Ea.	1.5	99.20
Windows, awning, average quality, 2′ x 3′ insulating glass	4 Ea.	3.5	706.65
Trim, colonial casing, windows, door & base	88 L.F.	3.0	38.35
Siding, vinyl embossed, 8″ wide, w/trim	40 S.F.	1.5	30.50
Flooring, vinyl sheet, .25″ thick	72 S.F.	2.5	196.00
Paint walls, ceiling & trim, primer & 2 coats	288 S.F.	5.0	24.40
Totals		40.5	$1768.20
Project Size 6′ x 12′	Contractor's Fee Including Materials		$3960

Enclosed Porch with Windows
Winterizing an existing porch like this one can increase the interior space of your home without the large expense of a complete room addition. Because the roof and support system are already in place, many do-it-yourselfers can handle the finishing tasks at their convenience, without having to deal with the challenges of a completely new structure.

ENCLOSED PORCH WITH SLIDING GLASS DOORS

Existing Porch Structure

Drywall Ceiling

1" x 6" Pine Trim

Indoor/Outdoor Carpet

12' Wide Aluminum Sliding Glass Doors at Each End

8' Wide Aluminum Sliding Glass Doors

Open, attached porch areas can be remodeled with a very standard approach, or converted to a more deluxe kind of interior space. This plan presents the latter type of improvement, and features insulated sliding glass doors to provide the benefits of natural light and fresh air. If you want to increase the light and ventilation still further, you might invest a bit more by adding skylights. Generally, this is a moderate to difficult project because of the size of the porch area and the specialized skills required to accomplish several of the tasks. Once the enclosure has been finished, it will provide years of enjoyable and practical service for you and your family, while increasing the value of your home.

Materials

As in other porch plans included in this section, it is assumed that a weathertight, sturdy roof and a solid foundation and support system are already in place before the work begins. The materials list, therefore, includes only those products which are required to fill in the walls, finish the interior, and otherwise enhance the porch's function and appearance. Because many variables exist, the particulars of an individual project will modify this estimate. The size, roof style, and the amount of reconditioning required for the existing structure will affect the overall cost, as will the type and extent of finish work that goes into the new room. The basic structural materials are readily available from building supply retailers, but some sliding glass door models may require special ordering.

Before any new materials are installed,the existing structure should be thoroughly inspected and evaluated. The roof should be dry and its sheathing solid and free from rot or deterioration. Carefully check the flashing along the seam between the roof and the wall of the house, and examine the underside of the roof's subsurface and rafters. If the roof is held up by a post-and-beam support system, check the condition and alignment of the supporting members. This plan depicts a concrete slab as the floor and foundation for the porch, but a concrete block or poured-in-place foundation with a wood floor may better describe your porch's arrangement. Regardless of the type, check and evaluate its condition before continuing. If deficiencies or weaknesses are found in the existing porch's components, correct them before proceeding with the project. Extensive reconditioning may require the services of a roofing or foundation specialist.

The sliding glass doors are the primary components of the conversion, so give careful consideration to their selection and installation. Generally, the extra expense for top quality window units is worthwhile, as they will provide years of reliable, weathertight service.

The most important aspect of the sliding glass door installation is the correct sizing and precise leveling, plumbing, and squaring of the rough openings. The units are available in various standard sizes, like the 6' and 8' models suggested in this plan. Odd sizes require special ordering and cost more because they must be custom made. The estimate given in this plan is for a high quality slider unit which, because of its expense, should be handled carefully, with plenty of time allowed for its installation.

The doorway from the porch area to the house may require some attention after the sliders and interior finish are put into place. If the porch area is to become a new room in the house, you may want to enlarge the existing doorway, build a rough frame with appropriate jack studs and headers, and then trim the opening. A slider unit or french doors can also be installed in this location. If the porch is to be winterized, but will still be considered more as an exterior area, the old doorway can be left as is with no additional work required. The exterior siding and any existing windows can be left in place or removed, depending on the extent of finish desired in the new porch. Your choice of treatment for this area will have a substantial impact on the cost of the project.

Level of Difficulty

Because of the specialty work involved in the sliding glass door installations, beginners and handymen with limited remodeling experience should consider hiring professionals to complete this task. Even experts and experienced handymen should seek some assistance. The components are expensive, and precise workmanship is required to ensure that the results of the installation are commensurate with the investment in materials. The rest of the project, with the exception of any extensive reconditioning work, should be within the reach of most do-it-yourselfers. Beginners should double the professional time for all work and seek advice when needed. Handymen and experts should add 50% and 20%, respectively, to the man-hours estimates for basic procedures, and 60% and 30% for the sliding door installations. All do-it-yourselfers will have to add both time and expense for extra interior finish work if the porch is to be integrated into the first floor room plan of the house.

What to Watch Out For

If the new glassed-in porch is to be used essentially as an interior facility, local building codes may require a minimum number of electrical outlets. Extra lighting fixtures and wall switches may also be desired by the homeowner. These necessities and amenities should be provided for before the ceiling and walls are framed and covered, to save time and money and to simplify the procedure. Remember that space may be required between the rough framing members of the slider units if wiring and switch or outlet boxes are to be installed in this location. Also, supply wires for the wall switches, outlets, and overhead lighting fixtures must be run above the finished ceiling and then fed to the electrical service panel. A qualified electrician should tie in the new circuit to the electrical supply and perform any parts of the installation which are too difficult for the do-it-yourselfer. Beginners should hire a professional for all of the electrical work.

ENCLOSED PORCH WITH SLIDING GLASS DOORS

Description	Quantity	Man-hours	Material
Remove existing door & enlarge opening	I Ea.	4.0	0.00
Frame opening into house, 2" x 4" studs	32 L.F.	1.5	8.90
Header over opening, 2" x 10" stock	20 L.F.	1.0	9.45
Trim at opening, I" x 6" jamb, stock pine	24 L.F.	1.0	9.60
Casing, stock pine, 11/16" x 2-1/2"	24 L.F.	1.0	21.20
Sliding glass doors, aluminum, 5/8" insul. glass, 8' wide, premium	2 Ea.	11.0	1113.20
Sliding glass doors, aluminum, 5/8" insul. glass, 12' wide, premium	2 Ea.	13.0	1318.90
Miscellaneous wood blocking for ceiling, 2" x 4" stock	48 L.F.	1.5	15.10
Insulation, fiberglass, kraft-faced batts, 6" thick, R-19	192 S.F.	1.5	90.60
Sheetrock at ceiling, 1/2" thick, 4' x 8' sheets, taped & finished	6 Sheets	4.5	58.10
Trim, cove molding, 9/16" x 1-3/4"	60 L.F.	2.0	163.35
Indoor/outdoor carpet, 3/8" thick	21 S.Y.	4.5	171.20
Paint trim, primer & 2 coats	50 L.F.	1.5	4.25
Paint ceiling, primer & I coat	192 S.F.	1.5	20.90
Totals		49.5	$3004.75
Project Size 12' x 16'	Contractor's Fee Including Materials		$6660

Enclosed Porch With Sliding Glass Doors

This glassed-in porch enclosure will add an attractive and comfortable new living space to your home. If the conditions of the existing roofed-over structure are right, this deluxe conversion can be performed for a reasonable cost.

LARGE LEAN-TO GREENHOUSE

One of the options for attached greenhouses is an exterior structure with its access limited to the outside. As long as some type of heating and ventilation system is employed to stabilize the air temperature inside, such a facility can serve as an attractive, yet practical, interior garden, independent of the household. In some cases, a doorway to the interior might be planned as another part of the project, to be completed at a later date. In this way, the homeowner can adjust to the energy demands of the greenhouse without interfering with the normal operation of the house's heating or air conditioning system. In other cases, a doorway between the inside living area and the greenhouse simply may not be desired.

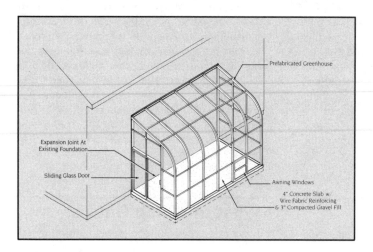

Prefabricated Greenhouse

Expansion Joint At Existing Foundation

Sliding Glass Door

Awning Windows

4" Concrete Slab w. Wire Fabric Reinforcing & 3" Compacted Gravel Fill

Materials

The construction supplies for this project consist of the concrete and other materials needed to form the slab, as well as the factory-prepared greenhouse kit, and the items required to attach it to the slab and house wall. Before purchasing the greenhouse kit, do some research and shopping to find out about brand names, designs, levels of quality, and prices of the various units. Some offer more operational accessories and better craftsmanship and engineering than others. As with the purchase of any home building products, it pays in the long run to buy a quality item.

The support system for this greenhouse installation is comprised of a 4" concrete slab which has been placed over a 3" bed of compacted gravel fill. Before the slab is put into place, the area must be dug out by hand to a depth of 7". Accurate measuring, squaring, and leveling of the form is a critical procedure in the operation, as the base of the greenhouse has fixed dimensions and the unit as a whole must fit snugly against the house wall. If the foundation is not true in its placement, the greenhouse will not sit properly on the slab or against the house wall; and, consequently, the enclosure may develop leaks. In climates where deep frost occurs, the

slab recommended in this plan may not be adequate, and a deeper foundation may be required. Any movement or heaving of the surface can cause the seams along the house and foundation to open, the mullions and weatherstripping in the greenhouse to separate, and, possibly, the glass panels to crack. Other floor and foundation systems could also be used; for example, redwood and pressure-treated pine are options for the base. These can be set in or on one of the following: concrete pedestals, concrete block foundations set on footings, or established supports like decks and patios. The cost for the greenhouse support system will vary from this model's estimate according to your requirements and preferences.

Once the slab or foundation and floor have been placed, the house wall is prepared to receive the greenhouse, and the kit is assembled. Even if you plan to keep the house siding as is, you may have to make a channel in the siding for the greenhouse frame and apply flashing and caulking where needed along the seams between the new structure and the house. If your house is painted a light color, you might consider applying two coats of dark, flat paint to the siding in the area to be enclosed by the greenhouse. Painting before the greenhouse is placed will save some time. You might also consider applying dark paint to the concrete floor. Both of these surfaces will absorb sunlight and provide radiant heat.

The greenhouse kit included in this plan features a sliding glass door, an awning window, and double-layered tempered glass in an aluminum frame. All of the hardware needed to interconnect the greenhouse's components and base fittings is included in the kit. Other accessories, such as screens, shades, additional awning windows, fans and heaters are available at extra cost. If the greenhouse is to be used exclusively as an exterior facility, some of these optional accessories, especially a fan and heater, may become necessities and, therefore, will add to the basic cost.

Level of Difficulty

Many experienced do-it-yourselfers can complete this project on their own, but beginners and less-skilled handymen may find some aspects of the undertaking out of reach. Basically,

the installation involves two challenging operations, the placement of the slab and the erection of the greenhouse itself. Both of these procedures require skilled and precise workmanship. Further, because the greenhouse kit is expensive and the structure intricate, mistakes can be costly and difficult to correct. In short, beginners should leave the slab and greenhouse installations to a professional and limit their efforts to such tasks as excavation and finish work. They should allow some added time for these tasks. Skilled handymen and experts who have masonry experience should add 50% and 20%, respectively, to the man-hours for the placement of the slab. They should add even more time for the greenhouse fabrication and erection to allow for patient and careful workmanship.

What to Watch Out For

Although all of the greenhouse projects in this section involve attached structures with shed roofs, other roof designs and building configurations are also possible. A gable roof design, for example, might be a better choice if the greenhouse will look or perform better with its length running at right angles to the house. If the greenhouse is placed on a wall with an east or west exposure, such an alignment may utilize available sunlight more effectively. In hot weather, the larger area of a vented gable roof will increase the ventilation and rate of exhaust in the greenhouse. In addition to attached greenhouses, factory-prepared freestanding models offer other options for greenhouse projects.

LARGE LEAN-TO GREENHOUSE

Description	Quantity	Man-hours	Material
Clearing & excavation for slab, by hand	1 Ea.	12.0	0.00
Gravel fill, 3" deep, compacted	140 S.F.	1.0	18.65
Edge forms, 4" high	32 L.F.	2.0	7.75
Expansion joint at existing foundation, premolded bituminous fiber	16 L.F.	0.5	9.30
Reinforcing, welded wire fabric, 6 x 6-10/10	140 S.F.	1.0	13.55
Concrete, ready mix, 3000 psi	2 C.Y.		135.05
Placing concrete	2 C.Y.	1.0	0.00
Finishing, broom finish	128 S.F.	1.5	0.00
Greenhouse, prefab., 8' x 16' x 11'-6" high, w/awning window & sliding glass door	1 Ea.	24.0	10,376.95
Flashing, aluminum, .016" thick	32 S.F.	2.0	25.25
Finish, grade & re-seed	1 Ea.	2.0	2.60
Totals		47.0	$10,589.10
Project Size 8' x 16'	Contractor's Fee Including Materials		$16,900

Large Lean-To Greenhouse

For the active year-round or seasonal gardener, this improvement can provide many years of enjoyable and practical service. Although this model is essentially an exterior facility, it can be easily incorporated into the house's interior with the addition of an entryway.

SUNROOM GREENHOUSE

Combination greenhouse-sunrooms have become popular home improvements because they combine the beauty of plants and open natural lighting with the practical benefits of passive solar heating and increased year-round interior living area. This plan demonstrates how a large greenhouse-sun room addition can be nestled into the corner between wings of a house. Because of its size and the deluxe products used in its construction, it is an expensive improvement, but one which will return more than the homeowner's investment in increased property value. It is a challenging project for all levels of do-it-yourselfers, and beginners and inexperienced handymen should consider hiring a contractor for much of the work.

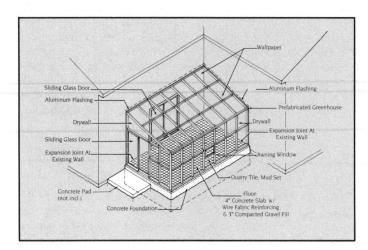

Materials

The materials required to construct this deluxe greenhouse-sun room consist of ready-mixed concrete for the foundation and floor, the factory-prepared greenhouse, and the basic building materials included in the finishing of the interior walls and entryway. Except for the greenhouse kit, all of the materials used in the project are readily available, so shopping for the best prices is usually worth the effort. Even ready-mixed concrete can be competitively priced, although a minimum charge is to be expected for a small order like this one. Remember that two separate deliveries, a few days apart, will be required to place the foundation, and, later, the slab.

Before the foundation work begins, however, a substantial amount of excavation must be completed. A perimeter trench must be dug to receive the form for the concrete. This task may have to be done by hand if the location of the site prohibits machine excavation. After the foundation has been allowed to set up for several days, a gravel subsurface, reinforcing, and expansion joints are installed, and the slab poured. The surface of the slab is troweled and then broom-finished to provide an acceptable base surface for the floor covering.

After the foundation and slab have been installed, the greenhouse itself is assembled on-site and secured to the foundation and house walls. This plan includes a quality factory-prepared unit with an insulated aluminum framing system and tempered glass panels. Be sure to do some research before buying this expensive component. There are many brand names and designs available in a wide range of quality and price. The extra cost of a fully insulated, well-made product will be justified by years of energy efficient, durable service. Most do-it-yourselfers will need some professional assistance with this installation. In any case, be sure that the final placement of the greenhouse is secure and weathertight before proceeding with the interior work.

Within the enclosure, the two walls of the house must be prepared to receive the finish materials, and the floor should be covered with its finished surface. In most cases, the exterior siding must be removed and, in this plan, a window opening enlarged and framed to receive a 6′ sliding glass door unit. If the new sun room is to be incorporated into the house's interior for year-round use, the opening can be enlarged even more and then trimmed with a jamb and facings. In this way you can deduct the expense of the slider unit, but you may have to add slightly to the cost of preparing the rough opening. A second doorway, through the other common wall, is another option you might want to consider. If you are tackling this task for the first time, be sure to seek some advice before you start. If the opening is greater than 6' in width, larger headers and, possibly, a beam or girder may be required to bear the load. The ceiling adjacent to the opening may also require temporary bracing during the procedure. After the opening has been made and sliders or a doorway frame installed, the walls are covered with 1/2" sheetrock or other suitable veneer and finished. This plan suggests 1/2" thick quarry tile for the finished floor. Its durability, low maintenance, and rustic appearance make it an ideal covering for plant and sunroom floors, but brick, flagstone, and other tile materials are viable options.

SUNROOM GREENHOUSE

Description	Quantity	Man-hours	Material
Site clearing, layout & excavation for foundation	I Lot	7.0	0.00
Concrete wall, 8" thick, 3000 psi, incl. form, reinforcing & sill plates, 42" high	100 S.F.	14.5	603.00
Gravel fill, 3" deep, compacted	200 S.F.	1.0	26.65
Expansion joints, premolded bituminous fiber	57 L.F.	1.5	33.15
Reinforcing, welded wire fabric, 6' x 6-10/10	200 S.F.	1.0	19.35
Concrete, ready mix, 3000 psi	3 C.Y.	0.0	202.55
Placing concrete	3 C.Y.	1.5	0.00
Finishing, broom finish	190 S.F.	2.5	0.00
Greenhouse, sunroom, prefab, 10'-6" x 18' x 10' high, double temp. glass, incl. sliding door & 1 awning window	I Ea.	32.0	11,491.35
Flashing, aluminum, .019" thick	46 S.F.	2.5	36.75
Remove window & siding for sliding glass door opening & end wall	I Job	6.5	0.00
Frame opening, 2" x 8"	20 L.F.	1.0	13.80
Door, sliding glass, aluminum, 6' wide	I Ea.	4.0	435.60
Drywall, 1/2" thick, for sides of opening	6 Sheets	3.5	58.10
Trim, jamb for door, 1" x 6" pine	40 L.F.	1.5	33.90
Crown molding stock pine, 9/16" x 3-5/8"	30 L.F.	1.0	39.95
Painting, trim, incl. puttying, primer & 1 coat	70 L.F.	1.5	4.25
Painting, walls, primer and 1 coat	200 S.F.	2.0	21.80
Flooring, quarry tile, mud set, 6" x 6", 1/2" thick	190 S.F.	22.0	643.75
Totals		106.5	$13,663.95

Project Size	10'-6" x 18'	Contractor's Fee Including Materials	$23,060

Level of Difficulty

This greenhouse-sun room project is a challenging undertaking which most do-it-yourselfers should leave, at least in part, to a professional contractor. The extensive concrete work and the erection of the greenhouse are jobs which require special skills and equipment and involve considerable liability if mistakes are made. Most do-it-yourselfers can handle the interior wall finish work, but some might consider hiring a mason or tilesetter to install the finished floor. As a general rule, beginners should limit their involvement to the finishing of the walls and should double the professional time for that operation. Handymen, too, should probably stick to the interior finishing at a rate of 50% over the estimated man-hours. If they attempt to lay the tile or brick floor, they should add 100% to the professional time to allow for slow and careful work. Experts should leave the foundation and slab installations to a specialist and consider hiring a contractor to erect the greenhouse. For the basic tasks, they should add 20% to the estimated man-hours, and for the finished floor, about 40%.

What to Watch Out For

In order for greenhouses and sun rooms to utilize the full benefits of solar energy, they must be properly located. For most installations, a south or west exposure is ideal because of the longer duration of available sunlight at all times of the year. East exposure is acceptable in some open locations, such as that of a waterfront home, but north exposures are generally unacceptable sites in this hemisphere. Another important consideration for locating the greenhouse-sunroom is protection from the wind. Wherever possible, an alcove, or in this case, the corner of an "ell", should be utilized.

Sunroom Greenhouse

This deluxe greenhouse-sun room will add beauty, increased living area, and comfort to homes which are spacious enough to accommodate it. Although the expertise of a contractor may be required for the construction of the exterior, do-it-yourselfers can save on installation costs by finishing the inside themselves.

GABLE DORMER 7' WIDE

2" x 6" Ridge Board
Building Paper
1/2" Plywood Sheathing
Asphalt Shingles
2" x 6" Rafters
2" x 4" Joists
Cedar Bevel Siding
1" x 6" Cedar Fascia
Cedar Plywood Soffit
2" x 4" Studs & Plates
Aluminum Flashing
1" x 6" Fascia
2" x 8" Trimmer Rafters
Wood Double Hung Mullion Window

In houses with the roof area to accomodate them, large gable dormers can significantly increase the amount of light and living space in second or third-floor rooms. Style, size, and location are crucial elements in dormer design. When placed on the roof of a house, they become a prominent feature, and the homeowner should make sure that they meet both aesthetic and practical needs. This double-window gable dormer plan demonstrates how a larger size dormer can be installed for a reasonable cost.

Materials

The materials used in this gable dormer plan include standard framing lumber, sheathing, and exterior finishing products. The exterior of a dormer is in some ways like a miniature wood-framed house in that it requires a wood support system, framed walls, and a roof. Because these materials, including 2" x 4"s, 2" x 6"s, siding, roofing materials, and the window unit, are usually in good supply, the do-it-yourselfer is encouraged to do some price comparing before buying. The first important procedure involved in this project is the laying out and cutting of the opening in the roof to receive the new structure. Because gable dormers are often installed in pairs and, sometimes threes, the location of the structures on the roof in relationship to one another is paramount to a successful design. Wherever possible, the longitudinal cuts for the roof opening should be made next to existing rafters. The width of the dormer, therefore, may have to be adjusted to fit the rafter spacing on a given roof. The roofs of most houses have rafters spaced at 16" on center, but in some homes they may be spaced at 20", 24", or even larger intervals. In the latter case, plan on increasing the cost of this operation, as additional

rafters and supports may have to be placed to restore the roof structure to safe standards. While the roof is open, check the condition of the other rafters and sheathing. If either of these components is questionable, have an inspection done by a professional. Any problems should be corrected before you proceed with the new installation. Placing a new dormer on a weak or deteriorated roof surface is a waste of time and money and can cause serious structural problems later on.

After the opening has been made, new support materials have to be placed, even on newer roofs. The most important of these supports are the trimmer rafters, which double the existing rafters next to the opening, and span the entire length from the ridge to the wall plate. The ends of the cut rafters must be capped with doubled headers. In both cases, the lumber should match the dimensions of the existing rafter material.

The walls, ceiling, and roof of the dormer are framed and covered after the opening has been fully prepared. Because of the number of angle cuts and the individual fitting required for many of the framing members, this procedure is time consuming and requires a patient approach by the do-it-yourselfer. If you are unfamiliar with the task, plan on making a few mistakes at first and allow some extra time for double checking the measurements and angles as you work. Remember, too, that the cutting will usually have to be done in an area remote from the dormer site, say, on the ground or a suitable surface inside the opening; so you will use up even more time going up and down a ladder or climbing in and out of the opening as the cuts are made. Plywood sheathing is placed on the dormer walls and roof after the framing has been completed. Be sure to scribe the angled side pieces accurately, as a tight fit is desirable. Remember, too, that the roofing, siding, and trim materials should match the products already in place on your house. Also, trim and structural features, such as the width of the fascia and the proportions of the soffit, should be duplicated as closely as possible.

Level of Difficulty

This gable dormer project is a difficult job which requires considerable carpentry skill and know-how to complete. Beginners and handymen whose remodeling experience is limited should not tackle it. The structure itself is a challenging

undertaking, and its inconvenient roof location makes it a bit more complex. Do-it-yourselfers who undertake this project should anticipate some problems inherent to roof work. Some of these include height, limited access to the site, and the awkward position from which power and hand tools must be operated. Two steps in the project are critical to the overall success of the installation. One is the adequate restoration of the roof support with trimmer rafters and headers after the opening has been cut. The other is correct roofing and flashing installation to restore weathertight conditions to the roof. The roofing work, particularly, may require the services of an experienced tradesman, and even expert do-it-yourselfers are encouraged to consult a qualified roofer before attempting this task. Generally, experts should add 50% to the professional time for all procedures, and more for the finish roofing and flashing jobs. Handymen should add 100% to the man-hours estimates and should hire a professional for the roofing work if they are inexperienced in this area. Beginners should not attempt any of the tasks in this project for the reasons given earlier.

What to Watch Out For

Because of their inconvenient roof location, dormers are notoriously difficult to paint and maintain. As a result, you will want to select finish materials which will cut the time and difficulty of painting, window washing, and other maintenance chores. For example, window units with removable sash may cost a little more initially, but the convenience of washing or painting from inside the house, rather than from the roof or an outside ladder, might make the extra expense worthwhile. In most cases, stained surfaces are easier to apply and maintain than painted ones. If you can match the trim color of your house with a stain, use it on the dormer instead of paint to reduce the scraping and application time of future paint jobs.

7' WIDE GABLE DORMER

Description	Quantity	Man-hours	Material
Roof cutout & demolition	1 Ea.	16.0	0.00
Framing, rafters, 2" x 6", 16" O.C.	108 L.F.	3.0	50.95
Ridge board, 2" x 8" stock	12 L.F.	0.5	5.65
Trimmer rafters, 2" x 8" x 18' long	36 L.F.	1.5	24.85
Studs & plates, 2" x 4" stock	120 L.F.	2.5	37.75
Sub-fascia, 2" x 6" stock	16 L.F.	0.5	7.55
Headers, double 2" x 6" stock	24 L.F.	1.5	11.35
Ceiling joists, 2" x 6", 16" O.C.	36 L.F.	0.5	11.35
Gable end studs, 2" x 4" stock	10 L.F.	0.5	3.15
Sheathing, roof & walls, 1/2" thick	7 Sheets	2.5	111.15
Building paper, 15 lb. felt	210 S.F.	0.5	7.65
Drip edge, aluminum, .016" thick, 5" girth	28 L.F.	1.0	5.10
Flashing, aluminum, .019" thick	62 L.F.	3.5	49.50
Shingles, asphalt, multi-layered, 285 lb./square	6 Bundles	4.0	115.80
Fascia, 1" x 6", rough sawn cedar, stained	28 L.F.	1.0	40.00
Soffit, 3/8" rough sawn cedar plywood, stained	14 S.F.	0.5	18.15
Window, double window, double hung, 5' x 3', vinyl-clad, thermopane	1 Ea.	2.0	423.50
Siding, cedar, beveled, rough sawn, stained	120 S.F.	4.0	288.95
Insulation, fiberglass, 3-1/2" thick, R-11, paper backed	140 S.F.	1.0	87.25
Totals		46.0	$1249.65
Project Size 6'-8" x 10'-6"	Contractor's Fee Including Materials		$3540

7' Wide Gable Dormer

This large gable dormer project is a challenging undertaking for all levels of do-it-yourselfers. Nevertheless, if you have good remodeling skills and are willing to work at a slow pace, you can complete this improvement at reasonable cost while adding to the value, living space, and appearance of your home.

SHED DORMER 12' WIDE

2" x 6" Rafters
1/2" Plywood Sheathing
Building Paper
Asphalt Shingles
Aluminum Drip Edge
2" x 4" Studs
Vinyl Fascia
Vinyl Soffit
2" x 6" Trimmer Rafters
Vinyl Siding
Wood Double Hung
Mullion Window
Vinyl-clad
Aluminum Flashing

Although they are not as intricate in design as gable dormers, shed dormers are an efficient means of increasing the living space and window area of second and third floor rooms. Also, although all dormer installations are challenging projects, shed dormers are generally easier to install than those with gable designs. Because of the simplicity of their roof lines, the framing and roofing operations, particularly, can be done more easily. These tasks can be accomplished by do-it-yourselfers with moderate to advanced skill levels. As long as the ridge height and area of the roof can accommodate the dormer, it can be installed.

Materials

The amount of construction material used for shed dormer projects is usually greater than for gable dormers because they tend to be larger structures. Yet, the same basic materials are employed in essentially the same sequence of operations. One of the reasons that they tend to be larger structures is that a shed dormer roof often extends from the ridge of the existing roof to a point near or directly over the exterior wall. Because the dormer roof is flat, not gabled or peaked, the amount of usable open space enclosed by the structure is increased, and maximum ceiling height is attained. As in most exterior house improvements, framing lumber of varying dimensions, plywood sheathing, roofing, siding, and various finish products are used in this plan. Because these materials are usually in good supply, the do-it-yourselfer can save by comparison shopping before buying. For an order this size, the difference can mean substantial savings. If you consolidate the order with one retailer, local delivery will usually be included.

The removal and reconditioning of the affected roof area is a critical operation in preparing the house for the new structure. The roofing, sheathing, and rafters must be torn out, the structural integrity of the old roof restored, and the rafter support for the dormer installed. In most cases, it is best to make the longitudinal cuts beside existing rafters, which are then reinforced with trimmers. These new supports must span from the ridge to the eaves. The existing rafters are usually spaced at 16" on center, but they may be located at odd intervals in some older houses. Be sure to match or exceed the dimensions of the existing rafters with the trimmer material. Any deficiences or weaknesses in the existing roof or its support system should be corrected before the framing of the new dormer begins.

The frame for the shed dormer consists of 2" x 4" walls and 2" x 6" rafters and ceiling joists. After the front wall of the dormer has been framed, placed, and temporarily braced, the joists and rafters are installed. As in other roof framing operations, the general rule is consistency of length, angling and notching, and spacing of the roof framing members. The framing of the side walls must be accomplished one piece at a time, with two different angles cut at each end of the studs to fit the roof lines. This process takes some time, so plan accordingly, especially if the task is new to you.

Once the framing has been completed, 1/2" plywood sheathing is applied and then covered with 15-pound felt building paper. The finish materials which are placed on the dormer should match the products already in place on the rest of the house. This plan suggests low maintenance vinyl siding and aluminum soffit and fascia coverings; but other materials, such as cedar shingles and clapboards and conventional wood trim, may be more appropriate for your house. A gutter and downspout for the shed roof have not been included in the plan, but it might be a good idea to add them if the dormer is located above a doorway. If the face of the dormer is a continuation of the house wall, a gutter and downspout will be necessary. The roofing should match the existing roof material, except where prohibited by the pitch of the roof. If the ridge is low and the pitch of the new shed roof nearly flat, rolled roofing of matching color might have to be used, as shingles are not recommended for roofs with shallow slopes. When selecting the window unit, try to acquire thermopane sash in the same design of your present windows.

Level of Difficulty

This dormer project is challenging even for experts and accomplished handymen and is out of the reach of beginners. Whenever you open a roof and tamper with major structural components, like rafters, you have to have the building skill to accomplish the work efficiently and correctly. All do-it-yourselfers should be prepared to cope with the inconvenience and difficulties associated with roof work. Skilled handymen and experts should be able to complete all of the tasks involved in the project. They should add 50% and 20%, respectively, to the professional time for all of the procedures. The new roofing may pose some challenges, and require some extra time, especially in the flashing and the restoration of disturbed sections of the old roof. Nevertheless, once the drip edge has been placed and the job correctly laid out, the roofing material should go on smoothly. Remember to allow extra time and to get some help for hauling bundles of roofing to the work area. As with most of the exterior wood structures outlined in this book, experience in using power tools is a prerequisite for tackling this dormer project.

What to Watch Out For

All dormer installations should be completed or, at the least, closed in as rapidly as possible to protect the inside of the house from the elements. If you are doing the job on your own, arrange to have an adequate amount of time available for several successive days of work. Although sudden weather changes cannot be predicted, you can reduce the chance of getting caught off guard by scheduling the dormer project during the warm and dry time of year. Nevertheless, always have an emergency cover ready to use in the event of a sudden rainstorm, and then hold off on the resumption of construction until the roof area dries. Be aware that wet roofs can be very dangerous. These basic precautions can prevent serious water damage to your house's interior.

12' WIDE SHED DORMER

Description	Quantity	Man-hours	Material
Roof cutout and demolition	1 Ea.	12.0	0.00
Framing, rafters, 2" x 6" x 12', 16" O.C.	12 Ea.	4.0	67.95
Trimmer rafters, 2" x 8" x 18' long	2 Ea	1.5	24.85
Studs & plates, 2" x 4" stock	192 L.F.	3.5	60.40
Sub-fascia, 2" x 6" stock	14 L.F.	0.5	6.60
Header, double, 2" x 8", 5' long	10 L.F.	0.5	6.90
Header, double, 2" x 12", 20' long	24 L.F.	1.5	26.45
Ceiling joists, 2" x 6", 12' long	12 Ea.	2.0	67.95
Sheathing, roof & wall, 1/2" thick, 4' x 8' sheets	9 Sheets	3.5	142.90
Building paper, 15 lb. felt	150 S.F.	0.5	5.45
Drip edge, aluminum, .016" thick, 5" girth	36 L.F.	1.0	6.55
Flashing, aluminum, .019" thick	24 S.F.	1.5	19.15
Shingles, asphalt, strip, 235 lb./square	6 Bundles	3.0	74.50
Siding, vinyl, double, 4" pattern	90 S.F.	3.0	68.60
Soffit & fascia, vinyl vented	36 L.F.	5.0	58.80
Window, double window, 4' wide x 3' high, double-hung, plastic coated, premium	1 Ea.	2.0	423.50
Insulation, fiberglass, 3-1/2" thick, R-11, paper backed	192 S.F.	1.0	51.10
Totals		46.0	$1111.65
Project Size 12' x 8'		Contractor's Fee Including Materials	$3490

> ### 12' Wide Shed Dormer
> This small shed dormer can increase bedroom area and other second or third-floor space without the expense of putting on a full addition. Although it is a challenging undertaking, many accomplished do-it-yourselfers can complete the project on their own for the cost of the materials and the investment of several days of their time.

SHED DORMER 20' WIDE

2" x 6" Rafters
1/2" Plywood Sheathing
Building Paper
Asphalt Shingles
Aluminum Fascia & Soffit
2" x 4" Studs
2" x 8" Trimmer Rafter
Aluminum Drip Edge
Cedar Bevel Siding
Aluminum Flashing
Wood Double Hung Mullion Window

Larger shed dormers provide the means to effectively utilize upper floor space. They are usually placed on the rear roofs of cape-style houses and other structures with gable roof designs large enough to accomodate them. Before you begin the planning for any shed dormer, large or small, take some time to measure your attic to see that you have enough ridge clearance to accomodate the dormer and enough roof and floor area to make the project worthwhile. A height of roughly 9' from the bottom of the ridge board to the floor of the room below or, in the case of an attic improvement, to the top of the ceiling joists is a reasonable minimum measurement. Once the minimum height requirement has been met, the width and length of the dormer can be determined according to the intended use of the facility, rafter spacing in the existing roof, and the location of partitions.

Materials

This plan presents a basic design for the exterior shell of an 8' x 20' shed dormer with no interior materials included, except wall insulation. Although the structure is basic in its design, a substantial number of exterior materials is needed to construct it. If you are doing the building on your own, get prices from several different suppliers and compare them before you place the order. Also, make sure that delivery is included in the final price, as the materials will have to be trucked. The process of constructing the dormer requires different materials for the various components as the structure is built, including 2" x 4"s and 2" x 6"s for the support system and frame, plywood sheathing, and various exterior coverings and finish materials.

The most critical step in the project is determining the location and laying out the section of roof to be opened for the new dormer. In most cases, the new structure will be located in an area which begins on the lower part of the roof and runs to the ridge board. This width measurement will vary with each case, depending on the size and pitch of the roof, aesthetic considerations,

and the desired amount of new living space. The length of the roof area to be opened depends on such variables as the location of existing interior partitions, the design of the new living space, and wherever possible, the spacing of the existing roof rafters. The cost of this shed dormer project is based on an 8' x 20' structure placed on a roof with a steep pitch, but costs will vary somewhat if the dormer dimensions are modified. Once the location has been determined and laid out, the roof section can be opened by removing the roofing, sheathing, and rafters.

After the opening has been made, the new work begins with the installation of trimmer rafters and the heading off of the cut rafter ends and, if conditions warrant, the placing of additional support. Again, each case will vary, and additional costs and time may be required to bring the roof and dormer support system to safe standards. The frame of the new dormer should not be placed until its support system has been correctly installed and fastened. Professional consultation or subcontracting will save you money in the long run if extensive roof support reconditioning is required. The framing and closing in of the shed dormer proceeds in much the same order as that of other wood-frame structures. The face of the dormer is framed with 2″ x 4″s and then braced temporarily while 2″ x 6″ ceiling joists and rafters are placed. The side walls are then framed and the entire enclosure sheathed with 1/2″ plywood. A layer of felt building paper is applied to the walls and, optionally, to the roof. The roofing material, in this case asphalt shingles, is then applied to the shed roof before the window units are installed and the finished siding applied. The roofing, siding, and window units will also vary with each installation, as the products which are selected for the dormer should match or approximate the materials already in place on the house.

If the materials differ from those listed in the estimate, the cost may be affected. For example, the cedar roofing included in this materials list costs more than asphalt shingles, and quite a bit more than asphalt roll roofing. The windows included in this plan are quality thermopane double-hung units; but standard single-pane units can be installed for less expense. Remember, though, that the cost for storm windows, if you choose to install uninsulated windows, will have to be added.

Level of Difficulty

This project is a major home improvement that demands a considerable amount of carpentry skill and know-how. Further, the roof location of the dormer increases the difficulty and adds significantly to the time and general inconvenience of the operations. In many instances, special equipment may have to be employed for roof and upper story work—staging, roof jacks, sturdy extension ladders, and pump jacks, to name a few. Some of these devices may have to be rented, so allow for their rental cost and plan ahead to ensure their availability during the construction period. Be sure that you get some instruction in their operation before you use them if they are unfamiliar to you. Generally, beginners should not attempt this or other dormer projects, as the necessary skills and location of the work are too demanding. Experts and handymen should add 25% and 75%, respectively, to the man-hours estimates and be willing to seek professional advice when necessary.

What to Watch Out For

This dormer project plan consists of a listing of the materials and the estimated installation time for only the exterior of the structure. As the work progresses, though, take advantage of opportunities to make the subsequent interior finishing easier. Some of these odds and ends will take a little more time and money during the placement of the dormer, but they can provide substantial labor savings later on. For example, electrical or plumbing rough-in required for the interior of the new enclosure may be prepared for or relocated. Attic locations with hard-to-get-at places for insulation may be more accessible before the dormer is closed in. Plywood decking for a new attic room may be easier to stack or to place while the roof is open.

20′ Wide Shed Dormer			
Description	Quantity	Man-hours	Material
Roof cutout & demolition	1 Ea.	20.0	0.00
Framing, rafters, 2″ x 6″ x 12′, 16″ O.C.	16 Ea.	5.5	90.60
Trimmer rafters, 2″ x 8″ x 18′	2 Ea.	1.5	24.85
Studs & plates, 2″ x 4″ x 8′, 16″ O.C.	240 L.F.	4.5	75.50
Sub-fascia, 2″ x 6″	22 L.F.	1.0	10.40
Headers, double 2″ x 8″ x 4′ long	16 L.F.	1.0	11.05
Headers, double 2″ x 12″ x 20′ long	40 L.F.	2.5	44.05
Ceiling joists, 2″ x 6″ x 12′	16 Ea.	2.5	90.60
Sheathing, roof & walls, 1/2″ thick, 4′ x 8′ sheets	12 Sheets	4.5	190.50
Building paper, 15 lb felt	240 S.F.	0.5	8.70
Drip edge, aluminum, .016″ thick, 5″ girth	44 L.F.	1.0	8.00
Flashing, aluminum, .019″ thick	40 S.F.	2.5	31.95
Shingles, Asphalt, Multi-layered, 285 lb./sq.	3 Sq.	2.0	57.90
Siding, cedar, beveled, rough sawn, stained	130 S.F.	4.5	313.05
Soffit & fascia, aluminum, vented	42 L.F.	6.0	71.15
Windows, double window, double hung, insulating glass, 4′ x 3′	2 Ea.	3.5	653.40
Insulation, fiberglass, 3-1/2″ thick, R-11, paper- backed	344 S.F.	4.0	91.55
Totals		67.0	$1773.25
Project Size 20′ x 8′	Contractor's Fee Including Materials		$5280

20′ Wide Shed Dormer

If the ridge height and roof area are adequate, a relatively large dormer like this one will reclaim wasted floor space. Although the project is fairly costly and time consuming, it remains an economical way of adding space that will return years of service while increasing the value of your home.

ROOM ADDITION 8′ × 8′

Aluminum Flashing

Asphalt Shingles

Aluminum Gutter

Awning Window

Vinyl Siding

Aluminum Downspout

Vinyl Soffit, Fascia, & Drip Edge

Entrance Door

Concrete Landing (not incl.)

Backfill, Finish Grade, & Re-seed

Concrete Block Foundation

Concrete Strip Footing

Room additions, like other projects involving attached structures, should complement the style and design of the house while meeting the need for new living area. Because of budget limitations, major remodeling projects like this one often require modifications in the structure's design and materials. This give-and-take process may lengthen the planning stages, but it helps ensure the livability, appearance, and value of the addition. This plan demonstrates how an 8′ x 8′ structure can be built for modest cost. Because the project is small scale and at first-floor level, do-it-yourselfers can take a hand in its construction and enjoy the benefits of lower costs.

Materials

It is possible to dig the foundation for this addition by hand to its required 4′ below-grade depth, however, machine excavation is a practical alternative, the cost of which is included in this estimate. The excavation should be wide enough to accommodate the footing and foundation walls and deep enough to rest on firm, frost-free subsoil. Once the footing has been carefully laid out and put into place, the concrete block wall can be built to the desired height. A formed and poured concrete wall is a slightly more expensive option.

The exterior of the structure is comprised of framing, sheathing, and finish materials common to wood-framed houses. The support for the floor of the room consists of 2″ x 8″ joists placed 16″ on center and covered with 5/8″ plywood sheathing. Before the floor frame is placed, a doubled 2″ x 8″ sill should be lagged or bolted into the top of the foundation wall. A little extra expense for pressure-treated lumber for the sill plate will provide protection against rot and deterioration. If pressure-treated lumber is not used, you might consider treating the sill lumber with wood preservative before the floor frame is placed. A vent should also be included in the foundation as protection against dampness and deterioration. When planning the roof frame, be

sure to match or complement the pitch of the house roof and the design of its soffit and fascia. This part of the project requires substantial carpentry skills and a basic knowledge of framing procedures. Seek advice and help if these tasks are new to you. The sheathing and exterior finish materials can be applied once the framing is completed. This plan includes economical asphalt strip shingles, vinyl siding, and aluminum soffits and fascias. If other finish products are more appropriate to the style of your house, these substitutions will alter both the cost of materials and the estimated time for installation. Most do-it-yourselfers can accomplish this roof work if they are given instruction on laying it out and flashing it correctly at the house wall.

Inside, many different surface coverings and trim materials can be used, according to your home's decor and practical requirements. For example, if this addition is to be used as a mud room and entryway, the low-maintenance vinyl flooring suggested in this plan might be a better choice than carpet. The possible wall and ceiling coverings include taped and finished 1/2″ drywall, wood paneling, or other sheet products. Be sure to take care of all the preliminary work, like the electrical rough-in, insulating, and the placing of underlayment, before you apply the finish surfaces.

Level of Difficulty

Because of its small size and first floor location, much of this 8' x 8' addition project can be completed by do-it-yourselfers. The foundation work should be left to the contractor; but the framing and finish work can be performed by homeowners with a moderate level of remodel-ing skill. Beginners should get help before starting new procedures and seek guidance as they progress. Homeowners should weigh the savings on labor costs against the investment of their time in jobs which require specialized skills and know-how. Siding, roofing, electrical work, and flooring can be done much faster and with better results by a specialty contractor than by the handyman who is unfamiliar with the tools, materials, and the ins and outs of its placement. Generally, beginners should add 100% to the man-hours estimates for the basic tasks and hire a professional for the time-consuming, techni-cally-demanding specialty operations. Handy-men should add 50% to the time for basic tasks and carpentry procedures and 70% for any spe-cialty work that is new to them. Experts should add about 20% to the professional time for all tasks in this project. Almost all do-it-yourselfers should hire a contractor to do the electrical rough-in, and even experts should leave the circuit tie-in to a qualified tradesman.

8' x 8' ROOM ADDITION

Description	Quantity	Man-hours	Material
Excavate, with machine, 4' deep	I Job	6.0	0.00
Footing, 8" thick x 16" wide x 20'	I C.Y.	4.0	106.00
Foundation, 8" concrete block, 4' high	96 Blocks	16.0	428.65
Frame, floor, 2" x 8" joists, 16" O.C, 8' long	80 L.F.	1.5	55.15
Floor sheathing, 5/8" plywood, 4' x 8' sheets	2 Sheets	1.0	34.05
Frame, walls, 2" x 4" studs & plates, 8' high	20 L.F.	3.5	71.40
Header over window, 2" x 8" stock	8 L.F.	0.5	5.25
Wall sheathing, 1/2" x 4' x 8' plywood	6 Sheets	3.0	95.25
Frame, roof, 2" x 6" rafters, 16" O.C.	80 L.F.	1.5	37.75
Ridge board & sub-fascia, 2" x 8" x 8' long	24 L.F.	1.5	16.55
Ceiling, 2" x 6" joists, 16" O.C.	48 L.F.	1.0	22.65
Roof sheathing, 1/2" x 4' x 8' plywood	3 Sheets	1.5	47.65
Siding, vinyl embossed, 8" wide, with trim	180 S.F.	6.0	135.05
Soffit, 12" wide vented, fascia & drip edge	35 L.F.	5.0	59.30
Roofing, standard strip shingles & felt paper	I Sq.	2.0	57.90
Flashing, aluminum stop flashing	20 S.F.	1.5	15.95
Gutters, 5" aluminum, .027" thick	16 L.F.	1.5	16.10
Downspouts, 2" x 3", embossed aluminum	20 L.F.	1.0	12.60
Wall insulation, fiberglass, 3-1/2" thick, R-11	180 S.F.	1.0	58.80
Ceiling, insulation, fiberglass 6" thick, R-19	50 S.F.	0.5	23.60
Window, clad awning type, 40" x 22", thermopane	I Ea.	1.0	225.05
Exterior door, wood, 2'8" x 6'8", prehung with lockset	I Ea.	2.0	372.70
Drywall, 1/2" x 4' x 8', standard, finished	10 Sheets	6.0	96.80
Underlayment, 3/8" particleboard	2 Sheets	1.0	31.75
Flooring, vinyl sheet, .125" thick	50 S.F.	2.0	196.65
Trim, ranch base & casing	50 L.F.	2.0	42.35
Paint walls, ceiling & trim, primer & 2 coats	320 S.F.	5.0	69.70
Electrical wiring, 4 outlets, I switch	I Lot	7.0	74.95
Backfill, finish grade & re-seed	I Job	13.0	12.10
Totals		98.5	$2421.90
Project Size 8' x 8'	Contractor's Fee Including Materials		$6680

What to Watch Out For

The type and placement of windows and doors are among the most important design features of any room addition. Although they are also some of the more expensive items in any home improvement project, it does not pay to compromise on the quality or design of these components. Whenever possible, purchase well-made thermopane window units. Not only do they provide on-going energy savings, but they usually include screens, and do not require the extra expense of storm windows. The door used in this plan is a new fixture; however, the old exterior door could be relocated to the entryway of the new room. Existing window units can be relocated in the same way to reduce the materials cost. If you choose to reuse the old door and windows, be sure that they are in good enough condition to make their relocation worthwhile. While cosmetic deficiencies are usually fairly simple to correct, structural defects involve a considerable amount of repair time.

8' x 8' Room Addition

This 8' x 8' addition can add to the comfort and convenience of your home. It is an approachable project for the do-it-yourselfer because it is relatively small in size and is conveniently located.

ROOM ADDITION
8' × 12'

Asphalt Shingles

Aluminum Flashing

Aluminum Flashing

Vinyl Soffit, Fascia, & Drip Edge

Cedar Bevel Siding

Aluminum Gutter

Picture Window

Steel Entrance Door

Concrete Foundation

Concrete Step & Landing (not incl.)

Concrete Strip Footing

Backfill, Finish Grade & Re-seed

Aluminum Downspout

The proximity of property boundaries, design of the existing house, and other factors often prevent the conventional construction of a room addition. In these circumstances, unusual designs may be called for, such as this 8' x 12' addition between the wings of the house. Although the structure is moderate in size, it is a challenging project for most do-it-yourselfers, as it calls for quite a few carpentry and building skills.

Materials

One of the benefits of placing the addition in a corner location is that two of the walls are already in place. Thus, you can save on the materials and labor which are normally required to frame and cover these walls. For the new construction, a 4' foundation is required on the remaining two sides. The other materials are standard framing lumber and interior and exterior coverings and finish materials appropriate to the style of the house. Before placing the order, do some comparative pricing at several building supply outlets. Also, because of the size of the order and the number and weight of materials, trucking is required, so make arrangements for delivery before you close the deal.

The foundation suggested in this plan is constructed from poured concrete, but concrete blocks can also be used and will function as well. The extra time and expense required to install foundation vents are well invested, as they will help to increase air circulation and prevent moisture from accumulating underneath the structure. In most cases, excavations and foundation installations for room additions are best left to the contractor. Accurate location and leveling of the forms and skillful concrete placement are vital to the successful completion of the project.

The shell of this addition is comprised of standard materials commonly used in exterior framing and finishing. After the sill, floor joists, and floor sheathing have been placed, the two exterior walls are framed on the deck and raised into position. The roof framing of corner structures can be tricky, so plan ahead and get some help if you think you will need it. After the roof structure has been completed, the gable end must be framed with 2" x 4"s, placed individually. The sheathing for the walls in this plan is 3/4" rigid styrofoam, but standard 1/2" plywood can also be used. The roof also requires plywood sheathing before it is covered with a layer of building paper and asphalt shingles. Because of the amount of flashing required, most do-it-yourselfers should consider hiring a professional to do the roofing work. Before the interior finish materials are applied, the exterior walls and the ceiling should be insulated at the recommended R-values for your area of the country. In colder climates, the floor should also be insulated before the sheathing is placed. Additional materials cost will have to be added to the project; but your floors will be warmer during the cold months, and your heating bill lower. After the electrical work has been roughed in, the interior finish materials can be installed. Cost will vary here according to your choice of products, the amount of trim, and decorative considerations. Standard 1/2″ drywall requires know-how and skill to install and finish, but most handymen can do the job if they are given some assistance at the outset. Underlayment should be installed beneath the carpet and laid at right angles to the floor sheathing, with no coincidental seams. All of these materials should match or complement the decor in the rest of your home.

8' X 12' ROOM ADDITION

Description	Quantity	Man-hours	Material
Excavate, with machine, 4' deep	1 Job	6.0	0.00
Footing, 8″ thick x 16″ wide x 20' long	1 C.Y.	3.0	88.30
Foundation walls, 8″ thick, c.i.p. concrete	2 C.Y.	12.0	296.20
Frame, floor, 2″ x 8″ joists, 16″ O.C., 8' long	120 L.F.	2.5	82.75
Floor, sheathing, 5/8″ plywood 4' x 8' sheets	3 Sheets	1.5	51.10
Frame, walls, 2″ x 4″ studs and plates, 8' long	20 L.F.	4.0	194.80
Header over window & door, 2″ x 8″ stock	18 L.F.	1.0	38.30
Wall sheathing, 3/4″ x 4' x 8' rigid styrofoam	5 Sheets	2.0	79.40
Frame, roof, 2″ x 6″ rafters, 16″ O.C.	169 L.F.	3.0	84.95
Sub-fascia, 2″ x 6″ stock	14 L.F.	0.5	6.60
Ceiling, 2″ x 6″ joists, 16″ O.C.	90 L.F.	1.5	47.20
Support beam, double 2″ x 10″	28 L.F.	1.5	52.85
Roof sheathing, 5/8″ x 4' x 8' plywood	7 Sheets	3.0	114.10
Siding, cedar bevel, 1/2″ x 8″, A grade	160 S.F.	6.0	452.55
Soffit, 12″ wide vented, fascia & drip edge	22 L.F.	3.5	37.25
Roofing, standard strip shingles & felt paper	2 Sq.	4.0	115.80
Flashing, at valley	20 S.F.	2.5	33.55
Gutters, 5″ aluminum, .027″ thick	12 L.F.	1.0	12.05
Downspouts, 2″ x 3″, embossed aluminum	10 L.F.	0.5	6.30
Wall insulation, fiberglass, 3-1/2″ thick, R-11	160 S.F.	1.0	52.25
Ceiling insulation, fiberglass, 6″ thick, R-19	100 S.F.	1.0	47.20
Door, steel 24 ga., 3' x 6'-8″, half glass, complete	1 Ea.	1.0	232.30
Picture window, 60″ x 48″, thermopane	1 Ea.	1.5	268.60
Drywall, 1/2″ x 4' x 8', standard, finished	10 Sheets	6.0	96.80
Underlayment, 3/8″ particleboard	3 Sheets	1.5	27.90
Carpet, 22 oz. nylon, with pad	12 S.Y.	3.0	237.85
Trim, ranch base & casing	70 L.F.	2.5	59.30
Paint walls, ceiling & trim, primer & 2 coats	320 S.F.	5.0	69.70
Electrical wiring, 4 outlets, 1 switch	1 Lot	7.5	74.95
Backfill, finish grade & re-seed	1 Job	13.5	12.10
Totals		91.5	$2973.00
Project Size 8' x 12'	Contractor's Fee Including Materials		$7470

Level of Difficulty

As in other complete room additions, this project requires a moderate to advanced level of skill in many construction procedures, including framing, roofing, siding, and exterior finish work. However, once the structure is closed in, the interior tasks can be completed one at a time over an extended period. This situation works to the benefit of all do-it-yourselfers who proceed patiently and learn as they go. Beginners can approach the interior work at a relaxed pace on weekends and evenings, but they should leave most of the exterior work on this project to contractors. The foundation, framing, roofing, siding, and other specialized tasks require skill and experience. For the more basic tasks, like painting, sheathing, and landscaping, beginners should add 100% to the professional time. Handymen should add 50% for all but the roof framing and finishing, electrical, and carpet installations. They should allow more time for these specialty tasks, and, depending on their ability, should hire professionals to do the work. Experts should add 20% to allow for a slow and patient installation process. All do-it-yourselfers should hire a contractor for the excavation and foundation work.

What to Watch Out For

The unusual roof lines of structures like this corner room addition provide a good situation for a skylight. Adding this amenity to the project will increase the cost, but the installation will be much easier and faster if it is done while the roof is being built, rather than later. Skylights are available in many sizes, models, and levels of quality. The good ones are expensive; but as with other window units, the extra cost for a quality product will be returned in energy efficiency and durability over the years.

8' x 12' Room Addition

Corner room additions such as this 8' x 12' design require imaginative planning and skillful installation, but offer a great potential for reward. When appropriately tailored to the roof lines and setting of your house, they can add an attractive exterior feature while increasing the living area and value of your home.

ROOM ADDITION
12' × 16'

If you have sufficient yard area and adequate distance to property lines, an "ell" configuration is usually the most convenient and appropriate design to use for a room addition. The new structure, though attached, is essentially a miniature house with its own foundation, frame, and interior and exterior finish. Care should be taken in determining its location, roof lines, and exterior trim to ensure that it will become an integral part of the existing house. Just as important are local zoning regulations, which should be checked before you begin any work. Like other room addition projects in this section, it's a major home improvement which requires considerable carpentry and building skills.

Aluminum Ridge Vent
Asphalt Shingles
Aluminum Gutter
Aluminum Downspout
Steel Entrance Door, Half Glass
Picture Window
Concrete Landing & Step (not incl.)
Cedar Shingles
Backfill, Finish Grade & Re-seed
Double Hung Window
Vinyl Soffit, Fascia, & Drip Edge
Concrete Block Foundation
Concrete Strip Footing

Materials

The materials in this plan, especially the basic subsurface components, are readily available at building supply outlets, and you can shop around for the best deal. For an order of this size, the savings can be considerable, with free local delivery a part of the purchase agreement.

Most do-it-yourselfers should have the excavation and foundation work for this addition done by a contractor. A substantial amount of earth has to be removed to allow for the 4' foundation depth. Additional expense should be figured in if some of the excavated material has to be trucked from the site. This plan suggests a concrete block foundation; but a formed and poured foundation can also be used. If you plan to install the foundation yourself, but don't have any experience with masonry, get some professional advice before you start. A poorly constructed or misaligned foundation can cause major problems during the construction of the facility.

After the foundation has been placed, the framing, sheathing, and exterior finishing tasks can be accomplished. A 2" x 8" sill plate is secured to the top of the foundation wall, and the 2" x 10" floor joists installed. Be sure to use

at least 5/8" plywood for the decking and to stagger the termination seams for additional floor strengthening. Standard 2" x 4" partitions with appropriate headers and jack studs are erected for the door and window opening and are then covered with 1/2" sheathing. If you are not experienced in framing, be sure to get some help for this part of the wall and roof work. The gable roof is basic in its framing design, but it requires skill and know-how to construct. The most critical aspect of the roof framing procedure is the layout of the rafter template, which must duplicate or complement the roof pitch and overhang features of the existing house. This plan also includes a 10' ridge vent strip, which should be installed as part of the finish roofing procedure. The final steps in the exterior work include finishing the soffit and trim, placing the door and window units, and applying the siding.

Within the new room, preliminary work on the floor, ceiling, and walls has to be completed before the finish products are placed. The subfloor has to be covered with appropriate underlayment if carpeting or resilient flooring is to be installed. The ceiling and walls should be insulated and roughed in for the desired electrical fixtures. Once the rough wiring is in place, the fixtures can be purchased and tied in later. When installing the drywall, always hang the ceiling pieces first and then the wall sheets. This plan calls for wainscoting constructed from 1/4"

paneling on the lower part of the walls. Before the paneling is put into place, 3/8" plywood backing is applied to the studs as a support, furring, and fastening subsurface.

12' x 16' ROOM ADDITION			
Description	Quantity	Man-hours	Material
Excavate, with machine, 4' deep	1 Job	6.0	0.00
Footing, 8" thick x 16" wide x 20' long	2 C.Y.	7.0	194.30
Foundation walls, 8" concrete block, 4' high	176 S.F.	31.0	805.00
Frame, floor, 2" x 10" joists, 16" O.C., 12' long	192 L.F.	3.5	132.40
Sill plates, 2" x 8" stock	48 L.F.	1.5	33.10
Floor, sheathing, 3/4" plywood 4' x 8' sheets	6 Sheets	2.5	102.20
Frame, walls, 2" x 4" plates, 12' long	144 L.F.	3.0	45.30
2" x 4" studs, 8' long	320 L.F.	5.0	100.65
Header over window & door, 2" x 8" stock	36 L.F.	2.0	24.85
Wall sheathing, 1/2" x 4' x 8' plywood	12 Sheets	5.5	190.50
Frame, roof, 2" x 6" rafters, 16" O.C., 8' long	208 L.F.	3.5	98.15
Ceiling, 2" x 6" joists, 16" O.C.	156 L.F.	2.0	73.60
Ridge board & sub-fascia, 2" x 8" stock	50 L.F.	2.5	34.50
Roof sheathing, 5/8" x 4' x 8' plywood	9 Sheets	3.5	153.40
Felt paper, 15 lb., on roof & walls	700 S.F.	1.0	25.40
Roofing, asphalt shingles, 285 lb. premium	3 Sq.	7.0	282.40
Flashing at wall .016" thick	16 S.F.	1.0	6.40
Ridge vent strip, aluminum	10 L.F.	0.5	26.25
Siding, no. 1 red cedar shingles, 7 1/2" exp.	370 S.F.	14.5	358.20
Soffit, 12" wide vented, fascia & drip edge	48 L.F.	7.0	81.30
Gutters, 5" aluminum, .027" thick	34 L.F.	2.5	34.15
Downspouts, 2" x 3", embossed aluminum	20 L.F.	1.0	12.60
Wall insulation, fiberglass, 3-1/2" thick, R-11	400 S.F.	2.0	130.70
Ceiling, insulation, fiberglass, 6" thick, R-19	200 S.F.	1.5	94.40
Door, steel 24 ga., 3' x 6'-8", half glass, complete	1 Ea.	1.0	232.35
Picture window, 60" x 48", thermopane	1 Ea.	1.5	268.60
Double-hung window, 36" x 48", thermopane	2 Ea.	2.0	423.50
Drywall, 1/2" x 4' x 8', standard finished	12 Sheets	8.0	116.20
Paneling, 1/4" thick for wainscot	5 Sheets	6.5	164.55
Plywood, 3/8" thick, backing for paneling	5 Sheets	3.0	77.45
Carpet, 24 oz. nylon, with pad	23 S.Y.	5.0	455.85
Trim, ranch base, casing & wainscoting	155 L.F.	6.0	168.80
Paint walls, ceiling & trim, primer & 2 coats	420 S.F.	4.0	91.50
Electrical wiring, 4 outlets, 1 switch	1 Lot	7.0	74.95
Backfill, finish grade & re-seed	1 Job	13.0	12.10
Totals		173.5	$5125.60
Project Size 12' x 16'	Contractor's Fee Including Materials	$13,140	

Level of Difficulty

Most of the exterior work on this addition demands considerable skill and know-how. Beginners, therefore, should plan to restrict their efforts primarily to the interior finishing. The exterior painting, landscaping, and other basic operations are tasks which beginners can tackle, but advanced procedures such as framing and roofing should be left to a contractor. Beginners should add at least 100% to the man-hours estimates for all of the tasks which they undertake. Handymen should attempt only those exterior operations which they feel comfortable in taking on. The roof framing and finish work are especially challenging undertakings which may require professional assistance. Handymen should be able to handle all of the interior operations, except the carpeting and electrical installations, with 50% added to the professional time. Experts should add 20% for all interior and exterior jobs.

What to Watch Out For

The existing house wall which is included in the addition requires considerable preparation before it can be finished to blend in with the new room. The exterior siding has to be removed and any structural alterations made before the drywall or other finish material is applied. If an acceptable entryway from the house to the new room already exists, no structural work is required and the rough opening can simply be trimmed with the appropriate materials. If there is no access or an existing entryway has to be widened, the wall will have to be opened and new structural members added.

12' x 16' Room Addition
This good-sized room addition will boost the value of your home by adding to its living space and enhancing its exterior appearance. With careful planning and professional assistance where needed, it is a manageable job for many do-it-yourselfers.

SECOND STORY ADDITION 8' × 12'

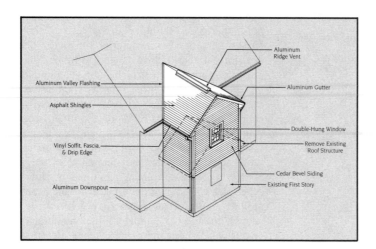

Aluminum Ridge Vent

Aluminum Valley Flashing

Aluminum Gutter

Asphalt Shingles

Double-Hung Window

Remove Existing Roof Structure

Vinyl Soffit, Fascia, & Drip Edge

Cedar Bevel Siding

Aluminum Downspout

Existing First Story

Second floor living space can be increased by means of attic conversions or the placement of dormers, but still more interior area can be created with a complete room addition. If the conditions are right and there is an existing attached structure on which to build, adding a second story may be the answer. Because of the difficulties in removing the old roof, the potential for hidden problems, and the need to work rapidly, most do-it-yourselfers should hire a contractor to perform the exterior work.

Materials

Conventional framing, sheathing, and finish products are placed on top of the supporting first-floor. What makes the installation of the new components difficult is the general inconvenience of the second-story location and the extra time required to complete any off-ground construction.

Before the new materials are placed, an extensive amount of preliminary planning has to be done, as well as preparation of the old structure to receive the new one. The first step is to evaluate the condition of the existing wood structure and its foundation. Even expert do-it-yourselfers should hire a qualified inspector if there is any question about its strength or ability to support the load of the new materials. Foundation work and added lumber may have to be included in the estimate to reinforce the original structure before the new work begins. The next step is the removal of the old roof covering, sheathing, and rafters. As in dormer installations, this procedure can be time consuming, yet expediency is important because part of the interior of the house will be opened to the elements. If you plan to do this part of the project without the services of a contractor, be sure to have plenty of help on hand to move the

job quickly. Whenever possible, try to salvage the old lumber and sheathing. If they are in good condition, they may come in handy later in the project.

After the roof has been removed, the existing ceiling joists become the floor joists for the new room. If they are 2″ x 8″s or larger, they are probably strong enough as they are; but if they are 2″ x 6″s, they will need some reinforcing. Check with a professional to determine the size of required reinforcement materials and the methods of installing them. The deck is then sheathed with 5/8″ plywood before the wall partitions are framed. Be sure to prepare the area of the existing house wall to receive the new framing. The roof is then framed with 2″ x 6″ rafters and a 2″ x 8″ ridge board tapered into the existing roof. The sheathing and finished roofing, selected to match the existing finish roof material, are then applied. After the window unit and siding are installed, the structure is ready for the interior work.

Before work can begin on the additions interior, the type of access must be determined. This plan assumes that a stairway to the new room will be placed off a finished second-story bedroom or hallway. Whenever possible, existing window openings should be utilized as part of the future rough opening for a door. If you cannot use an existing window opening, then the wall will have to be opened at a convenient place and headers and jack studs placed to rough in the entryway. If you want to open the entire wall or a large portion of it, more support will be required. Additional cost and time may have to be included in the estimate for the entryway installation, according to its type, size, and conditions of placement. As for the rest of the room, many different interior products can be installed to meet the practical and aesthetic standards of its intended use. When the rough electrical work and insulating have been completed, the walls and ceiling can be drywalled and finished.

8' x 12' Second Story Addition

Description	Quantity	Man-hours	Material
Remove existing roof structure & siding, etc.	1 Ea.	40.0	0.00
Frame, boxing at existing joists, 2" x 6" stock	32 L.F.	0.5	15.10
Floor, sheathing, 5/8" plywood, 4' x 8' sheets	3 Sheets	1.5	51.10
Frame, walls, 2" x 4" studs & plates, 8' long	32 L.F.	6.0	114.20
Headers over windows, 2" x 8" stock	12 L.F.	1.0	8.30
Gable end studs, 2" x 4" stock	12 L.F.	0.5	3.80
Wall sheathing, 1/2" x 4' x 8' plywood	9 Sheets	4.0	142.90
Frame, roof, 2" x 6" rafters, 16" O.C.	192 L.F.	3.5	90.60
Sub-fascia, 2" x 6" stock	24 L.F.	0.5	11.35
Ceiling, 2" x 6" joists, 16" O.C.	90 L.F.	1.5	42.45
Roof sheathing, 1/2" x 4' x 8' plywood	7 Sheets	2.5	119.25
Siding, cedar bevel, 1/2" x 8", A grade	270 S.F.	8.0	610.95
Soffit, 12" wide vented, fascia & drip edge	40 L.F.	5.0	77.40
Roofing, standard strip shingles & felt paper	3 Sq.	5.5	190.60
Ridge vent strip, aluminum	8 L.F.	0.5	21.00
Flashing, at valley	40 S.F.	2.0	31.95
Gutters, 5" aluminum, .027" thick	24 L.F.	1.5	24.10
Downspouts, 2" x 3", embossed aluminum	36 L.F.	1.5	22.65
Wall insul., fiberglass, 3-1/2" thick, R-11	260 S.F.	1.5	84.50
Ceiling, insul., fiberglass, 6" thick, R-19	100 S.F.	1.0	47.20
Window, double-hung, 3' x 3'-6", thermopane, plastic clad	1 Ea.	1.0	211.75
Drywall, 1/2" x 4' x 8', standard, finished	13 Sheets	7.0	125.85
Underlayment, 3/8" particleboard	3 Sheets	1.5	47.65
Carpet, 22 oz. nylon, with pad	12 S.Y.	2.5	237.85
Trim, ranch base & casing	70 L.F.	2.0	59.30
Paint walls, ceiling & trim, primer & 2 coats	420 S.F.	6.5	91.50
Electrical wiring, 4 outlets, 1 switch	1 Lot	7.0	74.95
Totals		115.5	$2558.25
Project Size 8' x 12'	Contractor's Fee Including Materials		$7730

Level of Difficulty

This project is one of the most challenging home improvements included in this book. The exterior operations require not only advanced carpentry and tool handling skills, but also fast and efficient work at roof level. As in the dormer project, expediency is a critical factor in any operation which involves opening a section of the roof. Here, the entire roof must be removed; the ceiling joists must be blocked off and, possibly, reinforced; and a new structure built and tied into the wall and roof of the existing house, all in a relatively short period of time. All levels of do-it-yourselfers, therefore, are encouraged to hire a specialty contractor for the exterior work. Even experts should consider professional help for the roof removal, and plan to have several experienced helpers on hand to assist with the framing and roofing tasks. Beginners and handymen should restrict their efforts to the interior work only and tack on an additional 100% and 50%, respectively, to the professional man-hours. Experts should add 30% to the time estimates for all exterior tasks which they feel they can handle, and 20% to the interior operations.

What to Watch Out For

If there is one guiding principle for room addition plans, it is that the new attached structure should blend with the house and complement its style, and not look "tacked on." Roofing and siding lines are particularly important in this blending process. This plan, for example, requires that the roof line of the new room align with that of the existing house, and that the courses of asphalt roofing meet precisely at the valley. The new siding should follow the same spacing of the structure below, and its course lines should align at the seam between the house and the addition.

8' x 12' Second Story Addition
If the conditions are right, this second-story room addition can add space to the upstairs of your house. Although it requires a considerable effort to construct, it provides an alternative plan to attic conversion or dormer installation.

SECOND STORY ADDITION 20' × 24'

If more interior space is needed, but restricted building area prohibits the construction of a ground-level addition, a large second-story structure may be the answer. This room addition plan demonstrates how nearly 500 square feet of new interior space can be created above a two-car, attached garage. Such a project is an expensive, time consuming undertaking which requires a major commitment on the part of the homeowner. The time schedule for the procedure has to be carefully planned to ensure expedient completion of the exterior enclosure. An architect can help you to determine the style, design, and structural aspects of the project.

Materials

This project involves the cost of roof removal and, in most cases, the strengthening of the support system for the new room. This expense is somewhat offset by the fact that a foundation already exists, and thus, you avoid the costs of its excavation and construction. Once the support system has been reconditioned to acceptable standards, the same materials used in other wood frame structures are employed in constructing this new room.

Before the new decking can be applied to this 20' x 24' room, the existing garage roof has to be removed and the ceiling joists reinforced to safe standards. If the existing joists are 2″ x 8″s or larger and are supported by a center beam, the amount of reinforcement will be minimal. If they are 2″ x 6″s, then a substantial amount of reinforcement will be required. The cost for this procedure will vary with each situation. After the 5/8″ plywood decking has been installed, the walls and roof are framed with standard 2″ x 4″ and 2″ x 6″ lumber and sheathed with 1/2″ plywood or comparable material. Care should be taken to blend the new structure to the old so that the roof line, the style of the overhang, and other design features complement one another.

The new exterior finish products should also be selected to harmonize with the style of the house. For example, premium asphalt shingles are suggested in this plan, but standard asphalt or cedar shingles can also be used. Tile and slate are two more possibilities. Some of the options for exterior walls are cedar shingles, clapboards, aluminum siding, stucco, or the cedar board and batten siding suggested in this plan. All of these materials vary in price, and the selection of one product over another will have a considerable impact on the estimated cost.

After the exterior has been completed and the structure made weathertight, a doorway or opening into the new room must be created. If you are completing the interior work on your own and are unfamiliar with cutting and framing a wall opening, get some advice before you start. The placement of a standard-sized 30″ or 32″ door requires 2″ x 8″ headers and jack studs for the rough opening frame, but a 6′ or 8′ wall opening necessitates more support and, possibly, temporary ceiling bracing during the installation procedure. Remember to allow time for stripping the siding on the wall where the entry is placed.

One of the advantages of this and most other room addition projects is that the interior work can be completed by the do-it-yourselfer, one task at a time, when convenient. The insulating, rough electrical work, and any partitioning are completed first, and then the ceiling and walls are covered and finished. Partitioning for closets or room dividers will add to the total cost and the installation time. A wide range of wall and ceiling coverings and finishes is available.

20′ x 24′ Second Story Addition

Description	Quantity	Man-hours	Material
Remove existing roof structure & siding, cut opening	1 Job	80.0	0.00
Frame, floor, 2″ x 8″ joists, 16″ O.C., 12′ long	540 L.F.	8.5	372.45
Floor sheathing, 3/4″ plywood, 4′ x 8′ sheets	15 Sheets	6.5	302.00
Frame, walls, 2″ x 4″ plates, 12′ long	264 L.F.	13.0	228.45
2″ x 4″ studs, 8′ long Headers over windows, 2″ x 8″ stock	24 L.F.	1.5	16.55
Wall sheathing, 25/32″ x 4′ x 8′ wood fiber board	22 Sheets	9.5	255.55
Corner bracing, 16 ga. steel straps, 10′ long	8 Ea.	1.0	50.35
Frame, roof, 2″ x 6″ rafters, 16″ O.C., 14′ long	238 L.F.	4.0	112.30
Ridge board, 2″ x 8″ stock	22 L.F.	1.0	15.20
Hip rafters, 2″ x 8″ x 18′	36 L.F.	1.0	24.85
Hip jack rafters, 2″ x 6″ stock, 16″ O.C.	336 L.F.	9.5	158.55
Sub-fascia, 2″ x 6″ stock	84 L.F.	2.0	39.65
Ceiling, 2″ x 6″ joists, 16″ O.C.	416 L.F.	5.5	196.30
Roof sheathing, 5/8″ x 4′ x 8′ plywood	30 Sheets	11.5	511.10
Roofing, asphalt shingles, 285 lb. premium	10 Sq.	23.0	941.40
Felt paper, 15 lb., on roof	1000 S.F.	2.0	36.30
Ridge vent strip, aluminum	14 L.F.	1.0	36.75
Siding, cedar board & batten, pre-stained	525 S.F.	16.5	749.60
Soffit, 12″ wide vented, fascia & drip edge	90 L.F.	12.0	174.25
Gutters, 5″ aluminum, .027″ thick	68 L.F.	5.0	68.30
Downspouts, 2″ x 3″, embossed aluminum	36 L.F.	1.5	22.65
Wall insulation, fiberglass, 3-1/2″ thick, R-11	525 S.F.	3.0	171.50
Ceiling, insulation, fiberglass, 6″ thick, R-19	480 S.F.	2.5	226.50
Casement window. 8′ x 5′, clad thermopane	1 Ea.	2.0	1292.30
Casement window, 24″ x 52″, clad thermopane	4 Ea.	4.0	948.65
Drywall, 1/2″ x 4′ x 8′, standard, finished	37 Sheets	20.0	358.15
Carpet, 26 oz. nylon, with pad	54 S.Y.	12.0	1070.25
Trim, ranch base & casing	186 L.F.	6.0	157.55
Jamb, 1″ x 6″ clear pine, at opening to house	1 Ea.	1.0	12.65
Paint walls, ceiling & trim, primer & 2 coats	1200 S.F.	19.0	261.35
Electrical wiring, 8 outlets, 2 switches	1 Lot	14.5	149.90
Totals		299.5	$8961.35
Project Size 20′ x 24′	Contractor's Fee Including Materials		**$23,160**

Level of Difficulty

This large second-story addition is one of the most challenging home improvement projects presented in this book. The removal of the roof and subsequent framing and roofing are difficult operations that must be completed as expediently as possible to protect the interior from the elements. All do-it-yourselfers, therefore, are encouraged to leave the exterior work to a professional and concentrate their efforts on the inside tasks. As noted earlier, the convenient location of the addition permits the do-it-yourselfer to work at his own pace. Do-it-yourselfers should be able to handle most of the interior operations, though they should leave the electrical and carpet installations to professionals. Beginners should add 100% to the man-hours estimate for all of the tasks they undertake. Handymen and experts should add 50% and 20%, respectively, to the estimate for the interior jobs, and more for the specialty work.

All do-it-yourselfers should hire an electrician to tie in the service for the new room.

What to Watch Out For

Painting is one exterior job that all do-it-yourselfers can accomplish to keep the costs down. If you install the aluminum soffit, fascia, and gutter products and the vinyl-clad windows suggested in this plan, the only thing you will have to paint is the siding. That, too, can be purchased pre-stained, but the chances of matching it to the color of the existing house are slim. Apply a minimum of two coats, one primer and one finish, to all new exterior materials which require painting. Skimping on the paint job is unwise, as it will not only detract from the appearance of the structure, but could also necessitate premature repainting and replacement of materials.

20′ x 24′ Second Story Addition

This 20′ x 24′ second story addition is a major home improvement which requires the services of a professional contractor for much of the structural and exterior work. However, most do-it-yourselfers can substantially reduce the cost of the project by completing the interior work themselves. The combined efforts of contractor and homeowner can result in a lot of new living space at a reasonable cost.

FIXED
BUBBLE SKYLIGHT

Fixed Bubble Skylight

Aluminum Flashing

Pine Jamb

2" x 6" Trimmer Rafter

2-2" x 6" Headers

Interior Casing

2" x 4" Curb

As in other exterior home improvements, the overall planning, layout, and design of a skylight installation must be determined with care. This plan features a small fixed bubble skylight which can provide an economical solution to lighting problems in an interior room or porch. Although this project involves the general inconveniences of roof work and the complications of roof hole-cutting, many do-it-yourselfers can complete the installation in a surprisingly short time.

Materials

Other than the skylight itself, the materials required to complete this project consist of the standard construction products needed to support the unit. These basic materials include lumber for adding strength to the rafters, flashing, incidental items for making the roof weather tight, and various interior trim products to finish the shaft and to refurbish the ceiling area affected by the installation. Because each project will present a different set of conditions, the type and amount of these materials may vary from the estimate. Slight increases or decreases in cost, therefore, are to be expected in installations of this type.

Before the prefabricated skylight unit can be placed, an extensive amount of preliminary work must be completed. The roof and ceiling areas to be opened must be carefully laid out, the holes cut, and support restored to the rafters and, if necessary, the ceiling joists. Determining the location of the skylight is a critical procedure for both practical and aesthetic reasons. Generally, a central location in the ceiling between existing rafters is ideal, as the hole-cutting is easier and trimmer rafters do not have to be placed. However, these conditions apply only when the unit you are installing is small enough to fit within your rafter spacing (usually 16"). In most cases, at least one rafter must be cut, and trimmers and headers installed to restore roof support. This operation can often be difficult and time consuming, as the trimmers may have to span a major portion of the length from the ridge to the top of the outside wall. The cutting of the holes in the roof and ceiling, the placing of the trimmer and header rafters and joists, and the installing of extra support can be difficult jobs which require know-how and moderate to advanced carpentry skills. Inexperienced do-it-yourselfers are advised to seek help if they are unfamiliar with these operations. Additional costs may be incurred during the preliminary phase of the project if extensive roof reconditioning is required. All do-it-yourselfers should have a professional contractor evaluate and, if necessary, correct any deficiencies in the structure of the roof before proceeding with the project.

The design and the size of the skylight unit should also be carefully selected so that it meets practical and aesthetic needs. This plan calls for a small fixed bubble, but a larger fixed unit or a ventilating model may be more appropriate for a given situation. In addition to the amount of light and ventilating capacity of the skylight, factors like the roof pitch, exposure, and exterior design of the fixture should also be considered. Generally, fixed dome skylights like this one are a good choice for well ventilated rooms, high ceilings above stairwells and hallways, and screened-in porches. As with other prefabricated building materials that will be exposed to the weather for many years, the quality of the skylight unit should be taken into consideration. Double-layered plastic bubbles like this one, for example, must be hermetically sealed to prevent condensation between the layers of plastic and to ensure efficient energy control. Most models include a base flange or provision for a curb and self-flashing. Be sure to follow precisely the manufacturer's guidelines when installing the skylight unit.

The time and material required to finish the interior of the skylight shaft will vary, as each installation will present a different set of conditions. This plan assumes that the skylight shaft extends only the thickness of the roof frame, as in attic rooms or basic porch locations where the ceiling follows the line of the roof. A longer shaft will be required, however, if the roof and ceiling are separated by attic space. In these cases, more materials and installation time will be necessary to build, insulate, and finish the shaft. The installation can also be more difficult when flared or angled shaft designs are needed or desired. Where long shafts are required, the extra cost and time will be considerable.

Level of Difficulty

With good conditions such as 16″ rafter spacing and no extra shaft requirements, most do-it-yourselfers can handle this skylight installation. Small, fixed plastic bubbles of this type tend to be relatively inexpensive, so there isn't the worry of working with very costly or complicated components. The units are often installed in porches and attics or on flat or gently sloping roofs, and while the hole-cutting is never easy, it is less difficult in these locations. As long as conditions are favorable, beginners can complete this installation with the addition of 150% to the professional time; but they should proceed cautiously and seek instruction beforehand from a knowledgeable person. For skylight placement on a steep roof or where long shafts and extensive preliminary work are necessary, beginners should consider hiring a professional installer. Handymen and experts should add 75% and 25%, respectively, to the man-hours estimate for all tasks. All do-it-yourselfers should build in extra time for the general inconvenience of roof work.

What to Watch Out For

Although they do not allow for increased ventilation, fixed skylights like this one provide many other advantages which make them the right choice for certain installations. One is that they are ideal for flat roofs and for roofs that tend to drain slowly, ice up, or collect snow. Once the sealed unit has been correctly placed and made weathertight, the chances of its leaking are minimal. A second advantage is the bubbled shape of the exterior which exposes more domed surface area to natural light. This feature makes them a good choice for roofs with northern exposures. A third advantage is that they are economically priced. For locations like porches and breezeways, they function as well as more sophisticated, operable windows for less cost.

FIXED BUBBLE SKYLIGHT			
Description	Quantity	Man-hours	Material
Roof cutout & demolition including layout	I Ea.	2.5	0.00
Trimmer rafters, 2″ x 6″ x 14′	28 L.F.	0.5	26.45
Headers, double 2″ x 6″ stock	8 L.F.	0.5	3.80
Curb, 2″ x 4″ stock	10 L.F.	0.5	3.15
Skylight, fixed bubble, 24″ x 24″	I Ea.	2.0	260.15
Flashing, aluminum, .013″ thick	9 S.F.	0.5	3.05
Trim interior, casing, 9/16″ x 3-1/2″	10 L.F.	0.5	8.45
jamb, I″ x 8″ clear pine	10 L.F.	0.5	9.10
Painting trim, incl. puttying, primer & I coat	20 L.F.	0.5	1.20
Totals		8.0	$315.35
Project Size 24″ x 24″	Contractor's Fee Including Materials		$780

Fixed Bubble Skylight
This basic fixed bubble skylight will dramatically increase the amount of light and sense of spaciousness in a bedroom, attic area, porch, or breezeway. If the conditions are right, it can be installed by most do-it-yourselfers for just the cost of the unit and a few basic construction materials.

VENTILATING BUBBLE SKYLIGHT

Ventilating skylights have some unique advantages; and when they are installed under the right conditions, they can greatly improve the appearance and air quality of an interior space. The large 52″ x 52″ ventilating bubble featured in this plan can considerably increase air circulation while providing nearly 18 square feet of window area. When the skylight is closed, the benefits of natural light continue, while the unit's double-layered insulating dome helps to keep the interior warm in winter and cool in the summer. Because of the large size of the skylight unit and the considerable preparation required to install it, this project is challenging. Beginners and handymen with limited remodeling experience should consider hiring a professional, at least for the more difficult exterior phase of the project.

Materials

The primary component in this remodeling project is the skylight unit, but several basic construction materials are also included in the plan. These are needed to restore the roof structure, to make the installation weathertight, and to return the interior to acceptable finished appearance. There are many styles and brand names of skylights available to the consumer in a wide range of quality and price. Therefore, it pays to do some research before you decide on the unit that meets your needs and budget requirements. Probably the most effective way of researching skylights and other major factory-made building products is to ask the retailer for references of people who have installed them. Consumer satisfaction is the best endorsement for any product.

The most challenging task faced in this skylight project is that of locating the fixture on the roof and ceiling, and the subsequent hole-cutting. Although only a few new materials are included in this preliminary work, the procedure is time consuming and demands considerable know-how to accomplish correctly and safely. To install a skylight of this size under normal conditions, about 20 square feet of roofing must be stripped, an equal area of sheathing removed, and two or, possibly, three rafters cut. If a finished ceiling is involved, a comparable area of interior covering will have to be removed and an equal number of joists cut. Temporary bracing may be required for the severed rafters and joists until the trimmers and doubled headers are placed. This plan suggests 2″ x 8″ trimmer rafters and headers, but 2″ x 6″s and even 2″ x 10″s may be needed if the existing rafters match these dimensions. Extra time and cost may be required for the preliminary work if extensive reconditioning and strengthening of roof framing members are needed.

Once the hole cutting and rafter trimming have been completed, the skylight unit can be placed in the opening and fastened into position. A unit of this size is heavy and awkward enough to cause problems in getting it to the site. You should have several workers available to help in getting it onto the roof and to position it from inside and outside of the opening. Remember that these expensive units are preframed, often prefinished, and fragile. Dropping or banging one can cause cosmetic damage at the very least, and worse, misalignment or breakage. After the skylight has been placed, the surrounding roof and perimeter seams are made weathertight with flashing, caulking, and reroofing. Re-using some of the old roofing can be a bit of a challenge, but it can also help to blend the new installation into the roof. Follow the manufacturer's guidelines and instructions throughout the placement operation, including the recommendations for proper flashing and weatherstripping.

The amount of interior finish material and installation time will vary according to the location and arrangement of the ceiling. If the finished covering is applied directly to the rafters, as in some attic and cathedral ceiling designs, the amount of finish material and the man-hours to install it will be fairly limited. In such cases, the hole is closed in with finished wood and then faced with trim. If, as in this plan, the finished ceiling lies below several feet of attic space and joists, the job becomes more difficult, costly, and time consuming. A light shaft must be built to span the attic space and joists to the level of the finished ceiling. A frame of 2 x 4's is normally used for the walls of the shaft. Finish material like sheetrock, pine boards, or paneling can then be applied to the inside of the shaft and appropriate casing used to trim the opening. Insulation of the recommended R-value for your area should be placed on the outside of the shaft walls. Further expense will be incurred for the shaft construction if special effects like flaring and angling are desired.

VENTILATING BUBBLE SKYLIGHT

Description	Quantity	Man-hours	Material
Layout, roof & ceiling cutout & demolition	1 Ea.	4.0	0.00
Trimmer rafters, 2" x 8" x 14'	28 L.F.	0.5	38.65
Headers, double 2" x 8"	18 L.F.	1.0	12.40
Curb, 2" x 4" stock	18 L.F.	0.5	5.65
Skylight, ventilating bubble, 52" x 52"	1 Ea.	3.0	580.80
Flashing, aluminum, .019" thick	21 S.F.	1.5	7.10
Shaft construction, 2" x 6" x 12' trimmer joists	24 L.F.	0.5	22.65
Headers for joists, 2" x 6" stock	20 L.F.	1.0	9.45
Framing, 2" x 4" stock	64 L.F.	2.0	20.10
Drywall, 1/2" x 4' x 8' sheets, taped & finished	2 Sheets	1.5	19.35
Painting, shaft walls, primer & 1 coat	64 S.F.	5.5	6.95
Insulation, foil-faced batts, 3-1/2" thick, R-11	64 S.F.	0.5	20.90
Trim, interior casing, 9/16" x 4-1/2"	18 L.F.	1.0	19.60
Painting, trim, primer & 1 coat	18 L.F.	0.5	1.10
Totals		23.0	$764.70

Project Size	52" x 52"	Contractor's Fee Including Materials	$1710

Level of Difficulty

This large skylight installation is a major project for do-it-yourselfers of all ability levels. If the project is complicated by the need to build a light shaft, the undertaking becomes even more challenging. Remember, too, that because the skylight unit is an expensive product, the risks of damaging it have to be weighed against the savings in labor costs when you install it on your own. Experts and skilled handymen can handle all procedures in the project, but they should add 25% and 75%, respectively, to the professional time estimate. They should allow even more time for placing the skylight itself, as careful handling and workmanship are important considerations. Any do-it-yourselfers who are inexperienced in roofing should get some advice on the task of replacing the disturbed roofing and applying the flashing. Beginners and less skilled handymen should leave all of the exterior work to a professional installer; but they may be able to handle the interior finish if the required ceiling work is minimal. They should double the man-hours estimate for all basic tasks, including painting.

What to Watch Out For

Determining the size, shape, and type of the skylight or sky window deserves ample consideration before the master plan for the project is finalized. For example, a large unit like this one can overwhelm a small room, and, conversely, skylights that are too small can look out of place on an expansive ceiling. Often, several medium sized units will look better and provide more flexibility for your ventilation, lighting, and aesthetic needs. Of course, more expense is incurred for more units; but if they are small enough to be placed between the roof framing members, installation cost for each one will be reduced. Remember that the exterior appearance of the skylight, especially on front roofs, is also important.

Ventilating Bubble Skylight
This large bubble skylight can improve the livability of your home by bringing in new light and ventilation. If the right design and roof location are chosen, this improvement can also enhance the exterior appearance of your home.

OPERABLE SKY WINDOW

Operable Sky Window

Existing Roof Structure

Shaft
2" x 4" Studs
1/2" Drywall

Aluminum Flashing

Framing
2" x 8" Trimmer Rafters
2-2" x 8" Headers
2" x 4" Curb

This project features a 48″ x 52″ top-of-the-line sky window with an operable sash. Units like this are equipped with insulated tinted glass and factory-prepared curbing. A wide selection of accessories is also available to suit the particular needs of each installation. This window addition can dramatically improve the lighting and ventilation in an interior space.

Materials

Only a small number of materials is required for this project, as the prefabricated skylight unit is designed for convenient installation. A considerable amount of preliminary roof work is necessary, however, and interior and exterior finish work will be required after the unit has been installed. The materials needed to complete these operations include inexpensive home building products, like framing lumber, flashing, and interior wood trim. These items represent only a small percentage of the total cost of the project, but they are necessary components. The trimmer joist/rafters, especially, are vital structural elements which will be used to restore ceiling and roof support after the opening has been cut.

Before you begin the task of opening the ceiling and the roof, take time to lay out the location of the window unit. Most of the popular brands of skylights are manufactured for easy placement between standard-sized rafter spacings. The frame of this 52″ skylight unit can be located in the space opened when two 16″ rafters are cut and partially removed. Whenever possible, locate the skylight between existing rafters, as you will save time and disturb the roof structure only slightly. Be sure to square the

layout and double check all measurements before the hole is cut. After trimmers and headers are installed, a curb may have to be fastened to the perimeter of the opening, depending on the manufacturer's recommendations. The instructions will also provide specific information for proper fastening and flashing of the window frame. Use accepted roofing methods for replacing the disturbed area with finished roof covering. Reusing salvaged pieces of the old roofing will neatly blend the new work with the existing roof.

In many instances, sky windows are placed in attic rooms, family rooms with vaulted ceilings, and in other rooms with slanted ceilings. The installation process is easier in these cases because the roof rafters and ceiling joists are often one in the same. After the skylight unit has been secured in its opening and made weathertight on the outside, the interior finishing is a relatively easy undertaking. The inside of the opening is trimmed with appropriate material, usually wood, and matching trim is applied for the casing.

In some instances, the interior finishing may be more difficult and costly. If, as in this plan, the roof and ceiling are separated by unused attic space and separate holes are required for the exterior and interior openings, you will have to build a light shaft between the two. The cost of this procedure and its degree of difficulty will vary with each situation, depending on the shaft's dimensions, finish, and design features. Usually, a 2″ x 4″ frame, sheathing, and insulation are required for the basic structure. Trim work and an appropriate covering are then applied to the shaft's interior to complete the procedure. If the bottom of the shaft is located on a horizontal ceiling, the opening could be flared to gain the maximum benefits of light and ventilation. Remember to figure in some extra time and cost for cutting and trimming the ceiling opening and joists as part of the shaft installation.

Level of Difficulty

If the basic conditions are right, the installation of this sky window can be a manageable project for do-it-yourselfers experienced in the use of tools and routine roof work. Beginners and less-skilled handymen, however, should not rush into the undertaking without considering the risks involved in roof hole-cutting and related procedures. Steep roofs and inaccessible attic locations can provide dangerous and troublesome conditions for inexperienced workers. Remember that you must also use power tools in awkward positions such as from a roof ladder. Because nearly 20 square feet of roof will be opened, rapid and effective work is required to cut the hole, trim it, place and flash the unit, and restore the finish roofing to weathertight condition within a few hours time. Experts and skilled handymen should be able to complete these tasks with 25% and 75%, respectively, added to the professional time. Inexperienced do-it-yourselfers should not attempt the exterior work and should double the estimated man-hours for finishing the interior. All do-it-yourselfers are reminded to allow extra time for handling this expensive and fragile skylight unit and for the general inconvenience of roof work.

What to Watch Out For

If a long light shaft is required for the installation of your sky window, you might want to put some extra effort into planning its design features. Although the length and width of the shaft's top opening are fixed, the sides, bottom, and length of its run can be creatively arranged to provide maximum practical operation and aesthetic appeal. One of the best ways to increase ventilation and light penetration is to flare the shaft by increasing the length and width of the opening at the ceiling end. This design requires more time and expertise to install because the rafters, joists, 2″ x 4″s for the frame, and sheathing must be cut at precise angles; but any additional cost for materials is small. Although this modification to the conventional shaft design will add some time and expense to the project, it can significantly improve its appearance and function.

OPERABLE SKY WINDOW

Description	Quantity	Man-hours	Material
Layout, roof & ceiling cutout, demolition	1 Ea.	4.0	0.00
Trimmer rafters, 2″ x 8″ x 14′	28 L.F.	0.5	38.65
Headers, double 2″ x 8″	16 L.F.	1.0	11.05
Curb, 2″ x 4″ stock	14 L.F.	0.5	4.40
Sky window, operating, thermopane glass, 48″ x 52″	1 Ea.	5.5	682.45
Flashing, aluminum, .019″ thick	14 S.F.	1.0	4.75
Shaft construction, 2″ x 6″ x 12′ trimmer joists	24 L.F.	0.5	22.65
Headers for joists, 2″ x 6″ stock	20 L.F.	1.0	9.45
Framing, 2″ x 4″ stock	64 L.F.	2.0	20.15
Drywall, 1/2″ x 4′ x 8′ sheets, taped and finished	2 Sheets	1.0	19.35
Painting, shaft walls, primer & 1 coat	64 S.F.	5.5	9.95
Insulation, foil-faced batts, 3-1/2″ thick, R-11	64 S.F.	0.5	20.90
Trim, interior casing, 9/16″ x 4-1/2″	18 L.F.	0.5	19.60
Painting, trim, primer & 1 coat	18 L.F.	0.5	1.10
Totals		24.0	$864.45
Project Size 52″ x 55″	Contractor's Fee Including Materials		$1850

Operable Sky Window

Installing a large sky window like the one featured in this plan can transform a gloomy interior area into attractive and pleasant living space. With the addition of a clever shaft design and the appropriate accessories, the installation can produce spectacular results.

BRICK PATIO IN SAND

There are many advantages to working with brick, concrete, and stone as building materials. They are durable, strong, and attractive; and they can be used in a wide variety of installations, from interior fireplace facings to exterior walkway and patio surfaces. Once you have learned some of the basic skills, acquired the fundamental hand tools, and gained some experience, working with these materials can be enjoyable and rewarding. If you are inexperienced with masonry tasks, it is best to start with a project that is small in size and not too demanding. This 6' x 12' brick patio plan presents such an opportunity. Also, because the bricks are set in sand, mistakes can be easily corrected, with little or no waste of materials.

4" x 8" x 1-1/2" Edging Brick
Patio Brick Laid Flat

Finish Grade & Re-Seed
4" Washed Sand Base

Clearing & Excavating

Polyethylene Vapor Barrier

Materials

Patio projects utilize the same basic materials, though they may vary in form, size, and method of placement. The first step is arranging some type of a form system to set the limits and the perimeter design of the patio. Then, a subsurface of sand, gravel, or concrete is put into place to establish a level base and support for the installation. Lastly, the surface material of brick, stone, or concrete is applied and then grouted or finished. All of these materials are readily available from building and masonry supply outlets, so it pays to shop for the best prices. In most cases, they have to be trucked, so be sure to arrange delivery as a part of the purchase agreement. The retailer may or may not charge you for curb delivery, depending on the size of the order the distance to the site. In addition to the masonry supplies, some basic hand tools are needed for all brick or stone patio installations. These include a stonemason's hammer, flat stone chisel, 3' or 4' level, square, and long tape measure.

Before the bricks can be set for this 6' x 12' patio, the area must be laid out, excavated, and prepared with a sand base. Minimal materials cost is involved in this stage of the installation process, but a significant amount of time is required to dig out the site to the required depth and to place the sand. If the area is level, the procedure is basic, but more time and expense may be involved if you have to contend with a slope. Be sure to dig out completely all vegetation, especially grass and other perennial plants that are hardy enough to re-establish themselves later on between the bricks. This plan suggests that a polyethylene barrier be placed below the layout of base sand to prohibit the growth of deep-rooting vegetation, but some hardy plants with shallow root systems may still establish themselves above the barrier if they are left unattended. The cost of the barrier is minimal and its benefits are many, so be sure to include it. Once the base sand has been leveled and tamped, and a course of perimeter bricks placed, the surface can be laid.

The bricks themselves are the most important and costly component of the project, so be sure to make the right selection. There are many different types, sizes, and grades of brick available, but not all of them can be used for paving purposes. In most cases, bricks that can be used for paving are referred to as "all purpose bricks," "hard brick," or "pavers," and are rated as "SW" (severe weathering). Bricks with a rating less than "SW" may crack and even disintegrate in time when exposed to water, icing, and constant freeze-thaw weather conditions. Be sure to verify the rating of the brick with your retailer before you buy it, as a softer, less durable product will necessitate premature replacement of the patio materials. Paving brick is more expensive than the softer "MW," or "NW" brick, but it will last longer if properly installed.

The method and pattern for laying the brick on the sand base should be carefully planned. One of the advantages of setting the bricks in sand is that trial and error will usually only cost you more time. As a general rule, patterns which require little or no brick cutting are desirable because they install faster and create minimal waste. Simple jack-on-jack and basket-weave patterns in various configurations require little or no cutting. There is some cutting involved, however, in the intricate running bond and herring-bone patterns, like the one illustrated. In short, the more imaginative the design, the more cutting is required, and the more waste of material is incurred. Once you have gotten the knack of "striking" brick and cutting it accurately, the waste will be minimal. However, some mistakes will occur as you learn this art, so allow for extra material if you are a beginner. A masonry saw can make the job easier. You might also seek professional advice or ask an experienced friend for help before you start.

After the brick has been set and leveled in the desired pattern, the seams are grouted with screened sand or stone dust and packed solid. Doing this process correctly takes time, but it is a vital operation in the project. If the sand grout is not packed tightly, the bricks will wobble and eventually become misaligned. Several treatments are usually required to solidify the surface. A light watering with a hose should follow each packing session. Be sure to kneel outside of the patio, whenever possible, when you work at grouting. If you have to walk or kneel on the newly placed bricks, use a piece of plywood to distribute your weight. Keep the new patio wetted down for a couple of weeks after it is finished, and regrout it from time-to-time.

Level of Difficulty

This project presents an excellent opportunity for all levels of do-it-yourselfers to acquire some basic masonry skills without the worry of wasting materials. As long as you take time to lay out the site, prepare it properly, and select a design that is commensurate with your ability, little can go wrong; and the result will be of professional quality. Beginners should allow an additional 75% to the professional time for simple patterns and 100% for more intricate designs. Handymen and experts should add 40% and 10%, respectively, to the man-hours for all tasks included in the project. All do-it-yourselfers should allow for additional time and materials if they choose patterns which require brick cutting and are unfamiliar with the procedure.

What to Watch Out For

The cost for the brick paving material in this 6' x 12' patio allows for a perimeter course of brick laid lengthwise on edge, and for surface courses laid flat. More material will be required if the pattern includes bricks laid in soldier or sailor style or in other vertical or angled arrangements. Sawtooth or sailor edging, for example, requires more perimeter bricks than standard horizontal edging. Extra material and installation time are also required for special patterns or angled surface courses. This herringbone design uses about 20% more brick than a basketweave or jack-on-jack pattern because some waste occurs when the bricks are cut.

BRICK PATIO IN SAND			
Description	Quantity	Man-hours	Material
Layout, clearing & excavation for patio, by hand	1 Job	4.5	0.00
Polyethylene vapor barrier, .008" thick	80 S.F.	0.5	2.90
Washed sand for 4" base	1 C.Y.	0.0	15.65
Grade & level sand base	72 S.F.	2.0	0.00
Edging brick 4" x 8" x 1-1/2", laid on edge	36 L.F.	1.5	31.35
Patio brick, 4" x 8" x 1-1/2" thick, laid flat, herringbone pattern	72 S.F.	11.0	197.75
Finish grade & re-seed	1 Job	1.5	5.85
Totals		21.0	$253.50
Project Size 6' x 12'	Contractor's Fee Including Materials		$1020

Brick Patio In Sand

This brick-in-sand patio project can enhance an entranceway or create a small outdoor sitting area at a modest cost. Because it is basic in design, small in size, and easy to install, you can benefit from the self-satisfaction and reduced cost of completing it entirely on your own.

BRICK PATIO IN MORTAR

The process of placing bricks in mortar on a concrete slab is more difficult than setting them in sand, but it is well within the reach of many do-it-yourselfers. If the slab is already in place and the laying of the brick is all that has to be done, the job is fairly easy. However, if you begin from scratch and must place the concrete slab first, the project becomes more difficult, costly, and time-consuming. Mistakes are not easily corrected when they involve mortar, bricks, and concrete, so work slowly and get help and guidance when needed as the project progresses. One of the advantages of a patio project is that its convenient location allows the do-it-yourselfer to do the work in stages at a comfortable pace.

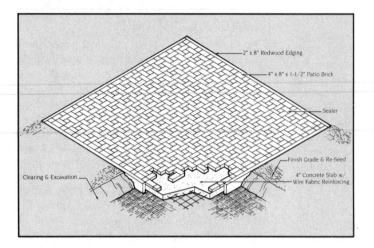

Labels on diagram: 2" x 8" Redwood Edging · 4" x 8" x 1-1/2" Patio Brick · Sealer · Finish Grade & Re-Seed · 4" Concrete Slab w/ Wire Fabric Reinforcing · Clearing & Excavation

Materials

The materials included in this project consist of the concrete and metal reinforcement for the slab, a 2" x 8" redwood border, the brick, and mortar mixed in various portions with sand. These are all common construction materials and, except for the ready-mixed concrete, can be purchased from most building and masonry supply retailers. It pays to shop for the best deal, especially on the brick, which is the most costly product included in this project. As for the ready-mixed concrete, some price comparing may help here as well; but because the amount of material required for this patio is relatively small, you may have to pay a minimum delivery charge to cover the supplier's trucking expenses. If you don't want to complete the project all at once, the slab can be placed and the brick surface applied at a later date, with full use of the facility between steps of the project.

Before the slab is placed, a substantial amount of excavating has to be done. The patio area should be carefully located, measured, squared, and then dug out by hand to a size slightly larger than that of the finished surface. Remember to leave room for the slab form and for the redwood edging. Some additional cost may be incurred for a layer of gravel if the slab is being placed on poor subsoil. This precautionary measure will help to reduce cracking and heaving of the slab during freezes. The form for the slab may be made from the 2" x 8" redwood border or from conventional lumber. The use of the redwood will save you time later on because once it has been placed, it is there for good as the trim for the finished patio. Be aware, however, that the edges may take some abuse during the slab placement. If you are fussy about its appearance, you might consider placing the border after the concrete has set up. Doing it this way will take more time, and extra expense will be incurred for the purchase of temporary form lumber. Be sure to square the form to its precise dimensions and then brace the corners and stake the sides to hold it firmly in place while the slab is poured. A slight pitch off level in one direction away from adjacent structures will help to drain the surface. Remember, too, that the pattern of bricks to be used on the finished surface has to be considered before the concrete is placed. An error of an inch or two can add time and expense later because of the extra brick cutting required to adjust for the error in measurement or square.

Once the form has been placed, and the reinforcing wire positioned, the slab is poured and finished. This process can be challenging if you are inexperienced because you have to work quickly and efficiently. Be sure to get some advice beforehand and to have plenty of help available on the day that the ready-mixed truck arrives. Getting prepared for the truck's arrival requires much organization and a set plan to minimize the time of the delivery. If the truck is tied up for too long, you will be charged extra. If the site is inaccessible to the truck, wheelbarrows will have to be used in the delivery. In some cases, ramps or wood tracks may have to be used as access routes to protect the landscaping from the weight and traffic of the wheelbarrows. After the delivery has been completed, the concrete is leveled and rough finished in preparation for the placement of the bricks.

The process of laying the bricks on the finished slab also requires basic masonry knowledge. The entire brick surface does not have to be completed in one session, so work very slowly at first with the anticipation of faster placement as you get better at it. Never mix more mortar than you will use in an hour of brick laying. If any brick cutting is required, do it before mixing the mortar or starting the brick placement for that session. As in all construction projects, keep an eye on level and square as you proceed. Investment in a stringline, long mason's level, and a good trowel will add to your efficiency and to the appearance of the finished patio. The time and money invested in an application of masonry sealer will be returned many times over in protection for the finished patio.

Level of Difficulty

This project is challenging for most do-it-yourselfers, but manageable if it is taken in small steps. With patient work, even inexperienced handymen can complete the patio with professional results. Seek advice and guidance as you proceed, and complete one phase before going on to the next. Impatience will only cause frustration, poor workmanship, and wasted time and materials. The most demanding part of the project is the placing of the slab, because a great deal of work has to be compressed into a four-hour period. Novices may consider hiring a contractor to form and pour the slab and could then follow up with the brick work. Experts and most handymen should be able to complete the entire project on their own. They should add 10% and 40%, respectively, to the man-hours estimate for the project. Beginners should add 75% to the professional time for all tasks. All do-it-yourselfers who are inexperienced in laying pavement bricks can expect a very slow work pace at first, with a gradual increase in productivity as the surface is laid.

What to Watch Out For

The border trim requires careful planning because it has both a practical and an aesthetic role in the overall design of the patio. Although special border features and materials usually cost more and take longer to install, they can bring the design of the patio to life and add lasting protection to the edge of the surface. This plan calls for 2" x 8" redwood edging, but there are other options for rot-resistant wood edges, such as cedar, locust, or pressure-treated pine. Patios which are recessed or terraced can be made even more attractive with appropriate wood edging. Bricks set in soldier, sailor, or sawtooth arrangements can also enhance the surface design while adding durability to the patio's edge. Be sure to point all joints in the edging, including those that are hidden by the backfill, to protect them from water penetration and to maintain the strength of the border.

BRICK PATIO IN MORTAR

Description	Quantity	Man-hours	Material
Layout, clearing & excavation for patio, by hand	1 Ea.	7.0	0.00
Edging, redwood, 2" x 8"	48 L.F.	2.0	41.85
Base, 4" thick concrete slab reinforcing, welded wire fabric 6' x 6' - 10/10	160 S.F.	1.0	15.50
Concrete, ready mix, 2000 psi. 4" thick	2 C.Y.	0.0	135.05
Place concrete	2 C.Y.	5.0	0.00
Patio brick, 4" x 8" x 1-1/2" thick, grouted, 3/8" joint	144 S.F.	25.0	327.55
Finish grade, & re-seed	1 Job	2.0	11.70
Sealer, silicone or stearate, 1 coat	144 S.F.	0.5	31.35
Totals		42.5	$563.00

Project Size	12' x 12'	Contractor's Fee Including Materials	$2050

Brick Patio In Mortar

The 12' x 12' brick-in-mortar patio presented in this plan will make an attractive and practical addition to the exterior of any home. Although its installation requires a moderate level of masonry know-how, the project can be completed in small steps and at a comfortable pace for do-it-yourselfers who are willing to learn as they go.

CONCRETE PATIO
12' × 16'

The primary advantages of concrete as a patio, walkway, or floor material are its strength and durability, but as an added benefit, it can also be shaped and molded into a variety of configurations and forms. It can take on many surface textures and can be colored it is being placed, or painted after it is installed. With imaginative planning and design, a standard concrete patio can be enlivened with the addition of colored stones, terracing, or redwood bordering or sectioning. Be sure to locate it appropriately and build in the proper drainage, expansion, and reinforcement controls required in all concrete and slab work. This 12' x 16' patio is a moderately challenging project. If the work is done in stages, experts, handymen, and many beginners can complete the project on their own.

Materials

The site has to be laid out and excavated, the forms built, the sub-surface and reinforcement placed, and the concrete poured and finished. As long as the grade on which the patio is to be built is level or gently sloped, and the subsoil easy to dig into, the project can be completed as estimated with no extra costs. All masonry work which involves mortar and concrete requires efficient organization and detailed preparation. Before you begin work, you will need some basic masonry hand tools: shovels, stiff rakes, a sturdy wheelbarrow, trowels, a float, and an edging or jointing tool. A stringline, square, 3' or 4' level, 16' tape measure, and hammer are required for the construction of the forms. Extra cost will be incurred if you have to buy some of these tools, but all of them are necessary to complete this project. The specialized concrete finishing tools, reinforcement materials, and pre-molded expansion joint can be purchased from a masonry supplier.

The excavation work required for this patio is substantial, as the 12' x 16' area has to be dug out by hand to a depth of at least 7" to allow for 3" of gravel fill for a subbase under the 4" slab. Be sure to dig out the edges of the cavity throughly to permit easy placement of the form and to allow some leeway for squaring and leveling. The form should be pitched slightly away from any adjacent structures, squared, and braced firmly with stakes and corner ties to its final position. The subsurface material, reinforcement wire, and expansion joint should then be placed in preparation for the concrete delivery.

The concrete for a relatively small job like this one may cost more per cubic yard than it would for a complete foundation or celler floor, because of the dealer's overhead for trucking costs. A minimum charge, therefore, is not unlikely. Be sure to work out all of the conditions of delivery with the retailer before the order is placed. The amount of time allowed for the delivery and the cost of additional truck tie-up time are important details that you should be aware of. Good organization and advance preparation will keep the costs down. If the site is accessible to the truck and the concrete poured directly from the chute, the job will go quickly, efficiently, and most economically. If it has to be transported from the street or driveway, then more time, man-power, and possibly, expense will be involved. Wheelbarrowing concrete is a physically demanding task which involves concentrated, rigorous work during the delivery period.

After the concrete has been put into place, several hours can elapse before the material hardens to an unworkable state. Always keep some fresh concrete handy during the screeding to add to low spots and to offset settling as the surface is finished. On warm days, you may have to work a little faster in the finishing process, but there still will be enough time to create the desired texture. If the surface sets up too quickly, it can be enlivened with mist from a hose. Do not give it the full spray of a hose at this time, however, as this may expose the aggregate and damage the finish. Also, do not overwork the surface during finishing, as too much troweling can cause the aggregate to settle and separate from the rest of the slab. Be sure to tamp the edges only enough to fill voids and to create a solid side surface. Control joints and rounded edges should be added after the finishing process.

Level of Difficulty

The most difficult procedures are the actual placement of the concrete and its subsequent finishing, both of which can be troublesome for inexperienced workers. Remember that several hours of intense, physically demanding work are involved in accomplishing this phase of the project. Beginners, therefore, should make arrangements to have at least one experienced person on the job during the pour and for some time after to oversee the operation. Novices should add 75% to the professional time for all of the preliminary tasks, like the setting of the form and placement of the reinforcing. Handymen with experience in concrete work and experts should add 40% and 10%, respectively, to the man-hours estimate for the entire project.

What to Watch Out For

Many alternatives to the conventional square, single-level patio are possible if the surrounding terrain is suitable and if you are willing to exercise your imagination and ingenuity. Terracing the patio is one example which is not so complex as it may seem. The same basic techniques used for single-level slabs are employed in multi-level installations, only in modular arrangements. Where the land slopes away from the house, two- and three-tier patio designs are an option, with interconnecting pressure-treated pine or redwood steps. Railroad ties and other rot-resistant border materials can be used to shore cutouts in the embankment. Single-level concrete patios can also be sectioned off in interesting configurations and grids with redwood or cedar dividers. Rounded corners and oval shapes are among the alternatives to conventional square and rectangular patio shapes. Masonite or 1/4" plywood can be used to form the curved edges. Custom-colored surface materials are also available on special order from concrte dealers and masonry suppliers if you want to mix them on your own. All of these variations from the standard patio design will add expense to the project, but they can enhance the facility's appearance.

12' x 16' CONCRETE PATIO

Description	Quantity	Man-hours	Material
Layout, clearing & excavation for patio, by hand	1 Job	12.0	0.00
Gravel fill, 3" deep, compacted	210 S.F.	1.5	13.35
Edge forms, 4" high	40 L.F.	2.5	9.70
Expansion joint at existing foundation, premolded bituminous fiber	16 L.F.	1.5	9.30
Reinforcing, welded wire fabric, 6' x 6'-10'/10'	210 S.F.	1.5	20.35
Concrete, ready mix, 3000 psi	3 C.Y.	0.0	202.55
Place concrete	3 C.Y.	4.0	0.00
Finishing, broom finish	192 S.F.	3.0	0.00
Finish grade & re-seed	1 Job	4.0	11.70
Sealer for concrete	72 S.F.	1.5	15.70
Totals		31.5	$282.65
Project Size 12' x 16'	Contractor's Fee Including Materials		$1270

12' x 16' Concrete Patio

Most do- it-yourselfers can complete this 12' x 16' patio plan if they are willing to put in several sessions of hard work. If you are unfamiliar with concrete construction, be sure to seek advice and arrange to have a knowledgeable person available to assist you during the slab placement and finishing. Your efforts will produce substantial savings and a home improvement that will give you and your family years of enjoyment.

FLAGSTONE PATIO
IN SAND

In addition to brick and concrete, many natural stone materials can be used to create attractive and functional patios. In geographical areas where material is quarried or close to an abundant supply, the cost for both rough and cut stone can be surprisingly affordable. Like brick and concrete, stone is durable and can maintain its appearance with little upkeep throughout years of wear. This plan features a 6′ x 12′ patio constructed from bluestone flags of random-sized squares and rectangles, set in a sand bed. Like the brick-in-sand patio outlined earlier in this section, this project can be completed by most do-it-yourselfers for just the cost of the materials.

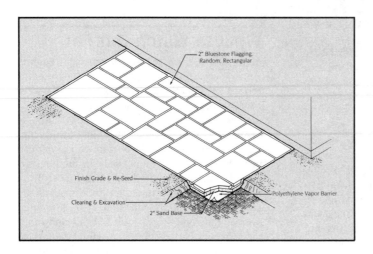

Materials

The basic materials used for patio projects of this type tend to be readily available from masonry suppliers, though the choice of stone may be limited. Flagstone, slate, and bluestone are the most common, but you may have to compromise on the size of the rectangular cut pieces if you plan to buy from the retailer's stock. Planning far enough in advance of the project will allow you to special order the type of stone and its size, but you may have to pay more for the custom cutting.

No special type of sand is required for the base, as long as it is not too fine to restrict drainage, nor too coarse to prohibit easy placement of the stones. Sand that has been screened and washed, like mason's sand, works the best and is usually the most economical. Only a small amount is needed to cover this 6′ x 12′ area to a depth of 2″ and to provide the grouting between the pieces of stone. If you live in an area where clean sand (not sandy soil) is naturally available, it can be used for the base. Be sure that you screen it first through 1/4″ wire screen to remove pebbles and organic matter. Money saved by acquiring or transporting the sand yourself should be weighed against the time and trouble required in its preparation.

Before the sand base is installed, the area for the new patio should be measured, squared, and staked out. Check the diagonal measurements of the rectangular area to be sure that they are equal. The site must then be excavated to a depth of about 4″ to allow for a minimum of 2″ of sand base and approximately 2″ of stone depth. A polyethylene barrier is placed under the sand to restrict grass and other hardy plants from growing between the stone. No permanent border strip is included in this plan, but a temporary form made from 2″ x 4″s may be used to keep the sand base intact and to ensure straight edges for the laying of the perimeter stones. After the sand has been placed, it is leveled with a straight piece of wood cut to the 6′ width of the surface. It should then be tamped and watered, allowed to set for a day or two, and then tamped and watered again. A third treatment may be required before the base is firm enough to receive the surface stones. The stones are then placed on the sand bed in the desired configuration or pattern. If you are installing rectangular flags of random size, as suggested in this plan, you might consider roughly laying out the entire patio, or a good portion of it, to get an idea of the trial-and-error fitting procedure. This preliminary layout will also give you a sense of how to place the material with maximum coverage and as little cutting as possible. By minimizing the cutting, you save time and avoid damaging or wasting the material. The permanent placement of the surface stones is easier and faster if they are uniform in their shape and thickness. Like bricks, stones of a generally consistent proportion can be placed on the leveled base with little fuss or readjustment. If there is much variation in thickness, the process takes longer, as each stone has to be leveled separately by adding or taking away sand. In most cases, rectangular bluestone flags maintain a consistent 2″ thickness, but common flagstone and other paving materials are apt to be irregular. The trouble-free placement of regular stones might be worth the extra investment as you save on installation time. If you have not cut stones before, be sure to get some advice or have an experienced person show you the technique. You may have to invest in a stone chisel or brickset because a conventional cold chisel or other substitute will not do the job as well. The damage to the flags resulting from incorrect cutting methods may cause considerable waste and, therefore, expense. Even with the right tools and technique, a 20% waste allowance should be expected for irregular flagstone.

The joints between the stone can be grouted as each section is laid, but it is better to wait until the entire surface is completed. The same material used for the base sand can also be employed for the grouting, though there are other alternatives. Preprocessed grouting, stone dust, and fine sand will cost more, but they can provide more effective packing for the stones and enhance the design of the patio. The grouting materials should be dampened after it has been swept into the joints with a stiff broom. Use a jointing tool, brickset, or similar device to pack the material, and then wet it again. Repeat this process several times until the grout is level

with the surface of the stones and tightly packed. Whenever possible, kneel on the ground outside of the patio when installing the grout.

Level of Difficulty

This project can be completed by homeowners who have the time to devote it. Working with regular stone flags is not a difficult undertaking, and the results can be very rewarding. The advantage of installing a sand-set patio is that you can work at a comfortable pace and rectify mistakes easily. The most difficult task in the project is the cutting of the stones; but with careful planning, even this job is within the reach of the do-it-yourselfer. Those who are inexperienced in stone cutting should get instruction in the technique before they begin the project. Beginners should add 75% to the professional time for the project; handymen 40%; and experts, 10%. Extra time should be allowed for the installation of stones with irregular shapes and/or thicknesses and for those which require extensive cutting.

What to Watch Out For

Patios which are constructed from brick or stone and set in sand are not as easy to maintain as those set in mortar. Some of the stones may have to be reset periodically, and the grout replenished because of frost heaving or loosening from foot traffic. Even though the plastic barrier will prevent deep-rooted plants from becoming established, smaller surface plants will grow between the stones during warmer times of the year. If you use an inert grouting material like stone dust or professionally prepared exterior grout, the problem will still exist, but the amount of growth will be reduced.

FLAGSTONE PATIO IN SAND

Description	Quantity	Man-hours	Material
Layout, clearing & excavation for patio, by hand	1 Job	4.0	0.00
Polyethylene vapor barrier, .008″ thick	80 S.F.	0.5	2.90
Washed sand for base, 2″ thick	1 C.Y.	0.0	15.65
Grade & level sand base	72 S.F.	2.0	0.00
Flagging, bluestone, snapped random rectangular, 2″ thick	86 S.F.	17.0	324.65
Finish grade & re-seed	1 Job	2.0	5.85
Totals		25.5	$349.05

Project Size	6′ x 12′	Contractor's Fee Including Materials	$1360

Flagstone Patio In Sand

This small flagstone-in-sand patio project provides an ideal opportunity for do-it-yourselfers to learn the basics of dry-set masonry. With time, patient work, and a modest investment for materials, the exterior of your home can be enhanced with this comfortable and attractive sitting area or entryway apron.

FLAGSTONE PATIO IN MORTAR

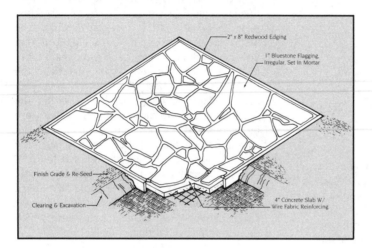

- 2" x 8" Redwood Edging
- 1" Bluestone Flagging, Irregular, Set In Mortar
- Finish Grade & Re-Seed
- Clearing & Excavation
- 4" Concrete Slab W/ Wire Fabric Reinforcing

Flagstone, bluestone, slate and other paving stones can be set in mortar to create attractive patio surfaces. Like brick, these materials offer the advantages of durability, low maintenance, and rugged beauty. They differ from brick in that they can be more expensive and often take longer to install because of their irregular sizes and shapes. This plan provides a cost estimate for the installation of a 12' x 12' irregular flagstone patio, including excavation, placement of the slab, and application of the finished surface. Because of the relatively large size of the patio and the number of masonry tasks required to complete it, beginners may consider hiring a contractor to do some of the work.

Materials

This plan calls for the basic masonry materials used in most mortar-set patios. The project is really two installations in one. The first involves excavating and preparing the site and then placing the slab; the second includes the placement of the flagstone in the mortar bed and the finish work. For both phases of the project, several basic masonry tools are needed. Some of these tools may have to be purchased or rented, and this extra cost may have to be figured in. As for the materials themselves, no additional costs should arise if the patio as planned is installed under normal conditions on level ground. Be sure to compare prices before you buy the materials to get the best deal.

Before construction begins, you will need to carefully determine the location of the patio and lay it out. Generally, level, well-drained areas near the house are best suited to patio installations. Conveniently located spots that are protected from the wind and exposed to moderate sun are ideal. Although only 6" of earth has to be removed, the excavation of a 12' x 12' area requires a considerable effort. Be sure to dig out several inches more than the patio dimensions so that you will be able to move the form freely

while setting it. If the subsoil condition is poor, you may have to allow for extra time and expense to place a layer of gravel or crushed stone under the slab. Set and brace the form precisely at square and pitch it slightly away from the foundation before you stake it into final position. Standard welded wire reinforcing or steel rods will add strength and reduce cracking in the slab. If the new concrete abuts the foundation or a concrete walk, an asphalt-impregnated expansion joint should be placed along the seam.

The slab can be put into place at any time after the form has been completed, but you may be rushing things if you try to build and set the form and place the concrete all in the same work session. The general rule to follow for the concrete delivery is "Be Prepared." Have all of the necessary tools, plenty of manpower, and a detailed plan of operation ready when the truck arrives. Disorganization and poor preparation can add time and, therefore, expense to the procedure, as you may tie up the truck for longer than the allotted delivery time. Once the concrete has been placed, you have about four hours to finish the slab, so work patiently, but methodically. The finish does not have to be troweled extensively because a rough finish is best for the bonding of the mortar.

Allow the slab time to set up and cure—usually three or four days—before proceeding with the second stage of the project, the placement of the mortar bed and flagstone. As in the brick-in-mortar patio project, the important aspect of this operation is to complete small, manageable sections at first, with increased production as the project progresses. Flagstone, however, does require more know-how, skill, and installation time than brick because its irregular shape necessitates cutting and fitting some pieces. Be sure to select flags of uniform thickness, as adjustments cannot be easily made for variations of thickness. Before laying a section of stones, place the pieces on the slab and position them by trial and error until you arrive at a combination that provides maximum coverage and joints that average about 3/4″ in width. Some cutting of the stone may be required, but only as a last resort. Then, remove the pieces in order and reconstruct the pattern in a nearby area. Moisten the slab in the area to be covered, spread the mortar to a thickness of about 1″, reposition the stones, and tap them into place with a mallet or a hammer and block of wood. Precisely maintain level as you lay the stones so that the finished surface will look neat and drain properly. After the entire surface has been set and the mortar has cured, grout is packed into the joints, pointed, and allowed to set up for a week before a sealer is applied.

Level of Difficulty

Because of the various masonry tasks required to complete this project, all do-it-yourselfers will find it a challenging undertaking. If you are inexperienced in placing concrete slabs, mixing mortar to the right consistency, and cutting and fitting stone, get some assistance and instruction before you start the project. Beginners might consider hiring a contractor to install the slab, then finishing the surface on their own. As long as you place the flagstone in sections small enough to complete in one hour at your work pace, you can't go wrong. Working in this fashion, the job may take a little longer to finish, but the results should be lasting and attractive. Beginners should tackle the slab placement only if an experienced person is on hand to assist. If the slab is installed incorrectly and the surface and edges are uneven, the flagstone placement will become a much more difficult and time-consuming operation. Beginners should add 75% to the man-hours for most of the tasks, and more for the flagstone placement. Handymen and experts should add 40% and 10%, respectively, to the professional time for all tasks, and more for the flagstone placement if they are inexperienced in stone cutting and fitting.

What to Watch Out For

The grouting for the flagstone can bring the surface of the patio to life, but it must be done neatly to achieve the desired effect. There are several methods which can be employed to quicken the pace of this time-consuming task and still produce neat results. One is to work with a trowel in one hand and a jointing tool in the other. A small portion of grout is placed on the trowel and scooped off as needed with the jointing tool. After a small section of joints has been filled, the grout is packed. If voids occur, extra mortar is added where needed and packed. A second method employs a small piece of sheet metal which is shaped into a "V" and carries a small amount of grout. The point of the "V" is placed on the joint and guided into the opening with a jointing tool or the point of the trowel. The packing and pointing of the grout is the same as for the first method.

FLAGSTONE PATIO IN MORTAR			
Description	Quantity	Man-hours	Material
Layout, clearing and excavation for patio, by hand	1 Job	4.0	0.00
Edging, redwood, 2″ x 8″	48 L.F.	2.0	79.00
Base, concrete slab, 4″ thick 6 x 6-reinforcing, welded wire fabric 10/10	160 S.F.	2.0	15.50
Concrete, ready mix, 2000 psi 4″ thick	2 C.Y.	0.0	135.05
Place concrete	2 C.Y.	5.5	0.00
Flagging, bluestone, irregular shapes, 1″ thick	170 S.F.	30.0	384.65
Finish grade & re-seed	1 Job	4.0	11.70
Totals		47.5	$625.90
Project Size 12′ x 12′	Contractor's Fee Including Materials		$2680

Flagstone Patio In Mortar

This patio project involves a considerable number of masonry tasks, all of which can be completed by most do-it-yourselfers. With patient fitting and mortaring of the flagstones, the resulting patio will be an attractive, functional, and lasting addition to the exterior of your home.

GROUND LEVEL DECK

2" x 4" Decking
Lag Bolts
Joist Hangers
Post Cap
Beam Hangers
2" x 6" Cap Rail
2" x 4" Rail
2-2" x 4" Posts
4" x 4" Posts
3-2" x 4" Treads
Concrete Landing
2" x 10" Stringers
2" x 6" Joists
2-2" x 6" Headers
Concrete Post Foundation

The addition of a deck is one of the easiest and most economical ways to improve the exterior of your home. Basic single-level decks are usually uncomplicated in their construction and are, therefore, manageable undertakings for homeowners who have limited building experience. This deck plan demonstrates how an attractive and functional facility can be constructed for a modest investment of both time and money. Because the deck is relatively small in area and built at ground level, it is an ideal project for beginners and handymen to gain experience in home improvement.

Materials

Most decks built at foundation or ground level are comprised of the same basic components. These vary in size and number, according to the method of installation, the dimensions of the stucture, its height above grade, and the complexity of its design. The materials used are basic decking products available at most building supply outlets, but they vary in quality and price, so do some comparison shopping before you buy. When you purchase the materials, select them yourself, if possible, looking for straight deck boards and sound support members. You should also clarify the conditions of delivery at the time of the purchase, since suppliers will make curb deliveries free of charge for a complete deck order.

All of the wood products for this deck are specially designed for use in exterior structures which are exposed to the elements. Pressure-treated deck materials are more costly then conventional, untreated components, but they are a much better choice. The additional expense for pressure-treated wood is worth the investment to guarantee the deck's longevity.

The support system for this 8' x 10' ground-level deck consists of footings, 4" x 4" posts, and the frame, which is comprised of 2" x 6" joists and headers. Before you begin the excavation for the footings, lay out their locations accurately to ensure a square and level support system for the rest of the structure. Several methods can be employed to establish the location of the support posts and their footings, but one of the most accurate is to approximate the layout with batter boards at the four corners, and then establish, by the use of stringlines, equal diagonals. Failure to place the footings and posts precisely at square with each other and with the side of your house will adversely affect the rest of the project. Double check the post locations before you set them in concrete and be sure to use cylindrical "tube" forms for the foundations. These are available at most building supply yards and are well worth the price. Review the layout of the 2" x 6" frame as well, to be sure that the doubled joists are correctly aligned with the 4" x 4" supports.

The decking suggested in this plan consists of 2" x 4"s laid across the frame and fastened with galvanized nails. However, decking materials of another thickness, width, or edge type can also be installed. Remember that the decking itself is the most visible component of the structure, so additional expense for aesthetic reasons may be a worthwhile investment. This deck plan includes a basic post-and-rail design for the railing system. It is one of the simplest railing designs to install, and it creates an attractive border with a 2″ x 6″ cap, which can double as a convenience shelf or a support for planters. More elaborate railings are also possible, but most of them require more materials and installation time. The system in this plan is very economical and basic in its design, but it is not child-proof. Safer, more expensive railings should be installed in decks that are high enough to create a safety hazard for small children. Stairway railings are not included in this plan because of its one-step access, but they should be installed at extra cost on deck stairways of more than one step. The posts for the railings should be constructed from 4″ x 4″s which are mortised into the frame and then fastened with lag bolts. Although the fitting of the posts takes a little longer and the lag bolts are more expensive than nails, the finished installation looks better, is more secure, and will last longer.

GROUND LEVEL DECK

Description	Quantity	Man-hours	Material
Layout, excavate post holes	4 Ea.	4.0	0.00
Concrete, field mix, 1 C.F. per bag, for posts, incl. 8″ dia. forms	4 Bag	7.0	102.90
Deck material, pressure treated lumber, Posts, 4″ x 4″ x 4′	16 L.F.	1.0	18.20
Headers, 2″ x 6″ x 10′	40 L.F.	1.5	24.70
Joists, 2″ x 6″ x 8′	72 L.F.	2.5	44.45
Decking, 2″ x 4″ x 10′	280 L.F.	8.5	115.20
Stair material, stringers, 2″ x 10″ x 3′	6 L.F.	0.5	7.10
Treads, 2″ x 4″ x 3′-6″, 3 per tread	12 L.F.	0.5	4.95
Landing, precast concrete, 14″ wide	4 L.F.	1.0	32.90
Railing material, posts, 2″ x 4″ x 3′	30 L.F.	1.0	12.35
Railings, 2″ x 4″ stock	52 L.F.	1.5	21.40
Cap rail, 2″ x 6″ stock	26 L.F.	1.0	16.05
Joist hangers, 18 ga. galvanized	7 Ea.	0.5	4.65
Nails, #10d galvanized	8 LB.	0.0	6.80
Bolts, 3/8″ lag bolts, long	18 Ea.	0.0	17.20
Totals		30.5	$428.85
Project Size 8′ x 10′	Contractor's Fee Including Materials		$1560

Level of Difficulty

Because this deck plan is basic in its design and constructed at ground level, it is an approachable project for beginners and less skilled handymen. A few basic carpentry skills, along with some experience in measuring, plumbing, and leveling, are required. Beginners should seek advice before they start and as the project progresses, and should double the professional time for all tasks involved in this project. Handymen and experts should add 30% and 10% respectively, to the estimated man-hours for the installation process.

What to Watch Out For

Because this deck is built at ground level with limited access to the terrain underneath, precautions should be taken to restrict unwanted vegetation from growing in this area. Some weeds and hardy grasses can establish themselves under the deck, eventually restricting ventilation and creating an eyesore. Decks which are built in sunny locations are particularly susceptible to this problem. To prevent this unwanted growth, remove about 3″ to 4″ of topsoil from the area to be covered by the deck and then cover it with a layer of polyethylene. Place enough gravel over the plastic to bring the entire area to grade level. This procedure will increase the cost of the job, but it will prevent a problem that is difficult to correct after the deck is in place.

Ground Level Deck

This basic deck project provides an excellent opportunity for inexperienced do-it-yourselfers to improve their construction skills. With some advice and instruction, they can complete this deck for the cost of materials, while adding an attractive, functional, and valuable addition to their homes.

ELEVATED DECK

2" x 4" Decking
2" x 6" Cap Rail
2" x 4" Rail
2" x 10" Stringers
Brick Landing
3-2" x 4" Treads
2" x 4" Seat Braces
3-2" x 4" Seat
2-2" x 4" Posts
4" x 4" Posts
2" x 8" Joists
2-2" x 8" Beam
Concrete Post Foundation

As in any other exterior home improvement, a deck's size and design should be determined by its intended use, the type and size of the house to which it will be attached, and budget limitations. Sometimes a large deck is most suitable for the needs and style of the house, but the cost of professional installation is prohibitive. This plan demonstrates how a 10' x 16' deck, complete with stairway and two-sided bench-railing, can be constructed for a reasonable cost by the do-it-yourselfer. Because the deck is only 4' above grade, it is still a manageable project for handymen who do not have extensive building skills.

Materials

The durability and ecomomy of pressure-treated lumber has helped to make decks a popular home improvement in recent years. The components of this deck are all constructed from pressure-treated products which are readily available at most building supply outlets. Shop around for the materials, both for quality and price. In making your selection, try to stay away from boards with excessive knots, voids, twisting, warping, or cupping. Make sure that you arrange delivery, as lumber for this size deck does require trucking. Such a purchase will probably warrant free curb delivery, providing the site is within a reasonable distance from the supplier.

The support system and frame for this deck plan consist of six 4" x 4" posts set in 3' concrete footings. The 2" x 8" joists are spaced 2' on center, with doubled support joists at 6' intervals, and doubled 16' headers. It is most important that you lay out the footing and post locations accurately, since the rest of the structure depends on their alignment. If you are inexperienced with the placement of footings and setting of support posts, do some research or seek professional help. Errant placement of the posts is difficult to correct once the concrete footing

has set, so double check all measurements as you go and be sure to use 8" diameter "tube" forms for the foundations. Before you begin construction of the frame, review the layout template to be sure that the doubled support joists will be correctly aligned when they are placed. The frame for this deck can be partially constructed on level ground and then raised into position to be finished. Be sure to square all corners and tie them with strapping before you lag the inside headers into the sill and start laying the deck.

Because 2" x 4" decking is used in this plan, fewer joists are required than for thinner deck boards. If you intend to use 1" boards, however, the spacing of the joists will have to be reduced to 16", their number increased, and the layout of the doubled joists changed accordingly. All of these modifications will affect the cost as will changing the pattern of the decking. Designs, like diagonal decking, create attractive surfaces, but they waste material and demand more installation time. If you are placing the decking in the conventional manner, be sure to measure accurately and make precise saw cuts; the cut-off pieces will be used later to fill out the courses. Use a spacer to keep the opening between courses at about 1/8" or slightly wider. This space is an important feature of the surface, as it allows for the drainage of rainwater, helps to ventilate the structure, and prevents the build-up of moisture-laden matter between the deck boards. Take time to align the nail heads by snapping chalklines before you fasten the surface, as they are one of the most visible features on the deck.

There are many options for the railing, bench, and stairway design. Standard 4" x 4" posts and 2" x 4" rails are used for the most economical railing system, but 2" x 2" balusters can also be installed at more expense to enhance the railing design or to make it child-safe. Costs can be cut by eliminating the bench altogether, or by reducing its length and limiting it to one side of the deck. Seek assistance from a qualified person if you have not installed a stairway before. Even though this one consists of only six steps, its assembly does require some skill and know-how. Safety is a primary consideration for any set of stairs, and consistent vertical spacing from tread to tread is one way of ensuring it. Proper support and correct placement of stringers and stairway railings are also critical safety considerations. Get some help when it comes time to accomplish these important carpentry tasks.

Level of Difficulty

This deck can be built by most handymen who have a reasonable level of skill in home improvement projects. Its 10' x 16' size makes it a major project, but the work time can be spread out because of the convenience of the location. A basic knowledge of carpentry is needed for the installation of all of the deck's components. If you are willing to work slowly and seek guidance as you progress, many of these skills can be acquired and developed as you go. In short, it is an excellent project for learning more about carpentry and building. Beginners can tackle this deck, but only if they are given thorough instruction before they start and plenty of guidance during the construction. They should plan on tripling the estimated times, even with professional assistance. Handymen should add 40% to the professional time for the framing and decking tasks and 75% for the footing, post, railing, bench, and stairway installations. Experts should add 10% to the estimated man-hours for all parts this project.

What to Watch Out For

No cost has been included in the estimate for the painting, staining, or finishing of the deck because none is required. The factory coloring of the pressure-treated lumber will gradually change to a natural wood color over several years' time. If you want to finish the deck, transparent stain looks good and requires little upkeep. Pressure-treated wood can be painted or coated with heavy-bodied stain, but regular maintenance will be needed to preserve its appearance. If you plan to finish the deck with any of these coverings, consider pre-painting or pre-staining the material with a base coat before construction and a finish coat after the deck is in place.

ELEVATED DECK

Description	Quantity	Man-hours	Material
Layout, excavate post holes	6 Ea.	6.0	0.00
Concrete, field mix, 1 C.F. per bag, for posts, incl. 8" dia. forms	6 Bags	10.5	154.35
Deck material, pressure treated lumber posts, 4" x 4" x 7'	48 L.F.	2.0	54.60
Headers, 2" x 8" x 16'	64 L.F.	2.5	39.50
Joists, 2" x 8" x 10'	120 L.F.	4.5	74.05
Decking, 2" x 4" x 12'	576 L.F.	17.0	236.95
Stair material, stringers 2" x 10" x 10'	20 L.F.	1.0	23.75
Treads, 2" x 4" x 3'-6", 3 per tread	70 L.F.	2.0	28.80
Landing brick on sand, no mortar	16 S.F.	3.0	131.65
Railing material, posts, 4" x. 4" x 3'	48 L.F.	2.5	19.75
Railings, 2" x 4" stock	96 L.F.	5.0	39.50
Cap rail, 2" x 6" stock	48 L.F.	1.5	29.65
Bench material, seat braces, 2" x 4"	108 L.F.	3.0	44.45
Joist hangers, 18 ga. galvanized	12 Ea.	1.0	8.00
Nails, #10d galvanized	15 LB.	0.0	12.70
Bolts, 3/8" lag bolts, long	28 Ea.	0.0	26.75
Totals		61.5	$924.45
Project Size 10' x 16'	Contractor's Fee Including Materials		$3250

Elevated Deck

Although this deck project involves a large-sized structure, it can be built by most handymen who are willing to invest the time, get help in starting out, and seek guidance as they go. By doing the work on your own, you can produce an attractive and functional home improvement for the cost of the material.

ELEVATED REDWOOD DECK

Because of its attractive grain and coloring and its ability to resist rot and deterioration, redwood has been popularly used as a deck material for many years. However, it is more costly than standard deck lumber and may be difficult to get, except by special order, in some areas of the country. This plan presents a deluxe 12' x 12' redwood deck with a built-in perimeter bench and bannistered safety railing. Although it is more expensive and has a more complex design than some of the other decks in this section, it is an improvement that will add beauty, comfort, and value to your home. Skilled handymen and experts should be able to handle the construction of this deck, but beginners and those with limited carpentry skills should hire a contractor to do much of the work.

2-2" x 8" Redwood Beam
Beam Hanger
Lag Bolts
2" x 8" Redwood Joists
2" x 4" Redwood Rails Top & Bottom
2" x 4" Redwood Decking
2" x 6" Redwood Cap Rail
2" x 10" Redwood Stringers
3-2" x 4" Redwood Treads
Concrete Landing
2" x 4" Redwood Seat Braces
2" x 6" Redwood Cap Rail
4-2" x 4" Redwood Seats
1" x 2" Redwood Balusters, 6" O.C.
4" x 4" Redwood Posts
Concrete Post Foundation

Materials

The materials used in this plan consist of the basic deck components in redwood, including 4" x 4" support posts, 2" x 8" joists and headers for the frame, 2" x 4" decking, and 2" stock in varying widths for the bench, railing, and stairway. Galvanized joist supports, 10d nails, and 3/8" lag bolts are also included in the design of the deck to ensure sturdy fastening, safety, and durability of the structure. Many other types of galvanized brackets, fittings, and fasteners are also available at reasonable extra cost if needed for special conditions or additions to this design.

Because this deck measures 12' in length, six footings and support posts must be installed. Be sure to square the four corners before locating the post positions. Also, make sure that you follow the plan and include six, not four, supports for this deck. Economizing by eliminating structural components, even for a deck, will cost you more money and aggravation in the long run because of sagging, loosening of the structure, and other conditions which require repair. As with any deck, but especially because this one is located 8' above ground, it is important that the deck frame be plumb, level, and square. Before fastening the joists, review the accuracy of the layout to be sure that the doubled joists are precisely aligned with the 4" x 4" support posts. This alignment must be exact to ensure safe bearing of the load of the structure. Before laying the decking, double check the frame for level and square. Then tie the outside corners temporarily to hold them at right angles while you place the surface material.

The 2" x 4" decking suggested in this plan provides an attractive and durable surface, but redwood boards of other widths can also be used. The deck boards may also be laid diagonally to add a different design feature to the surface. There is more waste of materials when the decking is installed in this way, so plan on about 25% in additional cost for the deck boards if you want them laid at 45 degrees. As you place the decking, allow proper spacing between courses, place the cupped side of the boards down, and use enough nails. To keep the rows of nail heads straight, lay the entire deck with minimum fastenings, and then complete the nailing by following chalk lines.

The built-in railing bench included in this deck plan can be altered to suit personal taste and the practical needs of the structure. The railing consists of 2" x 2" balusters set 6" on center, 2" x 4" rails and 4" x 4" fitted and lagged posts. The balusters take time to install and add considerably to the materials cost, but they are an important safety feature in any deck set this high off the ground. Check local ordinances for deck railing standards before you design the railing systems. Note that the stairway also includes balustered railings and wide treads for safe access. Skill and time is required to cut and install standard stringers. Risers can also be added for safety, but they will boost the cost and may conflict with the open and airy motif desired in most deck designs. If you are inexperienced in any of the finish carpentry tasks required in the project, especially the stairs, balustered railing, and bench, seek professional help.

Level of Difficulty

This deck project requires a considerable level of carpentry skill and building know-how. Several features of this model make it a more demanding do-it-yourself project than other deck plans included in this section. One is the expense of the redwood material, which may be twice the cost of conventional deck lumber. Mistakes in measuring, layout, and cutting can cost you more, so work slowly and carefully.

Another factor is the deck's height off the ground, which requires working from a step ladder and causes general inconvenience in some of the operations. A third challenging feature is the finish work required for the bench, railing, and stairway installations, all of which demand skillful carpentry. Beginners and less skilled handymen should not attempt to complete this project on their own. They should hire a contractor to accomplish the framing and finish work and add 100% to the estimated man-hours for tasks which they intend to take on. Handymen and experts should add 50% and 20%, respectively, for the support, framing, and decking jobs and 100% and 40% for the bench, railing and stairway installations. The increase in time for these finish tasks allows for a slower work pace. This helps to minimize the waste of materials.

What to Watch Out For

If the deck is 4' or less above level grade, the installation of the supports is accomplished fairly easily; but if the deck is higher than 4' or situated over sloping terrain, the job becomes more difficult. This redwood deck, although it is moderate in size at 12' x 12', is a challenging project because of its placement at 8' above ground level. Be sure to allow for extra time because of this inconvenience. Remember that the frame is built in place or in sections, and not conveniently laid out and constructed at ground level. Other materials also have to be raised to deck level before they are placed. Plan to use a stepladder for some of the railing work, as much of the layout and fastening can be accomplished more efficiently from outside the structure. One way of saving time on both the frame and railing installations is to work with a helper. With two workers, the joists can be placed without one person having to move from end to end of the frame as each piece is installed. The railing installation can proceed more efficiently with one worker inside the perimeter and another on a stepladder outside.

ELEVATED REDWOOD DECK

Description	Quantity	Man-hours	Material
Layout, excavate post holes	6 Ea.	6.0	0.00
Concrete, field mix, 1 C.F. per bag, for posts; incl. 8" dia. forms	6 Bag	10.5	154.35
Deck material, redwood, construction grade Posts, 4"x 4" x 12'	72 L.F.	3.0	163.80
Headers, 2" x 8" x 12'	48 L.F.	1.5	59.25
Joists, 2" x 8" x 12'	144 L.F.	3.5	177.75
Decking, 2" x 4" x 12"	504 L.F.	14.0	268.35
Stair material, stringers 2" x 10" x 16'	32 L.F.	1.0	35.25
Treads, 2" x 4" x 3'-6", 3 per tread	144 L.F.	3.0	76.70
Landing, precast concrete, 14" wide	4 L.F.	1.0	32.90
Railing material, redwood Posts, 2" x 4" x 3', doubled	120 L.F.	3.5	135.05
Railings, 2" x 4" stock	72 L.F.	3.0	38.35
Balusters, 2" x 2", 6" O.C.	240 L.F.	8.0	37.15
Cap rail, 2" x 6" stock	96 L.F.	3.0	118.48
Bench material, seat & braces, 2" x 4" stock	48 L.F.	1.5	25.55
Joist hangers, 18 ga. galvanized	12 Ea.	1.0	8.00
Nails, #10d galvanized	14 LB.	0.0	11.86
Bolts, 3/8" lag bolt	18 Ea.	0.0	17.20
Totals		63.5	$1360.00

Project Size	12' × 12'	Contractor's Fee Including Materials	$4630

Elevated Redwood Deck

This redwood deck is a challenging endeavor for most do-it-yourselfers, but it is an attractive structure which will add comfort and value to your home. If you work patiently and seek advice as you go, the results of your efforts will make the undertaking worthwhile.

L-Shaped Elevated Deck

One of the most exciting features variety of shapes and configurations can be used to style the facility to the house and surrounding terrain. Swimming pools, sloping grades, and unusual house layouts offer opportunities to install imaginative decks, custom-planned to complement the design features of the home. This L-shaped plan demonstrates how a deck installation can be modularized to create an attractive and functional facility. Basically, it consists of two separate decks which have been tied into one L-shaped structure, bordering two sides of the house. The same modular construction method can also be used for U-shaped, angled, and multi-level deck designs.

Materials

The materials used in the L-shaped deck plan are the standard pressure-treated products employed for other deck projects. The legs of the "L" are formed from two separate, but attached, deck frames, each with its own 4" x 4" post and footing support system. More time is required to lay out the footings for this deck because there are more of them, but the process is the same as with other decks of simpler design. The most important aspect of the footing and post placement is the establishment of a square and level support system for the rest of the structure. If you are inexperienced in this procedure, get some help from a knowledgeable person and take the job in steps, building the frame for the large 8' x 16' section first before laying out the footing and post support for the 8' x 12' section. By proceeding in this way, you can adjust for small errors in alignment of the section and prevent potential materials waste due to inaccurate layout.

The frame consists of 2" x 8" joists and headers which are assembled as two separate units. As in the layout for the footings and support posts, be sure to double check all measurements and make sure that the corners of each section are properly squared. Since this L-shaped facility is built only 3' off the ground, most of the frame for the 8' x 16' section should be built in place. If the adjacent terrain allows, it may be laid out and started on the ground and then positioned on the 4" x4"s to be finished in place. The 8' x 12' frame can be built in the same way.

The decking used in this L-shaped format consists of 2" x 4"s, but 2" x 6"s may also be installed on frames with 24" joist spacing. If thinner deck boards are to be installed, the joists will have to be placed at closer intervals and their number will be increased, so plan accordingly. Measure and cut the boards accurately, so that the shorter, cut-off pieces can be used to fill out the courses as the decking is placed. When laying the boards, place the cup side down and leave a space between courses. Also, keep a check on the gain at both ends and the middle as you proceed, to be sure that the decking is square to the frame. After all of the boards have been placed and fastened, snap a chalk line and saw the ragged ends to an even finished length.

The railing, bench, and stairway design offer the opportunity to add a distinctive and imaginative touch to the deck. This plan, for example, suggests using a corner bench design, but various other configurations are possible. The railing system, too, can be modified to suit the desired function and personal taste. In both cases, the cost of the project will be affected by alterations. A balustered railing design is an attractive addition to the deck's appearance and safety, but the added expense of the material used for the balusters, as well as their installation time, is considerable. Built-in benches also use a substantial amount of material, so plan to spend more money and allow more installation time if you are adding to the length or the number of benches. The ship's ladder stairway design enhances the open motif of the deck, but conventional stringers and treads can also be placed. The materials cost is the same for both stairway designs, but the cutting of the stringers takes a little longer. If you are not experienced in stairway building, read up on it and seek instruction before you start. Accurate layout of tread height is a must to ensure a usable set of stairs.

Level of Difficulty

As noted in the introduction to this deck plan, the carpentry skills required to complete this project are the same as for standard straight, square, or rectangular decks. A more intricate layout is involved in the alignment of the two sections; but if the project is taken in steps, the layout is simply a matter of more time, not more skill. Beginners, if they are given ample instruction and guidance, can do much of the work on this project, but they will need time to proceed slowly and must be willing to seek advice as they go. Handymen and experts should also allow additional time for the layout and placement of the support system for this L-shaped facility. Otherwise, the project should pose no challenges greater than those encountered in other deck projects. Beginners should triple the professional time estimates for most tasks; handymen should add about 60% to the estimates; and experts should add about 20%. If the facility is to be built more than 6' off ground, more time will be require for do-it-yourselfers of all ability levels.

What to Watch Out For

Modular decks of different shapes and levels are more expensive to build because they usually demand more material and installation time. But if your budget allows for a deluxe deck facility, the resulting structure can add considerably to the appearance and value of your home. Take some time to draw up the plans and do some reading on the subject before you decide on a deck design. Multi-level decks are not that difficult to build, particularly if they are close to ground level. U-shaped, angled configurations, and even hexagonal or octagonal designs, where appropriate, can be built to professional standards by do-it-yourselfers if they are willing to learn first and then work slowly. In addition to imaginative basic designs, other amenities like built-in planters, eating and serving facilities, and sitting areas can be included to enhance the deck's appearance and function. Of course, all of these extras add to the expense of the project, but if you are doing the work on your own, some of what you save on labor costs can be applied to the cost of materials for extras and deluxe design features.

L-SHAPED ELEVATED DECK

Description	Quantity	Man-hours	Material
Layout, excavate post holes	12 Ea.	12.0	0.00
Concrete, field mix, 1 C.F. per bag, for posts including 8" diameter forms	12 Bag	12.0	308.70
Deck material, pressure treated lumber Posts, 4" x 4" x 6'	84 L.F.	3.0	95.55
Headers, 2" x 8" x 16'	80 L.F.	3.0	49.35
Joists, 2" x 8" x 8'	96 L.F.	3.5	59.25
Joists, 2" x 8" x 12'	72 L.F.	2.5	44.45
Decking, 2" x 4" x 12'	720 L.F.	21.0	296.20
Stair material, stringers 2" x 10" x 6'	12 L.F.	0.5	14.25
Treads, 2" x 4" x 3'-6", 3 per tread	60 L.F.	2.0	24.70
Landing, brick on sand, no mortar	16 S.F.	2.5	42.60
Railing material, posts 4" x 4" x 3'	56 L.F.	2.0	23.05
Railings, 2" x 4" stock	136 L.F.	4.0	55.95
Cap rail, 2" x 6" stock	72 L.F.	2.5	44.45
Bench material, seats & braces, 2" x 4" stock	96 L.F.	3.0	39.50
Joist hangers, 18 ga galvanized	18 Ea.	1.0	12.00
Nails, #10d, galvanized	20 LB.	0.0	16.95
Bolts, 3/8" lag bolts, long	40 Ea.	0.0	38.25
Totals		74.5	$1165.20
Project Size 8' x 12' 6	Contractor's Fee Including Materials		$4310

L-Shaped Elevated Deck

This L-shaped plan demonstrates how deck construction can be modularized to create an attractive and practical exterior recreation and sitting area. Many do-it-yourselfers can complete this plan with professional results and considerable savings.

ROOF DECK

Wood Sliding Glass Door

2" x 6" Cap Rail

2" x 4" Rail

2-2" x 4" Posts

2" x 4" Decking

2" x 6" Sleepers - Wedged

Existing Structure Below

Not all houses can conveniently accommodate a roof deck, but those that can have the potential for a unique outdoor living area. This plan demonstrates how normally unused roof area can be turned into deck space. It is a challenging project for the do-it-yourselfer because of the general inconvenience involved in all roof work and because of the many carpentry skills that are required. Generally, a flat or gently sloping roof is best suited to a deck. A steeper roof can also accommodate a deck, but a different support system must be employed. The critical factor is the dormer or exterior wall, which must be able to accommodate a door for access to the proposed deck. Without this basic structural condition, the project cannot be accomplished without costly preliminary work.

Materials

Conventional deck materials and design are used in this roof deck plan, with the exception of sleepers which function as the deck frame and support system. As in the other deck plans presented in this section, pressure-treated lumber is employed for the basic components, including the sleepers, decking, and railing. If the roof is flat, the 2" x 6" sleepers can be laid on edge as in the example; but if the roof is slanted, they have to be sawn at an angle to compensate for the slope. Be sure to make the angled cut precise and consistent for all of the sleepers to ensure stability and equal load distribution. Some shimming will also be needed. Before you place the sleeper system, carefully check the condition of the roof and its rafters. If there are questionable areas, take steps to correct the situation, seeking professional advice and assistance if needed. Take care not to damage or puncture the roofing material during the deck installation process. Be sure to use proper caulking at points where the deck is attached to the roof.

After the sleeper frame has been placed, fastened, and squared, the decking and railing are installed as in any other deck. The 2" x 4" boards are laid with staggered end joints and with a space between courses to allow for drainage. The railing consists of doubled 2" x 4" posts, fitted and lagged into the sleeper frame, 2" x 4" rails, and a 2" x 6" cap. Great care should be taken in the design of the railing system for the roof deck; safety should be a primary feature. Check local building codes and regulations before construction begins to determine the minimum requirements for safety railings on off-ground decks. Adding balusters spaced at 6" or 8" along the railing on the open side of the deck, will increase the cost of the project, but the result will be a stronger, safer, and more durable railing.

The doorway to the roof deck should be installed before the deck is constructed to provide a convenient means of access to the roof site during construction. Many options are available in the choice of doors, so long as they are compatible with the structure and size of the wall. This plan includes the cost of materials for framing a 6' sliding glass door. The preparations will vary for other types and sizes of doors. Work carefully when cutting the opening to prevent excessive damage to the interior wall and exterior siding. Whenever possible, it pays to use an existing window space as part of the new door opening. You will have to enlarge and modify the rough window opening, but you will still be a step ahead in your door installation by using this approach.

Level of Difficulty

Beginners should not attempt to build this deck on their own unless it is to be located on a flat roof. Even then, they should seek professional advice before they begin the job. They should also leave the entire door installation to a professional, as the cutting of the opening and placement of the new unit involves considerable carpentry know-how. Handymen should be able to complete the deck construction in about twice the professional man-hours, but they should add more time if the roof area is not easily accessible. Plan to work slowly and seek guidance. Hole-cutting and door installation are not tasks for the handyman who is inexperienced in these areas. Experts should add about 30% to the

professional time for all tasks. They should allow a bit more time for the hole-cutting and door installation, as hidden problems tend to arise in these operations, especially in older homes. If electrical wiring is located in the wall, shut off the supply before cutting the hole. Hire an electrician to rewire the affected area if you are unfamiliar with electrical work. All do-it-yourselfers should consider the risks and inconvenience of working on a roof before they start this project, and make plans to acquire the appropriate equipment for safe and efficient roof work.

What to Watch Out For

Several important factors must be considered before installing a roof deck to prevent overloading the existing roof. Remember that the weight of the 8' x 16' deck will increase when in use. Be sure that the existing rafters and roof boards are in good condition and are sturdy enough to support more than the anticipated load. If additional support members are needed, they will have to be installed before you begin construction of the new deck. If you are in doubt as to how to reinforce the roof support, consult a contractor and hire him to do the work. The additional expense for his services will be well worth the investment to ensure proper and safe support for the new deck.

ROOF DECK

Description	Quantity	Man-hours	Material
Deck material, pressure-treated lumber			
Sleepers, 2" x 6" x 8'	112 L.F.	4.0	69.15
Header, 2" x 6" x 16'	16 L.F.	0.5	9.85
Decking, 2" x 4" x 12'	408 L.F.	12.0	167.85
Railing material, posts, 2" x 4" x 3', doubled	72 L.F.	2.5	81.90
Railings, 2" x 4" stock	72 L.F.	2.5	29.65
Cap rail, 2" x 6" stock	36 L.F.	1.5	22.25
Cut opening for sliding glass door	1 Ea.	15.5	0.00
Frame for door, 2" x 4" to support header	48 L.F.	1.0	15.10
Header, 2" x 8", doubled	14 L.F.	1.0	9.65
Door, sliding glass, stock, wood frame, 6' wide	1 Ea.	4.0	508.20
Nails, #10d galvanized	10 LB.	0.0	8.45
Bolts, 3/8" lag bolts, long	24 Ea.	0.0	22.95
Totals		44.5	$945.00
Project Size 8' x 16'	Contractor's Fee Including Materials		$2980

Roof Deck

If the conditions of the house are right, a roof deck addition can provide a unique dimension in exterior living space. For do-it-yourselfers who can handle some or all of the work, the project can be completed at a surprisingly reasonable cost.

OCTAGONAL REDWOOD GAZEBO

Gazebos can range from plain and rustic to very decorative and can be constructed from a wide variety of materials, from basic to deluxe. This model has 6' sides, a floor area of nearly 170 square feet, and a balustered railing. It is built of attractive, long-lasting redwood material. Because of its size and the skillful carpentry required in its construction, it is a challenging project. The extra expense of redwood underscores the importance of good workmanship. Beginners and inexperienced handymen are advised to hire a carpenter to complete some portions of the work. Despite the challenges and the expense of this project, the rewards are an attractive outside feature and years of pleasurable use for your friends and family.

Labels (left side):
- 3' x 3' Redwood Cupola
- Red Cedar Split Shakes
- 1" x 8" Redwood Fascia Board
- Redwood Balusters 6" O.C.
- 4" x 4" Redwood Posts
- 2" x 10" Redwood Joists & Headers
- 2" x 10" Redwood Stringers

Labels (right side):
- Roof:
  2" x 6" Redwood Rafters
  2" x 4" Redwood Collar Ties
  1/2" Plywood Sheathing
  Building Paper
- Aluminum Drip Edge
- 2" x 4" Redwood Railing Top & Bottom
- 2" x 6" Redwood Decking
- Concrete Piers
- 3-2" x 4" Redwood Treads

Materials

The materials used in this plan consist of basic products found in all exterior structures. The difference is that redwood is used instead of standard construction lumber for many of the components. Because redwood is not readily available in some areas of the country, you may have to special order it. In this case, the price may exceed the one given in the model's estimate. The plywood sheathing and the cedar for the roof are standard products generally available at building supply outlets, regardless of geographical location. When purchasing the materials, be sure to arrange delivery, as it is a large enough order to require trucking.

The most important procedure in the early stages of the project involves establishing the layout for the gazebo and accurately placing 3' concrete pedestals, which serve as its basic support. Because of the octagonal shape and the number of pedestals required, the operation is tricky; and careful planning and workmanship are crucial if the rest of the project is to go smoothly. Be sure to double check all measurements before placing the concrete. The use of "tube" forms will add to the cost of this procedure, but they will make it easier to place and level the pedestals accurately.

The next phase of the project involves the placement of the platform and 4" x 4" support posts. One method is to build the 2" x 10" frame in place and then mortise it into the posts so that short legs of about 6" extend below the frame onto the tops of the pedestals. Another way is to place the frame directly on the pedestals and set the posts beside the perimeter of the frame at each point. Still another is to plant the 4" x 4" legs in the concrete at rough height, level them by sawing after the concrete has cured, and then build the frame of the platform around them. Later, the 4" x 4" roof supports should transmit the load of the roof directly to the pedestals. The costs vary only slightly between these three methods.

After the 4 x 4's are positioned, they should be temporarily braced while the 2" x 6" headers for the roof perimeter are installed. The 2" x 6" roof rafters are difficult to place, as they must be precisely angled on both ends if they are to fit correctly. Ceiling joists are not called for in this plan, but they can be used in place of the collar ties if the new gazebo is to have a finished ceiling. Sheathing and finished roofing are applied after the roof frame is completed. Red cedar shingles are suggested in this plan, but any other type of finished roofing can be used, including tile, slate, and various grades of asphalt and cedar. Although the roof is relatively small, its installation can be challenging because of the hips and the triangular shape of the roof sections. Seek some assistance if you are an inexperienced roofer, and plan on allowing extra time for cutting and scribing the roofing material. Also be aware that considerable waste is expected on roofs of this design. The cupola can be placed at any time after the roof has been completed. Hiring a carpenter for this job might be a good idea, as extensive cutting of the base is required to install this expensive fixture.

The railing and steps of the gazebo also require skillful carpentry if you choose to follow the design of this plan. Here, a top and bottom rail are constructed with 2″ x 2″ balusters set at 8″ intervals. There are many other options, however, for the railing design. Fancy balusters, lattice, and wainscoting are some of the possibilities. Lattice and various trim styles can also be used for the opening above the rail and the fascia. Ornate trim designs tend to be more expensive than simpler styles, so compromises might be made to stay within a budget.

Level of Difficulty

The size, expense, and advanced carpentry skills required to construct this gazebo make it a challenging project, even for expert do-it-yourselfers. Beginners and handymen, therefore, should consider hiring a carpenter to complete the roof and some other aspects of the job. Mistakes can always be costly and time-consuming, but when redwood is involved, the price can be twice as high. The most challenging task in the project is the roof frame. The rental of staging may be an extra cost for this phase of the project. The detailed work of the finished roof and cupola may also be troublesome for many do-it-yourselfers. Generally, handymen and beginners should not attempt any of the roof work. They should add 50% and 100%, respectively, to the estimated time for all other tasks, and slightly more for fancy trim work which involves expensive materials. Experts should add 20% to the professional time for all jobs, and more for all aspects of the roof work.

What to Watch Out For

The gazebo outlined here is octagonal in shape, but six- and five-sided configurations are also authentic Victorian gazebo designs. The eight-sided structure presented in the book provides more platform space, but it also requires more materials and time to construct. The hexagonal and pentagonal types are slightly easier to build, because fewer pedestals are required; but the same kinds of complications still exist in angling the roof frame and applying its covering. However they may differ in size and shape, gazebos can be decoratively trimmed and authentically styled from the same kinds of materials.

OCTAGONAL REDWOOD GAZEBO

Description	Quantity	Man-hours	Material
Excavate, post holes, including layout	8 Ea.	8.0	0.00
Concrete, field mix, 1 C.F. per bag, for posts	8 Bags	4.0	98.35
Framing materials, redwood Posts, 4″ x 4″ x 12′	96 L.F.	3.5	218.40
Headers, 2″ x 10″ x 12′	48 L.F.	1.5	113.85
Joists, 2″ x 10″ x 16′	192 L.F.	6.0	455.35
Flooring, 2″ x 6″ x 16′	448 L.F.	12.0	552.95
Railing, top & bottom, 2″ x 4″	72 L.F.	2.0	59.25
Balusters, 2″ x 2″ x 3′	180 L.F.	7.0	69.70
Roof framing materials, redwood Headers, 2″ x 6″ stock	48 L.F.	1.0	59.25
Rafters, 2″ x 6″ x 10′	240 L.F.	7.0	296.20
Collar ties, 2″ x 4″ stock	24 L.F.	1.0	19.75
Fascia board, 1″ x 8″ stock	48 L.F.	1.5	87.15
Sheathing, 1/2″ plywood, 4′ x 8′ sheets	12 Sheets	4.0	190.50
Building paper, 15 lb. felt paper	250 S.F.	0.5	9.10
Drip edge, aluminum, 5″ girth	48 L.F.	1.0	8.70
Shakes, hand split red cedar, 18″ long, 8-1/2″ exposure	3 Sq.	12.0	290.40
Stair materials, redwood, stringers, 2″ x 10″ stock	16 L.F.	0.5	37.95
Treads, 2″ x 4″ x 4″, 3 per tread	24 L.F.	0.5	19.75
Cupola, stock unit, 1″ redwood, 3′ x 3′ base, 3′ high, copper roof	1 Ea.	2.5	363.00
Sealer, 2 coats, brushwork	1100 S.F.	10.0	119.80
Totals		85.5	$3069.40

Project Size 16′ x 16′	Contractor's Fee Including Materials	$7330

Octagonal Redwood Gazebo
This large, octagonal redwood gazebo is a home improvement that will enhance the atmosphere of your backyard landscape and expand your outdoor living space. While some aspects of the project may be out of reach for inexperienced do-it-yourselfers, it can still be your own personal creation, taking shape from the decorative features you choose to incorporate.

Costs shown in Home Improvement Cost Guide are based on National Averages for materials and installation. To adjust these costs to a specific location, simply multiply the base cost by the multiplier for that city. The data is arranged alphabetically by state and postal zip code numbers. For a city not listed, use the factor for a nearby city with similar economic characteristics. You May have to adjust for inflation. Cost figures given in this book are based on the value of $1 in 1989-90.

ZIP	CITY	MULT
ALABAMA		
350- 352	Birmingham	.83
354	Tuscaloosa	.86
355	Jasper	.83
356	Decatur	.85
357, 358	Huntsville	.86
359	Gadsden	.85
360, 361	Montgomery	.87
362	Anniston	.85
363	Dothan	.89
364	Evergreen	.89
365, 366	Mobile	.94
367	Selma	.89
368	Phenix City	.89
369	Butler	.89
ALASKA		
995, 996	Anchorage	1.30
997	Fairbanks	1.30
998	Juneau	1.30
999	Ketchikan	1.30
ARIZONA		
850, 852, 853	Phoenix	.96
855	Globe	.96
856, 857	Tucson	.95
859	Show Low	.96
860	Flagstaff	.96
863	Prescott	.96
864	Kingman	.96
865	Chambers	.96
ARKANSAS		
716	Pine Bluff	.86
717	Camden	.86
718	Texarkana	.86
719	Hot Springs	.86
720-722	Little Rock	.86
723	West Memphis	.90
724	Jonesboro	.90
725	Batesville	.86
726	Harrison	.86
727	Fayetteville	.88
728	Russellville	.88
729	Fort Smith	.88
CALIFORNIA		
900-918	Los Angeles	1.13
920, 921	San Diego	1.13
922	Palm Springs	1.15
923, 924	San Bernardino	1.15
925	Riverside	1.15
926, 927	Santa Ana	1.15
928	Anaheim	1.15
930	Ventura	1.14
931	Santa Barbara	1.15
932, 933	Bakersfield	1.13
934	San Luis Obispo	1.15
935	Mojave	1.12
936, 937	Fresno	1.14
939	Salinas	1.10
940, 941	San Francisco	1.21
943	Palo Alto	1.19
944	San Mateo	1.21

ZIP	CITY	MULT
CALIFORNIA (Cont.)		
945, 946	Oakland	1.21
947	Berkeley	1.21
948	Richmond	1.21
948	San Rafael	1.19
950, 951	San Jose	1.21
952, 953	Stockton	1.14
954	Santa Rosa	1.13
955	Eureka	1.15
956-958	Sacramento	1.15
959	Marysville	1.15
960	Redding	1.15
961	Susanville	1.15
COLORADO		
800-802	Denver	.99
803	Boulder	.99
804	Golden	.99
805	Fort Collins	.95
806	Greeley	.95
807	Fort Morgan	.95
808, 809	Colorado Springs	.96
810	Pueblo	.97
811	Alamosa	.97
812	Salida	.96
813	Durango	.97
814	Montrose	.96
815	Grand Junction	1.00
816	Glenwood Springs	1.00
CONNECTICUT		
060, 061	Hartford	1.02
062	Willimantic	1.02
063	New London	1.02
064, 065	New Haven	1.02
066	Bridgeport	1.01
067	Waterbury	1.01
068, 069	Stamford	1.01
DELAWARE		
197, 198	Wilmington	1.02
199	Dover	1.02
DISTRICT OF COLUMBIA		
200-205	Washington	.94
FLORIDA		
320, 322	Jacksonville	.88
323	Tallahassee	.81
324	Panama City	.81
325	Pensacola	.83
326	Gainesville	.88
327, 328	Orlando	.87
329	Melbourne	.86
330, 331	Miami	.90
333	Fort Lauderdale	.90
334	W. Palm Beach	.93
335, 336	Tampa	.89
337	St. Petersburg	.89
338	Lakeland	.86
339	Fort Myers	.88
GEORGIA		
300-303	Atlanta	.85
304	Statesboro	.85

ZIP	CITY	MULT
GEORGIA (cont.)		
305	Gainesville	.85
306	Athens	.85
307	Dalton	.89
308, 309	Augusta	.85
310, 312	Macon	.86
313, 314	Savannah	.86
315	Waycross	.83
316	Valdosta	.83
317	Albany	.84
318, 319	Columbus	.83
HAWAII		
967, 968	Honolulu	1.18
IDAHO		
832	Pocatello	.97
833	Twin Falls	.97
834	Idaho Falls	.97
835	Lewiston	1.05
836, 837	Boise	.96
838	Coeur D'Alene	1.05
ILLINOIS		
600-606	Chicago	1.03
609	Kankakee	1.02
610, 611	Rockford	1.02
612	Rock Island	1.03
613	La Salle	1.02
614	Galesburg	1.02
615, 616	Peoria	1.01
617	Bloomington	1.01
618, 619	Champaign	1.01
620, 622	East St. Louis	1.02
623	Quincy	.99
624	Effingham	1.02
625-627	Springfield	1.01
628	Centralia	1.02
629	Carbondale	1.02
INDIANA		
460-462	Indianapolis	1.00
463, 464	Gary	1.03
465, 466	South Bend	.98
467, 468	Fort Wayne	.94
469	Kokomo	.97
470	Lawrenceburg	1.01
471	New Albany	.95
472	Columbus	1.01
473	Muncie	.96
474	Bloomington	1.01
475	Washington	.98
476, 477	Evansville	.97
478	Terre Haute	.98
479	Lafayette	.96
IOWA		
500-503	Des Moines	.95
504	Mason City	.94
505	Fort Dodge	.94
506, 507	Waterloo	.95
508	Creston	.94
510, 511	Sioux City	.88
512	Sibley	.88

ZIP	CITY	MULT	ZIP	CITY	MULT	ZIP	CITY	MULT
IOWA (Cont.)			**MARYLAND** (Cont.)			**MISSOURI** (Cont.)		
513	Spencer	.88	217	Hagerstown	.94	654, 655	Rolla	.99
514	Carroll	.94	218	Salisbury	.94	656-658	Springfield	.90
515	Council Bluffs	.95	219	Elkton	.94	**MONTANA**		
516	Shenandoah	.95	**MASSACHUSETTS**			590-591	Billings	.95
520	Dubuque	.96	010, 011	Springfield	1.02	592	Wolf Point	.95
521	Decorah	.96	012	Pittsfield	.99	593	Miles City	.95
522-524	Cedar Rapids	.99	013	Greenfield	1.02	594	Great Falls	.95
525	Ottumwa	.99	014	Fitchburg	1.10	595	Havre	.95
526	Burlington	1.00	015, 016	Worcester	1.10	596	Helena	.95
527, 528	Davenport	.96	017	Framingham	1.12	597	Butte	.95
KANSAS			018	Lowell	1.07	598	Missoula	.95
660-662	Kansas City	1.01	019	Lynn	1.12	599	Kalispell	.95
664-666	Topeka	.93	020-022	Boston	1.12	**NEBRASKA**		
667	Fort Scott	1.01	023, 024	Brockton	1.02	680, 681	Omaha	.91
668	Emporia	.93	025	Buzzards Bay	1.02	683-685	Lincoln	.91
669	Belleville	.93	026	Hyannis	1.03	686	Columbus	.91
670-672	Wichita	.91	027	New Bedford	1.03	687	Norfolk	.91
673	Independence	.91	**MICHIGAN**			688	Grand Island	.91
674	Salina	.91	480	Royal Oak	1.08	689	Hastings	.91
675	Hutchinson	.91	480-482	Detroit	1.08	690	Mc Cook	.91
676	Hays	.91	484, 485	Flint	.97	691	North Platte	.91
677	Colby	.91	486, 487	Saginaw	.94	692	Valentine	.91
678	Dodge City	.91	488, 489	Lansing	1.02	693	Alliance	.90
679	Liberal	.91	490, 491	Kalamazoo	.98	**NEVADA**		
KENTUCKY			492	Jackson	1.04	890, 891	Las Vegas	1.07
400-401	Louisville	.93	493-495	Grand Rapids	.94	893	Ely	1.07
403-405	Lexington	.92	496	Traverse City	.94	894, 895	Reno	1.04
406	Frankfort	.94	497	Gaylord	.96	897	Carson City	1.04
407-409	Corbin	.94	498, 499	Iron Mountain	.97	898	Elko	1.04
410	Covington	1.01	**MINNESOTA**			**NEW HAMPSHIRE**		
411, 412	Ashland	.94	550, 551	St. Paul	1.01	030, 031	Manchester	.93
413, 414	Campton	.92	553, 554	Minneapolis	1.03	032, 033	Concord	.93
415, 416	Pikeville	.94	556-558	Duluth	.96	034	Keene	.93
417, 418	Hazard	.92	559	Rochester	1.00	035	Littleton	.93
420	Paducah	.94	560	Mankato	1.01	036	Charlestown	.93
421, 422	Bowling Green	.94	561	Windom	1.01	037	Claremont	.93
423	Owensboro	.94	562	Willmar	1.01	038	Portsmouth	.93
424	Henderson	.94	563	St. Cloud	1.01	**NEW JERSEY**		
425, 426	Somerset	.92	564	Brainerd	1.01	070, 071	Newark	1.09
427	Elizabethtown	.94	565	Detroit Lakes	.86	072	Elizabeth	1.09
LOUISIANA			566	Bemidji	.86	073	Jersey City	1.09
700, 701	New Orleans	.91	567	Thief River Falls	.86	074, 075	Paterson	1.11
703	Thibodaux	.91	**MISSISSIPPI**			076	Hackensack	1.11
704	Hammond	.90	386	Clarksdale	.87	077	Long Branch	1.09
705	Lafayette	.88	387	Greenville	.87	078	Dover	1.09
706	Lake Charles	.88	388	Tupelo	.85	079	Summit	1.09
707, 708	Baton Rouge	.89	389	Greenwood	.87	080, 083	Vineland	1.09
710, 711	Shreveport	.84	390-392	Jackson	.87	081	Camden	1.09
712	Monroe	.84	393	Meridian	.87	082, 084	Atlantic City	1.09
713, 714	Alexandria	.84	394	Laurel	.88	085, 086	Trenton	1.09
MAINE			395	Biloxi	.88	087	Point Pleasant	1.09
039	Kittery	.90	396	Mc Comb	.85	088, 089	New Brunswick	1.09
040, 041	Portland	.89	397	Columbus	.85	**NEW MEXICO**		
042	Lewiston	.89	**MISSOURI**			870, 871	Albuquerque	.90
043	Augusta	.90	630, 631	St. Louis	.99	873	Gallup	.90
044	Bangor	.90	633	Bowling Green	.99	874	Farmington	.90
045	Bath	.90	634	Hannibal	.99	875	Santa Fe	.90
046	Machias	.90	635	Kirksville	.90	877	Las Vegas	.90
047	Houlton	.90	636	Flat River	.99	878	Socorro	.90
048	Rockland	.90	637	Cape Girardeau	.99	879	Truth/Conseq.	.90
049	Waterville	.91	638	Sikeston	.99	880	Las Cruces	.90
MARYLAND			639	Poplar Bluff	.99	881	Clovis	.90
206	Waldorf	.95	640, 641	Kansas City	1.01	882	Roswell	.90
207, 208	College Park	.95	644, 645	Saint Joseph	.90	883	Carrizozo	.90
209	Silver Spring	.96	645	Chillicothe	.90	884	Tucumcari	.90
210-212	Baltimore	.94	647	Harrisonville	1.00	**NEW YORK**		
214	Annapolis	.94	648	Joplin	.90	100	Manhattan	1.21
215	Cumberland	.91	650, 652	Columbia	.99	103	Staten Island	1.21
216	Easton	.94	651	Jefferson City	.99			
			653	Sedalia	.99			

ZIP	CITY	MULT
NEW YORK (Cont.)		
104	Bronx	1.21
105	Mount Vernon	1.20
106	White Plains	1.20
107	Yonkers	1.15
108	New Rochelle	1.15
109	Suffern	1.15
110	Queens	1.21
111	Long Island City	1.21
112	Brooklyn	1.21
113	Flushing	1.21
114	Jamaica	1.21
115, 117	Hicksville	1.21
116	Far Rockaway	1.21
119	Riverhead	1.21
120-122	Albany	.96
123	Schenectady	.97
124	Kingston	1.15
125, 126	Poughkeepsie	1.15
127	Monticello	1.15
128	Glens Falls	.99
129	Plattsburgh	.99
130-132	Syracuse	.99
133-135	Utica	.93
136	Watertown	.93
137-139	Binghamton	.93
140-142	Buffalo	1.08
143	Niagara Falls	1.08
144-146	Rochester	1.01
147	Jamestown	1.08
148, 149	Elmira	.93
NORTH CAROLINA		
270, 272	Greensboro	.80
271	Winston-Salem	.83
275, 276	Raleigh	.83
277	Durham	.81
278	Rocky Mount	.83
279	Elizabeth City	.86
280-282	Charlotte	.82
283	Fayetteville	.83
284	Wilmington	.82
285	Kingston	.83
286	Hickory	.83
287, 288	Asheville	.82
289	Murphy	.83
NORTH DAKOTA		
580, 581	Fargo	.86
582	Grand Forks	.86
583	Devils Lake	.86
584	Jamestown	.86
585	Bismarck	.86
586	Dickinson	.86
587	Minot	.86
588	Williston	.86
OHIO		
430-432	Columbus	1.00
433	Marion	.98
434-436	Toledo	1.04
437, 438	Zanesville	1.00
439	Steubenville	1.01
440, 441	Cleveland	1.15
442-443	Akron	1.05
444, 445	Youngstown	1.02
446, 447	Canton	1.01
448, 449	Mansfield	1.01
450-452	Cincinnati	1.01
453, 454	Dayton	1.00
455	Springfield	.98
456	Chillicothe	1.01
457	Athens	1.00
458	Lima	1.06

ZIP	CITY	MULT
OKLAHOMA		
730, 731	Oklahoma City	.89
734	Ardmore	.89
735	Lawton	.89
736	Clinton	.89
737	Enid	.89
738	Woodward	.89
739	Guymon	.89
740, 741	Tulsa	.93
743	Miami	.93
744	Muskogee	.93
745	McAlester	.89
746	Ponca City	.93
747	Durant	.89
748	Shawnee	.89
749	Poteau	.88
OREGON		
970-972	Portland	1.04
973	Salem	1.03
974	Eugene	1.03
975	Medford	1.03
976	Klamath Falls	1.03
977	Bend	1.03
978	Pendleton	.97
979	Vale	.97
PENNSYLVANIA		
150-152	Pittsburgh	1.06
153	Washington	1.06
154	Uniontown	1.06
155	Bedford	1.06
156	Greensburg	1.06
157	Indiana	1.06
158	Du Bois	1.06
159	Johnstown	1.06
160	Butler	1.06
161	New Castle	1.06
162	Kittanning	1.06
163	Oil City	.98
164, 165	Erie	.98
166	Altoona	1.06
167	Bradford	.98
168	State College	.97
169	Wellsboro	.95
170, 171	Harrisburg	.97
172	Chambersburg	.97
173, 174	York	.97
175, 176	Lancaster	.97
177	Williamsport	.97
178	Sunbury	.97
179	Pottsville	.97
180	Lehigh Valley	1.04
181	Allentown	1.04
182	Hazleton	1.04
183	Stroudsburg	1.04
184, 185	Scranton	.94
186, 187	Wilkes Barre	.94
188	Montrose	.94
189	Doylestown	.94
190, 191	Philadelphia	1.08
193	Westchester	1.08
194	Norristown	1.08
195, 196	Reading	.94
RHODE ISLAND		
028, 029	Providence	.99
SOUTH CAROLINA		
290-292	Columbia	.80
293	Spartanburg	.80
294	Charleston	.81
295	Florence	.80
296	Greenville	.80

ZIP	CITY	MULT
SOUTH CAROLINA (Cont.)		
297	Rock Hill	.80
298	Aiken	.80
299	Beaufort	.81
SOUTH DAKOTA		
570, 571	Sioux Falls	.91
572	Watertown	.91
573	Mitchell	.91
574	Aberdeen	.91
575	Pierre	.91
576	Mobridge	.92
577	Rapid City	.92
TENNESSEE		
370-372	Nashville	.84
373, 374	Chattanooga	.88
376	Johnson City	.87
377-379	Knoxville	.86
380, 381	Memphis	.89
382	Mc Kenzie	.84
383	Jackson	.81
384	Columbia	.84
385	Cookeville	.84
TEXAS		
750	Mc Kinney	.97
751	Waxahackie	.92
752, 753	Dallas	.90
754	Greenville	.96
755	Texarkana	.96
756	Longview	.96
757	Tyler	.96
758	Palestine	.85
759	Lufkin	.85
760, 761	Fort Worth	.93
762	Denton	.96
763	Wichita Falls	.90
764	Eastland	.93
765	Temple	.90
766, 767	Waco	.87
768	Brownwood	.87
769	San Angelo	.87
770-772	Houston	.90
773	Huntsville	.89
774	Wharton	.93
775	Galveston	.93
776, 777	Beaumont	.96
778	Bryan	.90
779	Victoria	.86
780-782	San Antonio	.85
783, 784	Corpus Christi	.86
785	Mc Allen	.86
786, 787	Austin	.90
788	Del Rio	.86
789	Giddings	.90
790, 791	Amarillo	.90
792	Childress	.87
793, 794	Lubbock	.87
795, 796	Abilene	.88
797	Midland	.86
798, 799	El Paso	.83
UTAH		
840, 841	Salt Lake City	.94
843, 844	Ogden	.94
845	Price	.94
846	Provo	.94
VERMONT		
050	White River Jct.	.90
051	Bellows Falls	.90
052	Bennington	.90
053	Brattleboro	.90
054	Burlington	.90

ZIP	CITY	MULT
VERMONT (Cont.)		
056	Montpelier	.90
057	Rutland	.90
058	St. Johnsbury	.90
059	Guildhall	.90
VIRGINIA		
220, 221	Fairfax	.95
222	Arlington	.95
223	Alexandria	.95
224, 225	Fredericksburg	.95
226	Winchester	.95
227	Culpeper	.95
228	Harrisonburg	.95
229	Charlottesville	.88
230-232	Richmond	.88
233-235	Norfolk	.84
236	Newport News	.85
237	Portsmouth	.84
238	Petersburg	.88
239	Farmville	.88
240, 241	Roanoke	.84
242	Bristol	.85
243	Pulaski	.84
244	Staunton	.88
245	Lynchburg	.86
246	Grundy	.99

ZIP	CITY	MULT
WASHINGTON		
980, 981	Seattle	.97
982	Everett	.97
983, 984	Tacoma	1.05
985	Olympia	1.05
986	Vancouver	1.07
988	Wenatchee	.99
989	Yakima	1.05
990-992	Spokane	1.04
993	Richland	1.04
994	Clarkston	1.04
WEST VIRGINIA		
247, 248	Bluefield	1.00
249	Lewisburg	1.00
250-253	Charleston	1.00
254	Martinsburg	.96
255-257	Huntington	.98
258, 259	Beckley	1.00
260	Wheeling	.98
261	Parkersburg	.98
262	Buckhannon	1.00
263, 264	Clarksburg	1.00
265	Morgantown	1.00
266	Gassaway	1.00
267	Romney	.93
268	Petersburg	1.00

ZIP	CITY	MULT
WISCONSIN		
530-532	Milwaukee	.98
534	Racine	1.02
535, 537	Madison	.95
538	Lancaster	.95
539	Portage	.95
540	New Richmond	1.00
541-543	Green Bay	.97
544	Wausau	.95
545	Rhinelander	.95
546	La Crosse	.95
547	Eau Claire	1.00
548	Superior	1.00
549	Oshkosh	.96
WYOMING		
820	Cheyenne	.97
821	Yellowstone Nat'l. Park	.97
822	Wheatland	.97
823	Rawlins	.97
824	Worland	.97
825	Riverton	.97
826	Casper	.97
827	Newcastle	.97
828	Sheridan	.97
829-831	Rock Springs	.97

CANADIAN FACTORS
(reflect Canadian currency)

PROVINCE	CITY	MULT
ALBERTA		
	Calgary	1.05
	Edmonton	1.05
BRITISH COLUMBIA		
	Vancouver	1.08
MANITOBA		
	Winnipeg	1.02
NEW BRUNSWICK		
	Saint John	.95
	Moncton	.95

PROVINCE	CITY	MULT
NEWFOUNDLAND		
	St. John's	.96
NOVA SCOTIA		
	Halifax	.95
ONTARIO		
	Hamilton	1.06
	London	1.04
	Ottawa	1.04
	Sudbury	1.04
	Toronto	1.07

PROVINCE	CITY	MULT
PRINCE EDWARD ISLAND		
	Charlottetown	.96
QUEBEC		
	Montreal	1.05
	Quebec	1.05
SASKATCHEWAN		
	Regina	1.03
	Saskatoon	1.03

Index